Gender and Identity in Franz Grillparzer's Classical Dramas

Gender and Identity in Franz Grillparzer's Classical Dramas

Figuring the Female

Alicia E. Ellis

LEXINGTON BOOKS
Lanham • Boulder • New York • London

Published by Lexington Books
An imprint of The Rowman & Littlefield Publishing Group, Inc.
4501 Forbes Boulevard, Suite 200, Lanham, Maryland 20706
www.rowman.com

6 Tinworth Street, London SE11 5AL, United Kingdom

Copyright © 2021 The Rowman & Littlefield Publishing Group, Inc.

All rights reserved. No part of this book may be reproduced in any form or by any electronic or mechanical means, including information storage and retrieval systems, without written permission from the publisher, except by a reviewer who may quote passages in a review.

British Library Cataloguing in Publication Information Available

Library of Congress Cataloging-in-Publication Data

Names: Ellis, Alicia E., 1976- author.
Title: Gender and identity in Franz Grillparzer's classical dramas : figuring the female / Alicia E. Ellis.
Description: Lanham : Lexington Books, 2021. | Includes bibliographical references and index.
Identifiers: LCCN 2021009339 (print) | LCCN 2021009340 (ebook) |
  ISBN 9781793631718 (cloth) | ISBN 9781793631725 (epub)
  ISBN 9781793631732 (pbk)
Subjects: LCSH: Grillparzer, Franz, 1791-1872—Criticism and interpretation. | Grillparzer, Franz, 1791-1872—Characters. | Women in literature. | Gender identity in literature. | Feminist literary criticism.
Classification: LCC PT2274.W8 E55 2021 (print) | LCC PT2274.W8 (ebook) | DDC 832/.6—dc23
LC record available at https://lccn.loc.gov/2021009339
LC ebook record available at https://lccn.loc.gov/2021009340

For dhm
Without him, none of this would have been possible.

Contents

Acknowledgments	ix
Introduction: Grillparzer and the Figure of the Female	1
1 Sappho: The Gender of Belonging	31
2 Medea: The Construction of the Other	69
3 Hero: The Challenge of Virtue	107
Conclusion	151
Bibliography	159
Index	169
About the Author	177

Acknowledgments

This project began in a place that has taken me from one end of the scholarly world to an entirely different one. It was a memorable journey. It involved fitful starts, winding literary roads, and moments of insight. I had the opportunity to work with and learn from remarkable individuals who displayed incredible kindness, offered me unending support, and treated the project with discerning eyes. Many people have helped usher me along the way and I owe to them an enormous debt that cannot be understated. They listened to ideas just emerging, anchored me in the reading and writing, and told me when I needed to go further. I want to acknowledge their time, patience, and guidance:

I am thankful to the Provost's Office at Colby College for the sabbatical leave that gave me the time and space to complete this book. I also want to give special thanks to Karlene Burrell-McRae, Julie de Sherbinin, Arne Koch, Carleen Mandolfo, and Margaret McFadden for their deep integrity.

My dissertation advisor, Carol Jacobs, for sharing the richness of her intellect with me and for her unexpected and moving acts of kindness.

The members of my writing group at Colby College, "Vulnerable Bodies" —Nadia El-Shaarawi, Rebeca Hey-Colón, and Jay Sibara for the generative and intense work where their constructive and critical observations pushed the writing forward. I valued sharing our intellectual goals, the collaborative work, and the attentive and challenging readings of chapters. I am appreciative of Elena Monastireva-Ansdell, my colleague in Russian, who is unrelentingly gracious, generous with her time, and a talented interlocutor.

For the friendship and intellectual depth of my mentors and colleagues from the Pioneer Valley in Amherst, MA: Michele Barale, Ute Brandes, and Andy Parker from Amherst College when I was just an undergraduate; Michele Hardesty, Susana Loza, and Mary Russo from my years as faculty at Hampshire College; the German Studies Faculty Seminar at Five Colleges, Inc. for their helpful feedback on the project; and the Five College Fellowship Program for Minority Scholars for sponsoring a year of research.

My friends, Kimberly Juanita Brown, Sonya Donaldson, Nina Fischer, Jessica Hermosura, and Vonick Jean-Guillaume, who kept me going with their optimism, energy, and "let's get this done" attitude. A warm appreciation is due Jennifer Kinder and Davina Miller for their numerous acts of generosity and belief in this project. Their continued presence in my life is invaluable.

I would be remiss if I did not acknowledge the Grillparzer Society in Vienna for hosting me and granting me extensive access to Grillparzer's archive when this project was just finding its legs.

Michelle Boyd of the Inkwell Academic Writing Retreat for showing me how to put words to paper with care one summer in Nebraska; the National Center for Faculty Development and Diversity (NCFDD) and the Faculty Success Program for grouping me with some of the sharpest women—Hanne Levinson, Jenn McArthur, and Vanessa Muñoz—who practiced the craft of writing with me; Barton Byg, Mark Foster, and Paul North for asking the right questions; Margy Horton, for her close reading and thoughtful advice; and Lawrence Lan, for his superb technical skills.

To my family: my parents, Lawrence and Wendie, and my siblings, Ashli and Mark. I would not be where I am without their unflappable faith in me; the memory of my grandmother, Loleta Bowen, and my cousin, Susanne Hercules, infuses this book. They exhibited extraordinary strength and courage throughout their lives.

And for my partner in all things who was with me through this entire project. I am profoundly grateful.

Introduction
Grillparzer and the Figure of the Female

Gender and Identity in Franz Grillparzer's Classical Dramas: Figuring the Female explores how female speech resists the negating power of containment, regulation, and punishment in three of Franz Seraphicus Grillparzer's (1791–1872) classically inspired tragic dramas: *Sappho* (1818), *Medea* (1821), and *Des Meeres und der Liebe Wellen* (*The Waves of Sea and Love*) (1831).[1] Grillparzer's interpretations of the material from the ancient world explore the ways in which these female figures were excluded from formal discourse due to their gender and how they contested that exclusion through acts of transgressive narrative performance as sites of female agency. In Grillparzer's adaptations, gender tells stories about the role of the artist and domesticity in *Sappho*, violence and the claims of kinship in *Medea*, and Hero's desire and religious calling in *Des Meeres und der Liebe Wellen*.

The representations of the three female figures are measured and intentional recalibrations of narrative activity that renders visible what once was purposely concealed, underdeveloped, or defaced. These dramas neither evade the crises that follow the three heroines nor those that they themselves generate. Grillparzer allows the narrative problems centered always on gender and language to evenly unfold alongside the central concerns of the experiences of the female protagonists. His work creates connections and likenesses that make their gendered alterity a surprising but rewarding opening up of semantic opportunities. These opportunities are the correlation between one idea and the next, one sentence and the next, even of one woman and the next.

Gender and Identity in Franz Grillparzer's Classical Dramas asks ethical questions about how the three female protagonists live in a world that was not meant for them, how to live lives deemed unacceptable, and how to be recognized as not particular (partial). These questions about their worlds knock the certainty of a solidified knowledge off kilter and make it questionable, vulnerable even. When what was once rock solid becomes a question, an interrogation of those formal and embedded categories becomes inevitable. Grillparzer's dramas are about this vulnerability that reveal the incongruities and incompatibilities of the world that Sappho, Medea, and Hero inhabited.

Later discussions in this introduction position Grillparzer's work in a feminist context, and I argue throughout for readings of Grillparzer's dramas that are inflected with a nascent feminism materialized through female speech that is both autonomous and ventriloquial. This project centers discussions about what feminism looks like in Grillparzer's dramas and how his work emerges in ways that are often bound to feminist discourses that exist in our contemporary moment. I understand Grillparzer's dramas as open to feminist readings even if he is not what we would consider a feminist writer. This connection makes his contributions to European drama and, particularly, to Austrian letters stimulating to a modern reader because of the contact that it makes with contemporary feminist theory. The work of the feminist theorists Sara Ahmed and Judith Butler plays an important role in this study. Ahmed's contributions to a queer feminist theorizing allow for methodologies and findings that engage in nontraditional ways of thinking feminism. Her positioning of uncommon narratives in the same space for nuanced and significant observations and analyses of real-life, folk tales, and canonical texts evokes a new way of looking at the world in which women are viewed as problems. Judith Butler's remarkable work on gender, sex, the body, and performativity (e.g., *Gender Trouble* and *Bodies That Matter*) also inflects Grillparzer's dramas. Her suggestive and complex formulations around identity disturb the integrity and stability of those socially constructed structures of belonging and admission.

In *Bodies That Matter: On the Discursive Limits of Sex,* Judith Butler, following Barbara Christian, writes that literature or "literary narrative" is "a place where theory takes place."[2] If literature holds this significant status as a site of theoretical formation, then I contend that Grillparzer's work is about theories of textual identity that lead us directly to the work of feminism. To place Grillparzer in this critical tradition of theory-making and feminism is an exciting space for him to inhabit given his past minoritization. Grillparzer and his protagonists upset the proper reading of ancient texts with questions about how those structures function. The critical stance taken in each drama questions practices by interrogating that world. Grillparzer's dramas are, in many ways, about authority and who gets to authorize. They are a struggle against the abstract. They are the difficult descriptive work. Work that shows itself as work in which feminist theorizing can secure novel readings of older texts.

Yet the value of a literary work comes from its ability to adjudicate among meanings and not merely to represent them. We can only know what is real by how it shows itself in language and Grillparzer's female figures are structured by that language. Even then, the real is a site of contestation. His versions of these stories about Sappho, Medea, and Hero direct our attention to language as the primary way to understand literary history. That is, what does language mean and what is the way that it produces that meaning? The gathering of meaning in Grillparzer's three dramas shows us a world that already has a shape such that relations of meanings rather than meaning itself are revealed. Grillparzer relocates the attention in order to show those relationships. He is asking something of these known "texts" and also providing possible answers to those questions. The idea of representation or the copy as approaches to literary texts resonates in the dramas such that they become reappraisals of these stories about Sappho, Medea, and Hero. The textual experiences offer us representations of each through the complexity of his writing, their speech, and our reading.

In many ways, this project is narrowly guided by the work of Sara Ahmed's *Living a Feminist Life* as a way of approaching Franz Grillparzer's three classical dramas and the work that they do. Ahmed's study explores how feminist theory is produced from the ordinary and the mundane experiences of home and work. It shows how feminists become estranged from the world that they critique and how that critique can be transformative as they become what she terms "feminist killjoys" and willful subjects. Ahmed writes that the feminist killjoy is "willing to go against a social order, which is protected as a moral order, a happiness order is to be willing to cause unhappiness, even if unhappiness is not your cause. To be willing to cause unhappiness might be about how we live an individual life."[3] In their struggle to name and then remake the world around them, feminists must struggle with preexisting structures that are so embedded in the everyday as to be invisible. Their critique of the world in which they must live marks their struggle with those foundational structures that surround them. Here is where Sappho, Medea, and Hero come to the fore and this is where a reading of Grillparzer's work as open to feminist concerns can be located.

What does feminism have to do with three dramas written in the early nineteenth century? The content of Grillparzer's writing suggests that he understood what it might mean to go against the grain. Spending time on the ideas that Sara Ahmed formulates in *Living a Feminist Life* opens a new way of understanding how gender thinking might be done backward, a thinking backward, or an unthinking. I do not explicitly argue that Grillparzer was a feminist in the formal sense of the word but rather that his work can be read as a feminist intervention where gender and difference become the site of the constitution of his subjects. I suggest that he dramatized figures who, according to Ahmed, were "sensational" and that this idea of the sensational is one that is located in her revised definition of feminism.

Early in *Living a Feminist Life*, Ahmed writes:

> Feminism is sensational. Something is sensational when it provokes excitement and interest. Feminism is sensational in this sense; what is provocative about feminism is what makes feminism a set of arguments that is hard to deliver. We learn about the feminist cause by the bother feminism causes; by how feminism comes up in public culture as a site of disturbance.[4]

Yes. Grillparzer's heroines are scandalous and shocking but they are also remarkable and exquisite in the sense of what is intense and sharp. As troublemakers—characters who cause damage—Sappho, Medea, and Hero are also *sensible* beings. They are aware; they perceive:

> Feminism often begins with intensity: you are aroused by what you come up against. You register something in the sharpness of an impression. Something can be sharp without it being clear what the point is. Over time, with experience, you sense that something is wrong or you have a feeling of being wronged. You sense an injustice. You might not have used that word for it; you might not have the words for it; you might not be able to put your finger on it. Feminism can begin with a body, a body in touch with a world, a body that is not at ease in a world; a body that fidgets and moves around. Things don't seem right.[5]

If we take this definition as a point of departure, is there a way to make a claim for a feminist reading of these three ancient figures that does not do a disservice to the literary life of these texts? This is what is at stake in *Gender and Identity in Franz Grillparzer's Classical Dramas*. It is about understanding the consequences of female life or perhaps what the risks of having a female life are. For Sappho, Medea, and Hero are harmed women and Grillparzer's texts show that injustice, that wrongdoing. If feminism can begin with a fidgeting body in touch with a world, then it is the case that Sappho, Medea, and Hero are indeed feminist figures, examples of those bodies and lives that have endured and remembered.

In these three classical dramas, the female figures assume the role of radical subjects and this radicality has a direct relationship with language. Words degrade the women, and the ways in which they craft their speech in response to that humiliation becomes a kind of linguistic insurgency that posits them as willful and excessive. This suggests that Grillparzer, often considered nonpolitical, might have been concerned with and excited by emergent narratives of women's rights or the *Frauenfrage*.[6] Grillparzer, possibly engaging with nascent narratives of women's rights such as in the writing of Wollstonecraft (1759–1797),[7] attempts to revise and reimagine these classical female figures, imitatively lending them voice by giving concrete form to their [female] discursive reality as a form of politics.

We see this political side, for one thing, through the mirror of the past. Grillparzer's dramas demonstrate that these ancient texts are themselves morally ambiguous, rather than explorations of the outright failures of the characters in the texts. You could say he radicalizes the act of interpretation in the reception of classical texts, abrogating context, and exploiting it at the same time to speak to a nineteenth-century audience. Grillparzer's dramas reveal to us how adaptation and interpretation become literary vehicles for exploring a range of social practices. The past, one might say, is the safest and perhaps also the best arena for adjudicating the present—because distant, because not threatening, because of its association with high culture. And the themes that emerge from extant ancient texts include the role of the artist, the sacred, and erotic desire. It is my assertion that Grillparzer read these dramas on an incline—a line of sight that was discordant rather than integrative. The posture of his revisions redirects the energy of the three dramas toward gender and language as central to their interpretations. In no way was Grillparzer alone in his engagement with ancient materials nor with female characters. The figure of the female often appeared as lead protagonists in the works of the two Weimar Classicists, Johann Wolfgang von Goethe (1749–1832) and Friedrich Schiller (1759–1805) as well as earlier, in Lessing's eighteenth-century bourgeois dramas, and then again later, in Hebbel in the nineteenth century.[8]

While Grillparzer found resources for social critique in these ancient dramas, that does not mean that he thought this was their basic intention. Over the course of three dramas, Grillparzer dissects and even denies the ability of the ancient works to explain complex structures, affirm knowledge, and uphold the certainty of the self for Sappho, Medea, and Hero. He often vacates classical concerns about form and calls into question the generic conventions of the tragic drama through a lack of strictly demarcated acts and scenes such as in *The Waves of Sea and Love*. In these dramas, Grillparzer claims and reinscribes ancient stories which are demonstrations of the moral and ethical failures of tragic discourse as a possible center for female self-possession.[9]

This book is not as interested in how Franz Grillparzer lived or moved in his world. It wants to understand what he *did* with this writing of three female figures from antiquity. This study is not a close reading of Grillparzer's interior world but rather how his writing is at play with concepts related to gender thinking through a contemporary lens. I do not argue that this gender thinking is either fully developed or even consistent. What I do want to demonstrate is that these three dramas interrupt the conventional. I intend to show that in these dramas Grillparzer's tendency is toward what Sara Ahmed calls "the wrong sort."[10] These wayward women struggle for life in spaces that show them over and over how very wrong they are. Yet they resist this understanding of themselves as unwelcome difficulties that must be (re)solved. Instead they insert themselves into the world of trouble. They stay with the trouble and agitate and irritate. They ask questions. They ask the wrong sorts of questions.

Franz Grillparzer is most commonly associated with a type of apolitical nineteenth-century literary production termed *Biedermeier* that lasted from 1815 to 1848.[11] Nonpolitical and conservative subject matter were considered the hallmarks of Biedermeier culture.[12] This designation is no longer one that is given much credence in the scholarship. However, in the nineteenth and early twentieth centuries, it heavily influenced the way that certain literature was written, consumed, and interpreted. Although the term itself has a historical reference and was applied to literature as well as to interior design, for example, it was used derogatorily to describe a mood that was centered on the domestic. Rather than the world of political action, this mood signaled a turn inward to the private sphere or a quiescence. The emphasis on the private realm and domesticity were features of the period and authors such as Annette von Droste-Hülshoff, Jeremias Gotthelf, and Eduard Mörike were often invoked as Biedermeier writers along with Grillparzer. Even though Grillparzer was linked with this form of writing, itself an outdated mode of inquiry, his literary output clearly demonstrates his interest and engagement with the world of historical knowledge and contemporary events.

Although Grillparzer has not enjoyed sustained attention in American Germanistik over the centuries,[13] this study demonstrates that Grillparzer's accomplishments in dramatic writing disprove the earlier formal assessment of him as a Biedermeier artist and warrants his reevaluation as one of the greatest Austrian dramatists. In "Grillparzer's Attitude toward the State, the Nation and Nationalism," Dagmar Lorenz opens with this noteworthy statement that lays the foundation for a recalibration of Grillparzer studies: "Grillparzer contributed more than any other poet to the nineteenth-century discourse on Austria and Austrian identity. Even though he was often misunderstood or deliberately misrepresented for ideological purposes, his work was most influential in shaping post-Napoleonic Austrian identity."[14] Lorenz convincingly argues that "Grillparzer . . . represent[s] psychological and natural processes without forcing them into a system or explaining them to the last detail."[15] Lorenz's assertion that Grillparzer didn't explain processes down to the last element is exemplary for its attention to the dramatist's method of writing. Her treatment of Grillparzer's Austrian identity distances him from dated theorizations of the Biedermeier period and is an important aspect of the conflicted relationship to Weimar Classicism and the limitations that Grillparzer ascribed to that project after extensive readings of Schiller's classical aesthetic principles, journals, and literature, which he held in high esteem along with the important writings of Goethe such as the erotic *Römische Elegien* (1795) and the essay, "Über Laokoon" (1798).

Grillparzer criticism has tended to be uneven and a site of contention.[16] Assessments of the dramatic writing developed along thematic categories. While these classifications changed over time and were highly dependent on the theoretical resolve of the critics, many will agree that the historical or national drama, the comedy, and the classical play were the most significant in his oeuvre. Grillparzer was also an essayist, prose writer, and poet. Whether it is content, style, or chronology, evaluations of Franz Grillparzer have distinguished between his fate tragedies, character tragedies, and classical tragedies. Grillparzer's first stage production, *Die Ahnfrau* (The Ancestress) (1817), made him famous as a writer of the *Schicksalstragödie* (fate tragedy). The case of *Die Ahnfrau* details how a generational curse destroys a family plagued by ghosts, infidelity, and the threat of incest. The plot and catastrophe of *Die Ahnfrau,* inspired by the Spanish Baroque dramatist, Pedro Calderón de la Barca (1600–1681), were filled with superstition, mysticism, and murder. As William C. Reeve noted, *Die Ahnfrau* is exceptional for "the false hero, patriarchal supremacy, female ambiguity, and dream versus reality."[17] This early drama sets the tone for Grillparzer's later fame as an Austrian writer and, in some ways, also sets the stage for his later antique dramas. Grillparzer's dramatic work is variegated and thematically rich. For example, in the character drama, the development of the play is structured around one central figure and his or her personal downfall. Grillparzer's *König Ottokars Glück und Ende* (*King Ottokar's Fortune and End*) (1823) is the story of the thirteenth-century Bohemian king, Ottokar, who through his own poor choices and excessive pride, loses his power, his influence, and is eventually killed on the battlefield. For the purposes of this study, considerations of Grillparzer's oeuvre will focus solely on the three classical tragedies which display an interest in themes located in the *Schicksalstragödie* with some thematic overlap with the character drama.

Grillparzer uncovered the problems of speech, subject formation, and its necessary deformation in the dramas—both the classical and the historical character drama. For example, Sappho is introduced to us as the famous poetess who has won the highest laurels in a lyrical contest, yet she is unable to keep that identity intact and appealing once she is at home on Lesbos with her lover, Phaon. Sappho is both famous and radically different. This distortion of who she is—poet and lover—becomes central to our understanding of her. Sappho is a subject formed by her poetic gifts at the same time that she becomes undone by the perception of that ability by her love interest. Her poetic gift makes her simultaneously attractive and undesirable. Her genius and her gender cannot exist in the same body or voice and thus she cannot be understood as a true and comprehensible subject. In *Sappho*, this is conceived as successive phases of enlightenment and doubt that are threaded throughout the drama. In the case of *Medea*, this deformation is equally significant since it hinges on how Medea is treated once she arrives on Corinth with Jason. Indeed, Medea is fully aware of how she is conceived of as a witch and a barbarian and the denial of her humanity by the Greeks. Her disavowal by that community indicates that her lack of stability and safety is undeniable even as she continues to resist the structural conditions that force her expulsion. In Hero's case, she is both a symbol of the proper performance of a religious role that belongs to the family structure and the defiant and desiring priestess who withdraws from family duty to be the representative of a virginal life devoted to the goddess.

The speech patterns of Sappho, Medea, and Hero are parallel yet distinct. They follow a similar arc, from (1) having tenuous kinship bonds and an uneasy place within a social structure that is imposed on them as the proper form of existence; to (2) perceiving things and growing increasingly conscious of themselves, the world, and its injustice, and vocalizing their thoughts and feelings in opposition to the world's unjust structures; to (3) persisting, against opposition, in viewing the world as the problem rather than themselves, and using their speech to resist it, to refuse assimilation; to (4) a final speech act of suicide, murder, and a *Liebestod* that completely negates their social integration, defying the world's injustice, and asserting some measure of autonomy. They differ in the particular structures they're oppressed by and rejected from, the volume and intensity with which they resist, and the way their final dissolution unfolds.

If Grillparzer was writing tales of willful women across three dramas, then they must have engaged their worlds as an activity or an understanding. I am suggesting that these works be read as feminist recuperations and that the female protagonists are instances of a feminist will. It is both an exertion and a projection. It also functions as an interference—a rupture. It is the interruption of dominant political and social structures—whether formal or informal. The three female characters share an affinity for trouble. Each of the three disturbs existing patterns of the social recognitions that organize life. What Grillparzer succeeds in doing is in writing oppositionally. He dramatizes the experiences of willfulness as a condition and willfulness as the remedy. Grillparzer's work does not provide successful models of survival, but it does reveal a cluster of female figures who reject the lives that have been pressed onto them. They refuse to conform to the proper forms of existence. This is a mediated willfulness that is written in the language of the problem. Grillparzer's writing does not unburden the characters of their problem-causing natures. Rather, he solidifies their otherness through a form of work centered around the idea of the question.

Once their consciousness has been attuned to the wrongs that have been committed, the three female figures turn their attention to addressing those wrongs in ways that process that injustice or harm. The three women turn toward the problem through the use of language instead of away from it. What they have at their disposal are words that make the problems linguistically tangible and explorable—articulating what it is that pushes them back and out. What is unjustifiable in each of their stories gains resonance through their command of language as a theoretical practice. The differences in the valences of their self-portrayals do not mitigate the ways in which their language perceives and understands gender and power.

While all three women participate in forms of culture, they are still denied full entry into those spaces because they complicate and confuse the social worlds that they attempt to inhabit. While they try to "get along," they also try to redescribe the space and thus become what Ahmed terms, in more precise terms, feminist killjoys:

> However she speaks, the one who speaks as a feminist is usually heard as the cause of the argument. She stops the smooth flow of communication. It becomes tense. She makes things tense. We can begin to witness what is being locked in this dynamic. The problem is not simply about the content of what she is saying. She is doing more than saying the wrong thing: she is getting in the way of something, the achievement or accomplishment of the family or some *we* or another, which is created by what is not said.[18]

But that is not all there is to the feminist killjoy and while the purpose of this book is not to graph Sara Ahmed's theories onto readings of Grillparzer's dramas, I find her highly useful for thinking about how female life or feminist life can often develop in a nonlinear fashion that can either be a conscious decision or an accident. In Ahmed's discussion of Virginia Woolf's *Mrs. Dalloway* (1925), I find an energy that can be applied to Sappho, Medea, and Hero: "We might sense how a life has a shape when it loses shape. . . . Perhaps feminist consciousness also means becoming aware of one's life as a marvel or even marvelous. Being estranged from one's own life can be how a world reappears, becoming odd. You might become conscious of a possibility once it has receded."[19] As women who slowly become unattuned to a set of requirements, Sappho, Medea, and Hero eventually leave their lives. That is, they leave the lives that have alienated them. "The shape of a life can feel like a past tense; something we sense only after it has been acquired . . . But we might also know this: we can leave a life. It is not too late to leave a life."[20] Whether conscious decision or accident, Sappho, Medea, and Hero disavow their lives and acknowledge that estrangement.

This reluctance of Grillparzer's heroines to submit to the lives that they have received demonstrates that they are unassimilable, they are errant, they violate the law, and they are, in very tightly focused and differentiated ways, strangers in the social world. Because they resist and oppose the traditional institutions that structure their worlds, the three are in a constant struggle to maintain themselves and their own sense of self through speech in the endlessly performative nature of social existence.

VENTRILOQUISM AND FIGURATION

What might it mean to take "the occasion to speak"? It could refer to time and opportunity but also gesture to the conditions under which one is able to speak. However, it could also be directed at the audacious desire to represent the self through language. It is in the interest of the self that one speaks, to make the self-intelligible. If one initiates speech and, in this way, "speaks for" the self, is it not a step in the direction of autonomy? What happens if one speaks for someone else?[21] Can this giving "voice" to the other be both liberatory and repressive? Whose voice is being represented in the speaking for? Is it the represented other or the speaker? Finally, what might occur if the occasion for speaking is a displacement of voice or a denial of agency of this someone who is spoken for? I suggest that we might think about ventriloquy, a performative speech act, as the way to engage in the complex negotiation of representing elsewhere at the very moment of speech in Grillparzer's three tragedies. These are multi-layered processes of speaking and reading as interpretative models for understanding how Grillparzer carefully curates the three women but also refrains from concealing their voices.

The dramas show us the writer, Grillparzer, also performing the role of reader. The historical "readings" of the three female representations are forms of reception. The reality of their lives is realized or made real retrospectively from the point of reception. Since reception reveals previously hidden and marginalized facets of a text, I take Grillparzer's interventions as a reappropriation of the text in service of a recovery and radicalization of female voices. Yet what are the problems of men's words in women's mouths? Grillparzer's impersonation of female figures at the margins of the known world might be a problematic ventriloquism that could be read as a form or practice of writing that reproduces gender alterity for the sake of allowing new configurations of speech to become visible. Grillparzer engaged in deliberate, announced, and extended revisits of prior works and stories through hybrid articulations that serve as theories of response rooted in the texts. The case can be made that the dramatist created a linguistic space where the possibilities for female speech could be channeled. However, his is the appropriation of subjectivity in the service of a self that is already at the center of literary and historical discourse as white, male, and European. But Grillparzer writes about decentered figures who were already found in the literature. They are not invisible. They are marked as part of literary history. In this act of "reading," these female figures become living subjects in Grillparzer as reader. It is our task to then understand how Grillparzer participates in the creation or rather expansion of the stories of Sappho, Medea, and Hero through his dramatic responses to their earlier representations in the classical world.

Gender functions as performance in language, ventriloquism is a mode of imitated gender performance in language, and figuration is a way of relating one (ventriloquized) textual gender performance to earlier textual gender performances in a way that produces new meanings for each text. The chapters in *Gender and Identity in Franz Grillparzer's Classical Dramas* explore dramatic texts which "speak for" or on behalf of the female other and thus engage in complex interventions in the ways that voice, gender, and agency are articulated and organized. The occasion to speak belongs to Grillparzer where he figures these female voices as a ventriloquism of his own response to classical discourse and the themes that he wants to excavate. Grillparzer's role is one that presumes a kind of silence on his part—he is the listener. Yet the effacement of his voice only amplifies the fact that he is speaking for voices that should have been muted in the social world but were not.[22] These are not merely female voices but they also belong to the other in society such as the poor, the imprisoned, the mad, and the stranger. Although the female figures in these dramas take on lives of their own, they do remain animated by Grillparzer's intentions because of his proximity to their stories.

Gender is one of the supposedly stable categories used in identity construction to make the self-legible; however, because gender is by nature a performance, one that is carried out in language, it (gender performance) may be unstable, fragmentary, or incoherent. Because gender is a performance, it may be imitated by an "outsider," from a distance. We can understand these imitated gender performances using the metaphor of ventriloquism, which captures how artists adapt old, "speechless" materials, both tangible and intangible, and give them new life, meaning, and voice. Ventriloquism is a way to think about Grillparzer's crafting of proxy gender performance in the language of his classical dramas: as a male writer, he ventriloquizes (imitates or impersonates) female figures from a historical distance. Male poets and writers have long imitated female voices in dramatic discourse, but Grillparzer does this in a new way—one located in a feminist voicing—for which the ventriloquism metaphor is particularly helpful. This metaphor is complicated in that it is unclear whether the speechless materials (the "dummy" that is made to speak) are really being given voice and amplified, or if, rather, the artist is merely projecting his own voice or a fragment of himself through the medium of the dummy/raw materials as a masquerade.

A (ventriloquized) textual gender performance can take on new meanings as a figuration of earlier texts—that is, when a ventriloquized textual gender performance in, say, a nineteenth-century drama by Grillparzer, is a recapitulation and revision of a drama from classical antiquity, both texts create new meanings by being considered alongside each other. Figuration is a way of relating literary texts across time, such that (1) the older text is situated in a larger context that produces new meanings beyond its original meaning, and (2) the newer text is crafted as a fulfillment of the old that somehow points beyond both the old and new text to an imagined future. In the case of Grillparzer's figurations in the classical tragedies, the figuration raises questions and generates possibilities regarding gender—specifically, how female figures from the past of classical antiquity can be given voice in the present moment in a way that re-construes the classical narrative as part of a trajectory toward the agentification of the female.

This conceptual framework—a web of concepts and assumptions around gender, ventriloquism, and figuration—provides a heuristic for analyzing how, in Grillparzer's three dramas, a male writer can imitate (ventriloquize) female voices from an androcentric classical past, in a way that imagines or creates new discursive spaces for female figures to represent, assert, and construct themselves in language. This web of concepts will not only help us get at the heart of what Grillparzer is doing in these plays—it might also serve as a portable literary theory or lens for exploring how other texts might be able to ventriloquize across time through figuration.

In *Art and Ventriloquism* (2006), David Goldblatt writes that "Ventriloquism is an act in which *things* talk—in which things are made to talk by one who is present to them. It is a language-game in which talking to oneself and talking through intermediaries has an important place."[23] While Goldblatt is primarily concerned with the interpretation of artworks as a conversational exchange in a poststructuralist critique, the way in which he understands how art necessitates speaking in the voice of no ordinary "other" is significant for an analysis of Grillparzer's dramas. This other is both the artist who is speaking and the artist who is listening. There is an uncomfortable slippage between these two domains. Meaning is created through that slippage in which things that are not typically allowed conversation—the socially muted—can speak. Goldblatt elaborates on this creation of meaning through the ventriloquial exchange in which every text and every voice exists in reference to another text or voice:

> We ask of artworks what artists ask of the world, "What does it say to you?", as a way of approaching the question, "What have you to say about it?" In an unbridled, personal anthropomorphism we speak for things, as if things were speaking to us, reading their meanings for us, in voices of their own which are, at the same time, of course, only our altered voices dislocated. The ventriloquist's audience becomes part of the total context of the act—a kind of witness and judge of the ventriloquist's performance.[24]

What is a text prepared to do or to say? This is also a way of asking what does Grillparzer want his ventriloquism to articulate as a meaningful form of reality. Since "figure" is also the word that ventriloquists use to refer to the dummy that is manipulated, I want to think of Grillparzer's "figures" as both the women who speak and also as figures that refer to the world around them through a dialogic relationship with others. In *Ventriloquism Explained: And Juggler's Tricks, Or Legerdemain Exposed: With Remarks on Vulgar Superstitions: In a Series of Letters to an Instructor* (1834), one compelling definition of the ventriloquist is that he is "wel-known [sic] to have the power of modifying his voice in such a manner as to imitate the voices of different persons, conversing at a considerable distance from each other, and in various tones."[25] Grillparzer's appropriation of female voices makes two important gestures that are contained in this definition of the ventriloquist: imitation and distance. Thus, his ventriloquism of the ancient canon in which the female is central to the text is a revision of gender, speech, and agency in which things do talk—both a talking to oneself as Goldblatt noted and the talking through intermediaries or agents.[26] Grillparzer's dramas, for a brief moment, suggest that the female protagonist can operate at the margins of social convention in the complicated game of ventriloquism—the voice and its origin. Grillparzer did not invent these women, but he revises these stories as heuristic devices to create new figurations that are not complete and settled. Instead, they keep calling back to the original at the same time that they are creating a new way of being that is both uncontrollable and sensational.

Yet, appropriation and dislocation remain central to Grillparzer's work in which many voices beyond those of the women are also speaking. By dislocation, I mean that the interaction between speaking subjects—these figures—takes place across time and space which interferes with the here and now of ventriloquism. The figures that Grillparzer voices are the key to understanding ventriloquism. If the verb *to figure* means "to make" or "to fabricate," then is it not also certain that these women are created to fulfill the terms of the ventriloquized relationship? Yet these figures also arrive from a past (the classical world) in order to be fulfilled by the present writing (Grillparzer's revisions).

While Sappho, Medea, and Hero may have voices that are well-known in the classical repertoire, it is Grillparzer who has granted them this new ability to speak more fully in the dramas. In his revisions, these three figures "talk back"—they are defiant sources of "telling" that challenge social and cultural inequities around the idea of the female. Thus, "talking back" in Grillparzer's dramas *is* a challenge to literary antecedents since there is no ability to talk back unless one has been first addressed. Medea is exemplary in this instance because she has been addressed by multiple writers that range from Euripides and Seneca to Heiner Müller and Christa Wolf. In another context, Mikhail

Bakhtin wrote that the author "... does not speak in a given language ... but he speaks, as it were, through language, a language that has somehow more or less materialized, become objectivized, that he merely ventriloquates."[27] The social institutions in which Sappho, Medea, and Hero find themselves preexist them since the three are already scripted through classical discourse. In the nineteenth century, Grillparzer's protagonists enter a world already formed in which expectations about femininity structure the ways in which they are allowed to access social spaces.

While Grillparzer's work depends on the classical precursors, his formulation of female identity reaffirms the basic instability of the language in which their social identities are constituted. However, Grillparzer updates and changes these gender scripts. Grillparzer theorizes gender but to get at questions of identity even when identity as such is provisional, coalitional, and contested. As I wrote earlier, while his heroines are "talking back" in each drama, Grillparzer is also speaking on their behalf. The narrative authority is with him and the agency which the characters might have been granted in Grillparzer's representations must also be understood in the context of male authentication. However, ventriloquy is difficult to understand in the context of Grillparzer. Is his work subversive or is it conservative? Does Grillparzer challenge normative values based in patriarchy or does he simply repeat them? Does the success of his dramas reside in their performative reading of identity? And what are the contradictions in Grillparzer's generic choice? If drama is itself performance or a presentation of a performance, how does Grillparzer then embed gender performance into what is already "a doing"?

These issues move us in the direction of further questions about performativity offered in Judith Butler's *Gender Trouble: Feminism and the Subversion of Identity* where she argues that "As a shifting and contextual phenomenon, gender does not denote a substantive being, but a relative point of convergence among culturally and historically specific sets of relations."[28] Desire, recognition, and alterity are very much a part of *Gender Trouble* as is the constitution of the subject, how identity, and in particular gender identity, is constructed by and in discourse. If we take Butler's reading as a way out of ventriloquism, then can we say that Grillparzer's work on gender is a script that is always performed as "sets of relations" that converge around questions of language? If performative gender is a set of behaviors that are continuous and compulsory how might Grillparzer's dramas of gender perform differently—that is, against that script? If performativity is the process of historical repetition, how do Grillparzer's dramas both represent a distant past but also his present? And how might his repetition also be generative—disobedient to the normative ways in which gender is done and subjects are formed?

If representation is about the granting of visibility, then Grillparzer's dramatization of Sappho, Medea, and Hero would suggest that there are political stakes in his work. Butler writes that "representation is the normative function of a language which is said either to reveal or to distort what is assumed to be true about the category of women."[29] Visibility is then about legal or civic inclusion as a subject. If this is true then practices of inclusion and exclusion are political acts that exert a force on the concept of representation. While the three female figures are formed as subjects in Grillparzer's work, they must still overcome the hurdle of admittance to representation. This is the unexpected tension in the three dramas. Grillparzer might have been attempting a recuperative female poetics but it is one already hindered by the very real representational politics that curtail the introduction and continuing viability of the "female" as subject. Becoming female in Grillparzer's works is as much about inhabiting a body[30] as it is about exhibiting a self that performs the compulsory deed.[31]

Simone de Beauvoir's *The Second Sex* might be an informative way to also think about representation. If as Beauvoir wrote that "one is not born a woman, but, rather, becomes one,"[32] Butler suggests that even if gender is a construction that is a culturally bound compulsory mandate, there is no coterminous mandate that the "one" who becomes a woman is necessarily female. Butler's reading of Beauvoir in this moment helps us to move closer to Grillparzer's own efforts in his choice of protagonists: "If 'the body is a situation,' as she [Beauvoir] claims, there is no recourse to a body that has not always already been interpreted by cultural meanings."[33] These cultural meanings, the residue of the ancient world inherited by contemporary literary discourse, inform Grillparzer's own representation of female subjects. That is, his dramas rely on the identities of the characters as gendered subjects and he interprets them as female in order to represent something that can only be done through the figure of the female. This is about language—the figure of the female as a marker of discourse and its possibilities and limitations. Although Butler's work defies easy categorization, it is most interested in the formation of identity and subjectivity, tracing the processes by which people become subjects when they "assume" the sexed/gendered/raced identities constructed for them.

Gender is also part of a political schema that encompasses discussions of identity in Grillparzer. If gender is regulated, performed, and embodied, then it, along with identity, is also incomplete and subject to erasure. Late in *Gender Trouble*, Butler asks if there is "a political shape to 'women,' as it were, that precedes and prefigures the political elaboration of their interests and epistemic point of view?"[34] Another provocative aspect of Grillparzer's writing of Sappho, Medea, and Hero is the way in which he endows them with a politics that may not look, at first glance, to be so. If the shape of gender suggests the socially constructed, then gender is defiantly performative and produces social conditions and practices that are bound up with a politics about female participation in discursive processes. The performativity of these three representations are part of a complex negotiation of personal relationships and civic directives. Since gender is not performed alone and is always performed for someone, I suggest that it is Grillparzer and his ventriloquism of these female voices that amplify and encourage the social and material conditions of their existence in language.

Turning for a moment to eighteenth-century criticism on the classical world, I want to think for a moment about Lessing's work with ancient materials "in his attempts to recalibrate the 'modern.'"[35] In reference to Lessing's *Laocoon* (1766) and, more specifically to Sophocles *Philoctetes* (409 B.C.), David Wellbery writes that the voice of the critic is one of an ethically motivated emotion: "They [the critics] have intentional content, they are attuned to the specifics of situation, they are tied to desire and belief."[36] Thus, if we also take Grillparzer as a critic, then he is also involved in a complex evaluative space where he must productively combine elements of emotion and language in these three dramatic works. Wellbery goes on to write that "The critic emerges here as a grammarian of emotion, demonstrating that there is in the play [*Philoctetes*] no 'single thread' of sentiment, but rather an intricate 'weave' of conditioning factors, motivations, investments, focal objects, and past actions shaped into the unifying contour of the dramatic plot."[37] This might help us think about what Grillparzer aspired to in his revision of the three female figures as a "grammarian of emotion." He is the critic and his felicity to the demands of his dramas about Sappho, Medea, and Hero demonstrate his strong sentiments about the work that he commits to paper and his obligation "to get it right" in his dramatic plots. His primary role here is in the representation of these women—how they speak and how to then portray that speech. This connection to desire and belief is carried out across these three dramas as a linguistic awareness that modifies the ways in which Grillparzer depicts his protagonists through an intricate weaving that Wellbery details. To engage with classical materials is in some way to self-consciously reinterpret and revise them in a critical move that transforms the materials. Grillparzer is doing something with the classical materials rather than just repeating those stories. His work is about an approach to the voice of the female that is located in a critical cross-gendering of his writing. At every moment, Grillparzer writes with intention: his work is directed toward a subject. He wants to say "something" about identity by representing women's voices in ancient discourse through nineteenth-century literary production, which I argue, is an emergent feminist theorizing.

Again, what happens to men's words in women's mouths? How does Grillparzer speak for and through a represented other? What does a female voice mean in Grillparzer's dramas? Are his dramas about Sappho, Medea, and Hero merely elaborations of female worlds that emerge from the imagination of a man? And, to cite Butler, "Are the specificity and integrity of women's cultural or linguistic practices always specified against and, hence, within the terms of some more dominant cultural formation?"[38] Here, I would suggest, that while Grillparzer cannot write outside of his own literary-discursive system, his work is a provisional attempt at bringing these distortions of the category of the female into the critical language of feminist theorizing.

These voices and what they express as poetess, witch, and priestess craft a response to the claims of the classical world. However, this study is not about the status of the classical world on the nineteenth-century imagination. This is Grillparzer's response to Sappho, Medea, and Hero and because these dramas are about them, Grillparzer is necessarily caught up in a space of representing where he cannot evade the issue of gender and language—and, to a latent feminist impulse. There is a cost to wanting to address Greek models. The cost is that to have them you encounter a culture whose public art at least represents the figure of the female very differently than Grillparzer's contemporary world.

Several things are at work in Grillparzer's dramas. These three plays are rich examples of how representations can be about creating new narratives and also serve as reformulations of the past. He poses a question about the materiality of writing and of reading in each drama by theorizing gender as a social practice that is embedded in language as "desire and belief." These are tragedies that contain their own commentary yet they also have to be *thought through*. This thinking through is about how the opening or even disturbances of meaning are expressions of or engagements with identity. Grillparzer's aim was to recover and recontextualize tragic understanding through the representation of female figures as ventriloquial figurations that would serve as modes of imitated gender performance.

I want to take this moment to refresh the idea of the tragic where an arc between, on the one hand, conflict and crisis and, on the other hand, gender and sexuality exists. What else might this concern be or what is the logic that governs Grillparzer's texts? Certainly, his understanding of tragic resolution in the nineteenth century is different from the writer in the ancient world. His texts are extractions and repetitions from one place and time to another. Social and cultural imperatives inform his writing as do the ways in which sex, gender, and desire are played out across each drama as manifestations of cultural authority. I read this as Grillparzer's revision of female characters into cultural figurations—accessing something that was hidden or that remained unexplored. In the end, these three figures serve as clarifications of rather than as impediments to cultural practices. Speech becomes the vehicle in which they are figured for reality through Grillparzer's cultural inscription. Read together, these three dramas could be said to enact a kind of coalitional figuration of gender that is political, linguistic, and feminist. The basic structure of these ancient figurations is that of a literary reality that steps forward from the model of tragic discourse. Thus, Grillparzer demonstrates that the uncontainable, unintelligible, and inordinate reproduce the proof of their troubled and troubling existence by speaking as themselves—through Grillparzer, that is.

Grillparzer's writing constitutes subjects and shifts discursive practices to female experiences that are lived dramatically and that are the achievement and marker of fundamental literary realities. The figurations that surfaced from Grillparzer's female heroines recreate and disfigure ideas about containment and exclusion, art and life, the sacred and the profane, the erotic and the violent, and civic and state duty versus that of personal inclination. This is all managed through the female figure—represented, perhaps overrepresented—in Attic tragedy. Helene Foley also details the presence of women on the ancient stage as destabilizing and disruptive:

> While women in daily life appear to have been confined to the internal spaces of the household, to public silence, and to non-participation in the political life of Athens, women play an exceptionally prominent role in drama. They speak for themselves, lay claim to a wide-ranging intelligence, criticize their lot, and influence men with their rhetoric denied to them in life.[39]

Following Foley, one might even wonder if Grillparzer were not espousing a female radicality that emerges as a revolutionary politics of female truth that signals that his writing is very much at play with the intersection of subjection, subject formation, and presentation in female experiences of life. Here, culture and belonging come together to dramatize mechanisms of influence (and exclusion from such processes of influence) as well as how the role of political networks, home and host, space and time, and center and periphery come together in the service of typology—that is, a foreshadowing of later events in the stories of the three figures. The cost of exclusion from these relational processes and the dramatization of the forms of individuation that the female figures undergo as nineteenth-century literary reinventions are narrative formulas that encounter the conventions of tragic drama, both antique and contemporary.

The unfolding of the dramatic discourse around each female figure is the presentation of each as a philological reality—literary representations of human action. Long denied subjective reality, Grillparzer's ventriloquized female figures engage in a novel presentation of what it means to be a woman that insists on speaking the tensions and conflicts of personal experience even as she longs for acceptance and rootedness, a crucial aspect of how socially constructed designations are still privileged as the only viable ones.

These dramatizations are achieved through the interplay of female identity in direct conflict with the imagined social world of the fifth century BC (and even earlier in the case of Sappho) and its gendered expectations as explored by Grillparzer in the early nineteenth century. His dramas stand in the midway point between empathy and criticism. Grillparzer tried to represent reality as it *was* but also as it *should be* by revealing the contradictions inherent in that reality. He troubled the inevitability of the catharsis that had been sanctioned and codified by classical tradition by suggesting that there was no single version of cathartic reality. Thus, his versions offer a counternarrative to that of the canonical. His ambiguous stance on the outcome of the traditional tragic drama did not assume that catharsis was indeed inevitable and the final pronouncement. Grillparzer's alternative reading of reality is one that blends difference with desire. Yet Grillparzer was concerned with overcoming something in his dramatic work. Perhaps he wanted to convey that catharsis undermines criticism of tragic drama? Or that identification with the tragic figure is a deferral of criticism? Hence, for Grillparzer, catharsis is a kind of social awakening but it is aimed elsewhere. While that elsewhere may be about the social and sociality, it could also point to the construction of meaning in the radical absence of sociality. None of his female protagonists actually participate in the social (e.g., Hero is sequestered in her tower-temple on the island of Sestos in *Des Meeres und der Liebe Wellen*). Each drama begins and ends with the absolute negation of social integration as the result of the initiation and fulfillment of the tragic catastrophe. Grillparzer recognized the helplessness of his heroines and perhaps that is where we can locate the elsewhere of Grillparzer's texts—in the opposition to the ideological force of the canonical tragic discursive project. Without dismantling the original stories, Grillparzer inserted a critique of that story-world of nonnegotiable truth by implicitly questioning the status of genius, canon formation, and theories about the disinterested timelessness of the arts. These narrative acts serve to dis-unify the action of the drama and create spaces that shudder with ambivalence about the story that has just been offered. Grillparzer's literary engagement with these female voices is also about the management of processes of attention, perception, memory, and compassion articulated at each moment of conflict.

STRUCTURE OF CHAPTERS

The issues at stake in this discursive framing are multiple even though they remain focused on a handful of closely related themes: (1) the constructive and reconstructive work of gender; (2) the dual and competing gestures of inclusion and exclusion; (3) and the dilation or amplification of discourse.

The back and forth movement between a set of thematic problematics *is* the story of these three women. These dramas are demonstrations of sites of social conflict and spaces of personal ambivalence even though not all the dramas are united by these three motifs. I do not address all texts equally. I am selective about the narrative shifts and dislocations and how they (re)present the problem of narrative attention and linguistic performance. My approach is not intended to depoliticize or dehistoricize the texts in question but instead, insist that the textual involvement and investment reside elsewhere.

Chapter 1, "Sappho: The Gender of Belonging," is a reading of the poetess whose story is particularly stimulating due to the limited material we have on her. Even as the most famous woman poet of antiquity, nothing is known with certainty about Sappho's life. All that is reliably known is that she lived on the island of Lesbos[40] between the second half of the seventh and the first half of the sixth century.[41] It is true that the overwhelming majority of classical Greek literature has been lost, and what has been preserved is as good as random. Yet, Sappho is a historical figure even if her biography and bibliography are substantially lost to us.[42] Sappho's life and works were effaced from the literary and historical record after a long history of admiration and allusions to her and her poetry. An excess of speculation and a dearth of actual evidence about her exist into the present day. Sappho is a fragmentary transmission—piecemeal and cryptic. If we retreat to the references to Sappho by other ancients, even in those accounts, she remains a fragment.[43]

From the time of Classical Athens to the contemporary moment, the dominant tendency has been to read Sappho's poetry through conjectures about her life. In this treatment of Grillparzer's *Sappho*, I perform a close reading of the drama by looking at moments where Sappho's grief is articulated and how she manages the uneasy dynamic between lyrical prowess and domestic happiness as a woman in possession of social and political power. From the seventeenth century onward, fictionalizations of Sappho's biography became the dominant prevailing form of reception of her person and her work. In German, as elaborated by Herder in the late eighteenth century, Sappho became the model of a harmonious original genius.[44] As a further example, Sappho in the eighteenth century "was enlisted in the service of competing discourses under the auspices of 'fornication versus respectability,' 'ardency versus gentleness' and 'masculine versus feminine.'"[45] In the same accent, Renate Schlesier argues that European literature and scholarship from the nineteenth century focused on the social status of the intellectual woman and the valuation of female sexuality.[46] Grillparzer's *Sappho* is shaped, in many ways, by the social and intimate unintelligibility of her lyrical voice. The drama is a presentation of a woman who has become essentially a dash in the literary world. Sappho's oeuvre is mere residue and opens to all speculation. This interpretation is endless, multiple, and yet closed. Sappho is a woman who has become estranged from her life. She only recognizes that fact at the end—the contours that have given shape to her life cannot rescue her. I devote a great deal of this chapter working through the text of *Sappho* since it establishes the themes of the later plays: inclusion and exclusion; the work of gender; and the amplification of discourse. All three of these dynamics are at work in *Sappho* and make their way into the stories of Medea and Hero.

Chapter 2, "Medea: The Construction of the Other," suggests that there is an appealingly subversive element to Grillparzer's dramatization of the witch from Colchis that is central to the competing gestures of inclusion and exclusion. Adapting his Medea from the plot of Euripides' *Medea*, first performed in 431 BC,[47] Grillparzer announces his heroine as a revolutionary figure. Medea possesses powers beyond male authority and understanding while also enduring the pain of faithlessness and abandonment by Jason. As Marianne McDonald wrote, "suffering in Euripides leads to arming: it teaches the victim to imitate the victimizer."[48] Later, McDonald also states, Medea "is not simple, and neither are her interpretations. She overflows constricting categories."[49] Euripides' *Medea* is dangerous. She is isolated, stripped of value and significance, cast aside, and enraged. She has lost her cultural and genealogical affiliation as well as her husband and children. Yet, in the face of this rejection, Medea refuses to release her claims on those around her, the objects of her craft that define her, and the figures who would banish her. Similar to Euripides' Medea, Grillparzer's Medea is armed.

The difference in Grillparzer's Medea is as a socially unintelligible entity: the non-Greek. She is cast as uncivilized, a barbarian, an exile, a potential pollutant—a wretched being who is to be excluded. Yet, while Medea is excluded from forms of belonging in the trilogy,[50] she inhabits a space of ambivalence that both conceals and reveals her difference. She is the stranger and a colonial subject—designations produced in order to recognize her as the other in a potential multicultural and postcolonial reading that goes beyond the scope of this study.[51] Her genealogy and defiance of the laws of kinship mark her as socially abhorrent to the Greeks, a figure of abjection.[52] Her resistance to this ostracism emerges from her insistence on representation and recognition, statuses that are multiply complicated and troublesome. She will not stop insisting on her legitimacy—her own exemplary standing. Her challenge to social mechanisms tests the viability and vigor of a male practice of power and social control, which regulate and abridge all segments of life, in particular, female life. These are usages based in patriarchal systems designed to limit the participation and standardize the behavior of women.

While Sappho cannot formulate a poetic identity that will anchor her to the external world of prose, in *Medea*, Grillparzer reintroduces us to the monstrous witch of myth, a woman who deforms kinship and authority on the physical and linguistic levels. Medea understands that the conflict is not between barbarism and civilization but rather between assimilation and identity—that is, the social operation of coercive power in language. The struggle is also about whose version of reality will prevail in formulating the meaning of language. Medea, unlike Sappho and Hero, will not die and allow a return to a certain kind of normalcy that is heteronormative, homogenous, and safe. As a central move, Medea has deformed what it means to *mean* and how life can and should be managed in the face of forces meant to contain and abridge those very possibilities. Medea's murder of the new bride of Jason and then her own sons is the ultimate act of rebellion in a world that refuses to make room for her.

Chapter 3, "Hero: The Challenge of Virtue," on *Des Meeres und der Liebe Wellen* is not a close treatment of the story of the doomed lovers, Hero and Leander, but rather, a reading of the way that Hero lives in a confusing context that is at once unknowable but also heavily overdetermined. This is a drama in which the classical is not an achievement of excellence but rather a lesson to be learned. In many ways, this chapter functions as a coda to *Sappho* and *Medea*. As Grillparzer's final completed classical play, it appears on first reading to reject the pessimism that pervades the first two dramas by not following the pattern of *Sappho* and *Medea*. In *Des Meeres und der Liebe Wellen*, Hero and Leander love each other unlike the animosity that comes to define the relationships of Sappho and Phaon and Medea and Jason. Yet the ending—the death of the two lovers—suggests that, for Grillparzer, the only possible way of making sense of the classical world was to understand it as a failure, or, at the very least, an unresolvable moment. This failure is about the ways in which female identity is threatened by social and political power that does not allow her to be a coherent presence in a livable world. Leaving a life is about figuring out something about that life. It's an unraveling of an existence. Thus, Hero's story, like that of Mrs. Dalloway, is about flight; it is about a way out of compulsory forms of relationality that practice power as their primary movements. This undertaking—the removal of the self from an oppressive system appearing in the shape of an idealized but constricted mode of living—is one that is critical of the very form of that power. Hero's flight then is a critique of that power. Her refusals are forms of social expression that think about the politics of private life that frustrate the achievement of power.

This reading of Grillparzer's classical dramas offers a syncretic interpretation indebted to ideas about the discursive possibilities around female intelligibility and identity undergirded by a feminist impulse. The arrangement of characters and events and the introduction of locations and themes are opportunities for evaluating the abundance of textual meanings about gender rather than coming to a conclusion as if narrative meanings were unbroken or undivided structures. The cultural position of each female troublemaker is central to her "presencing" as a discursive subject. Thus, the chapters will consider visibility and accommodation as central to discursive figuration and how each figure understands herself as a matter of speech.

The socially constructed worlds of these three characters become lived realities: Sappho is the alienated poetess; Medea is the rejected witch; and Hero is the isolated priestess. It is in these sites where discursive gaps become filled with the feminine. Burdened with overdetermined designations, they either knowingly plunge or inadvertently stumble into these gaps—a deliberate error or a rhetorical misstep.

Into this abyss the formation of emotional properties is as boundless as the process of narrative continuity and discontinuity in *Sappho*, *Medea*, and *Des Meeres und der Liebe Wellen*. Grillparzer's Medea, Sappho, and Hero strive for self-representation in their dramatic speech—even when it flouts accepted patterns for gendered behavior and defies conventional knowledge about the place of women in the private and public spheres. Their impassioned, melancholic, and disaffected attempts at speaking or telling their stories upset cultural concepts of whole and integrated conventional identity and call attention to the status of self-representation as a rebellious act of female linguistic creation and re-creation.

I have introduced into this discourse the idea that Grillparzer wrote his three female heroines in ways that created a theorizing feminism—even if it did not understand itself as such. The feminist impulse that drives Grillparzer's dramas remains central to my analyses of each dramatic heroine—the stories that he tells and retells. There are different ways to be and to write and Grillparzer was conscious of this in these three classical plays. In "Whose Counting?," Sara Ahmed poses the question of what counts as feminist theory:

> ... first, it suggests to me that some theories and not others count as feminist; second, it suggests that the demarcation of feminist theory as an entity is not a simple act, but one that involves a set of criteria about "what is feminism" as well as "what is theory" that are always in dispute. That is, the question "what counts as feminist theory?" suggests that *somebody is doing the counting*.[53]

Here is where Grillparzer is situated for many who study his dramatic work on female heroines, and, in this case, his classical female figures who produce those spaces of critical relationships. Where does Grillparzer fit in terms of questions of feminism and theory? Throughout this study, I read the three dramas as theoretical formulations whose narrative structures are designed to manage identity and instances of difference. While I don't argue that Grillparzer was *actively* pursuing a firm theoretical model for these three figures through his ventriloquism, I emphasize that his very act of writing recalibrates the social operations of the feminine through a sustained engagement with the female figures as theoretical formulations. Grillparzer's work is oppositional in that the experience of female willfulness is a condition and also the remedy and that this is a process of refusal. The dramatist is working along two axes. One that uses the classical world to revise known stories as a literary practice and the other that calls those stories into question as a theoretical practice. In the same piece, "Whose Counting?" Ahmed writes that "In some sense, then, feminist theorizing will always operate in a double register: it will both contest other ways of understanding the world (those theories that are often not seen as theories as they are assumed to be 'common sense'), as it will *contest itself*, as a way of interpreting the world (or of 'making sense' in a way which contests what is 'common')."[54] This double register is where I believe Grillparzer's dramas reside.

NOTES

1. All references to the texts are taken from *Franz Grillparzer Werke in sechs Bänden*, ed. Helmut Bachmaier, vol. 2, *Dramen 1817–1828*, and vol. 3, *Dramen 1828–1851* (Frankfurt am Main: Deutscher Klassiker Verlag, 1986). All English translations are from Franz Grillparzer, *Plays on Classic Themes*, trans. Samuel Solomon (New York: Random House, 1969).

2. Judith Butler, *Bodies That Matter: On the Discursive Limits of "Sex"* (New York: Routledge, 1993), 182.

3. Sara Ahmed, "Feminist Killjoys (And Other Willful Subjects)," *Scholar and Feminist Online* 8, no. 3 (Summer 2010), http://sfonline.barnard.edu/polyphonic/ahmed_01.htm. Ahmed writes that "Feminist consciousness could be understood as consciousness of unhappiness, a consciousness made possible by the refusal to turn away. My point here would be that feminists are read as being unhappy, such that situations of conflict, violence, and power are read as about the unhappiness of feminists, rather than being what feminists are unhappy about."

4. Ahmed, *Living a Feminist Life*, 21.

5. Ahmed, *Living a Feminist Life*, 22.

6. See Matthew McCarthy-Rechowicz, *Franz Grillparzer's Dramatic Heroines: Theatre and Women's Emancipation in Nineteenth-Century Austria* (Cambridge: Legenda, 2018), 14–24. As McCarthy-Rechowicz notes, "the discussion of women Grillparzer knew serves to: show how women's rights were being debated at this time in Austria; demonstrate that women Grillparzer knew engaged actively with these debates in writing. . .and suggest that Grillparzer was more open to intellectual 'emancipated' women in real life than his diaries might make us think" (17). McCarthy-Rechowicz goes on to detail in his introduction how Grillparzer depicted women through contemporary studies of his work which, in most cases, were female characters.

7. Mary Wollstonecraft, *A Vindication of the Rights of Woman with Strictures on Political and Moral Subjects* (London: J. Johnson, 1792). In the "Introduction," Wollstonecraft wrote, "I shall first consider women in the grand light of human creatures, who, in common with men, are placed on this earth to unfold their faculties; and afterwards I shall more particularly point out their peculiar designation." Later in the same section, the author addresses women as rational creatures who do not exist in a state of 'perpetual childhood' but can stand alone despite their so-called inferiority. Also important were Olympe de Gouge's *Déclaration des droits de la femme et de la citoyenne* (1791), Johann Gottlieb Fichte's *Grundriß des Familienrechts* (1796), and Theodor Gottlieb von Hippel's *Über die bürgerliche Verbesserung der Weiber* (1792), as cited in McCarthy-Rechowicz, *Dramatic Heroines*, 24–26.

8. Johann Wolfgang von Goethe (1749–1832), *Iphigenie auf Tauris* (1779) and *Die natürliche Tochter* (1801–1803); Christian Friedrich Hebbel (1813–1863), *Judith* (1840), *Maria Magdalena* (1844), *Herodes und Mariamne* (1850), *Julia* (1851), and *Agnes Bernauer* (1855); Gotthold Ephraim Lessing (1729–1781), *Miss Sara Sampson* (1755), *Minna von Barnhelm oder das Soldatenglück* (1767), and *Emilia Galotti: ein Trauerspiel in fünf Aufzügen* (1772); Johann Christoph Friedrich von Schiller (1759–1805), *Kabale und Liebe [Luise Müllerin]* (1784), *Maria Stuart: ein Trauerspiel* (1800), *Die Jungfrau von Orleans: eine romantische Tragödie* (1801), and *Die Braut von Messina* (1803).

9. Influenced by the writing and travels of the art historian Johann Joachim Winckelmann (1717–1768), the Weimar Classicists must have been taken by the early texts that inaugurated art history and the obsession with the antique world and with the 'south' or a neo-Hellenism in *Gedanken über die Nachahmung der griechischen Werke in der Malerei und Bildhauerkunst [Reflections on the Imitation of Greek Works of Art in Painting and Sculpture]* (Dresden und Leipzig: Im Verlag der Waltherischen Handlung, 1756) and *Geschichte der Kunst des Alterthums [The History of Ancient Art]* (Dresden: In der Waltherischen Hof-Buchhandlung, 1764) as the inspiration for a new dramatic practice that would flow into and influence social life.

10. Sara Ahmed, *Living a Feminist Life* (Durham, NC: Duke University Press, 2017), 6.

11. This term refers to the Restoration, a period between 1815 and 1848 that began with the *Wiener Kongress* led by Austrian statesman Klemens von Metternich and concluded with the primarily democratic European revolutions of 1848. For a spirited discussion of the term and its relationship to the periods also known as *Vormärz* and *Junges Deutschland*, see Lee Jennings, "Biedermeier," in *A Concise History of German Literature to 1900*, ed. Kim Vivian (Columbia, SC: Camden House, 1992), 240–61.

12. For a comprehensive study of this period, see Friedrich Sengle, *Biedermeierzeit: Deutsche Literatur im Spannungsfeld zwischen Restauration und Revolution, 1815–1848* (Stuttgart: J. B. Metzler, 1971–1980). For new interpretations, see Robert Pichl and Clifford A. Bernd, eds., *The Other Vienna: The Culture of Biedermeier Austria; Österreichisches Biedermeier in Literatur, Musik, Kunst und Kulturgeschichte* (Vienna: Lehner, 2002). This volume devotes more than half of its contents to

Grillparzer's work and offers interesting historical, cultural and political counter-narratives to or rethinking of the prevailing definition of Biedermeier. For a broad overview of the term Biedermeier that includes a discussion of class and wealth, censorship and artistic production, see Donald G. Daviau's chapter, "Biedermeier: The Happy Face of the Vormärz Era," in Pichl and Bernd, *The Other Vienna*, 11–27.

13. Clifford Albrecht Bernd, "Grillparzer: Austrian Playwright or Weimarian Classicist? An American Perspective on *König Ottokars Glück und Ende*," in *Aneignungen, Entfremdungen: The Austrian Playwright Franz Grillparzer (1791–1872)*, ed. Marianne Henn, Clemens Ruthner, and Raleigh Whitinger (New York: Peter Lang, 2007), 111–18. Bernd writes: "Prior to World War I, there had been little academic interest in Grillparzer in the United States. . .Following World War I. . .Grillparzer, who had been all but excluded from German literary studies before the war, was suddenly actualized as a result of the Weimarian [Goethe and Schiller] mask that was placed upon him" (111, 112). Because he was a playwright of the nineteenth century rather than the much earlier eighteenth century like Goethe and Schiller, Bernd asks if Grillparzer could be viewed as an original playwright in the Weimarian tradition or rather as a "second-rater" (113). Bernd goes on to analyze Grillparzer's place as perhaps a belated Weimarian, an imitator of Goethe and Schiller but, in the end, assesses Grillparzer's greatness as that of "an original Austrian playwright." Using *König Ottokars Glück und Ende* and its focus on a single character as his example to think about the ways in which the dramas of Weimar classicism were structured around the conflicts between constellations of characters, Bernd determines that while he [Grillparzer] "cannot be elevated to the status of Weimarian classicist, not even a belated one, it is nevertheless rewarding to reflect on him in light of the Weimarian theater" (117). In the end, Bernd decides that Grillparzer was a captivating and original playwright because of his divergence from Weimarian theater.

14. Dagmar C. G. Lorenz, "Grillparzer's Attitude toward the State, the Nation, and Nationalism," in Henn, Ruthner, Whitinger, *Aneignungen, Entfremdungen*, 1. Lorenz's analysis of Grillparzer is founded on his rejection of nationalist aesthetics in favor of a multi-nation state system which embraced plural identities and a worldly sensibility.

15. Lorenz, "Grillparzer's Attitude toward the State, the Nation, and Nationalism," 6.

16. Ian F. Roe offers a comprehensive and welcome assessment of the twentieth-century scholarship on Grillparzer in *Franz Grillparzer: A Century of Criticism* (Columbia, SC: Camden House, 1995). See particularly Chapter 1, "Major Trends in Grillparzer Criticism," 1–33. Equally valuable is his evaluation of what he terms *Classicism* in the same study in which he treats the three dramas that preoccupy this current project. See Chapter 2, "Classicism," 34–54. He provides an extensive bibliography of critical scholarship on Grillparzer that begins in 1872 and brings the reader to 1994.

17. William C. Reeve, "Grillparzer's *Die Ahnfrau*: Das Leben ein Traum," in *Modern Austrian Literature* 39, no. 1 (2006): 1.

18. Ahmed, *Living a Feminist Life*, 37.

19. Ahmed, *Living a Feminist Life*, 47.

20. Ahmed, *Living a Feminist Life*, 47.

21. For a separate and compelling articulation and review of 'speaking for another' offered on feminist scholars, ethnic minorities and postcolonial critics, see Linda Alcoff, "The Problem of Speaking for Others," *Cultural Critique* 20 (Winter 1991–1992), 5–32. Alcoff writes of the 'discursively privileged' [of whom Grillparzer is one] in her long essay and spends some time thinking through the "recognition that there is a problem in speaking for others. . . . First, there is a growing recognition that where one speaks from affects the meaning and truth of what one says, and thus that one cannot assume an ability to transcend one's location. In other words, a speaker's location (which I take here to refer to their *social* location, or social identity) has an epistemically significant impact on that speaker's claims" (6–7).

22. Alcoff, "The Problem of Speaking for Others," 11. Alcoff again offers a trenchant observation for the purposes of Grillparzer's speaking for the other and my own understanding of his project: "I would argue that when we sit down to write, or get up to speak, we experience ourselves as making choices. We may experience hesitation from fear of being criticized or from fear of exacerbating a problem we would like to remedy, or we may experience a resolve to speak despite existing obstacles. But in many cases we experience having the possibility to speak or not to speak" (11).

23. David Goldblatt, *Art and Ventriloquism: Critical Voices in Art, Theory and Culture* (London: Routledge, 2006), xii.

24. Goldblatt, *Art and Ventriloquism*, xiii.

25. Harry Houdini Collection and McManus-Young Collection (Library of Congress), *Ventriloquism Explained: And Juggler's Tricks, Or Legerdemain Exposed: With Remarks on Vulgar Superstitions; In a Series of Letters to an Instructor* (Amherst, MA: J. S. and C. Adams, 1834), 54.

26. Goldblatt, *Art and Ventriloquism*, xii.

27. Mikhail M. Bakhtin, *The Dialogic Imagination: Four Essays*, ed. Michael Holquist, trans. Caryl Emerson and Michael Holquist (Austin: University of Texas Press, 1981), 299. See, in particular, the essay, "Discourse in the Novel," 259–422.

28. Judith Butler, *Gender Trouble: Feminism and the Subversion of Identity* (1990; repr., New York: Routledge, 2010), 14.

29. Butler, *Gender Trouble*, 2.

30. I want to be clear that these chapters are not about bodies as such but rather that the writing wants to disengage with the category of woman as body/corporeality and man as disembodied/existential.

31. In opposition is the work of Luce Irigaray who argues for the inadequacy of the entire system of representation as it stands. Butler understands Irigaray's work as moving in the direction of the idea of the *unrepresentable*: "women represent the sex that cannot be thought, a linguistic absence and opacity. Within a language that rests on univocal signification, the female sex constitutes the unconstrainable and the undesignatable." Butler, *Gender Trouble*, 13.

32. Simone de Beauvoir, *The Second Sex*, trans. E. M. Parshley (New York: Vintage, 1973), as quoted in Butler, *Gender Trouble*, 11.

33. Butler, *Gender Trouble*, 11.

34. Butler, *Gender Trouble*, 175.

35. Avi Lifschitz and Michael Squire, "Introduction," in *Rethinking Lessing's Laocoon: Antiquity, Enlightenment and the 'Limits' of Painting and Poetry*, ed. Avi Lifschitz and Michael Squire (Oxford: Oxford University Press, 2017), 30.

36. David Wellbery, "*Laocoon* Today: On the Conceptual Infrastructure of Lessing's Treatise," in Lifschitz and Squire, *Rethinking Lessing's "Laocoon,"* 81. See also Paul A. Kottman, "Art and Necessity: Rethinking Lessing's Critical Practice," in Lifschitz and Squire, *Rethinking Lessing's Laocoon*, 327–44. The essays by both Wellbery and Kottman argue for Lessing's interest in different media as one that solicits 'the aesthetic imagination': Lessing's essay is an attempt to grapple with the special ways in which the practice of art makes the world intelligible (56). In a similar fashion, Kottman writes that one of Lessing's concerns was a ". . . broader sense of what art *does*—namely, through its solicitation of our imagination, art makes intelligible some feature of our world or our shared lives together that would otherwise remain unintelligible" (328). It is Grillparzer's great achievement that his heroines continually grapple with the unintelligible in their lives and do so with language that is charged and defiant.

37. Wellbery, "*Laocoon* Today," 82.

38. Butler, *Gender Trouble*, 5–6.

39. Helene P. Foley, "The Conception of Women in Athenian Drama," in *Reflections of Women in Antiquity*, ed. Helene P. Foley (New York: Gordon and Breach, 1981), 133.

40. In *Women in Ancient Greece*, Sue Blundell writes: "The word 'lesbian' is a modern invention: it only began to be used to denote a female homosexual in the late nineteenth century." Sue Blundell, *Women in Ancient Greece* (London: British Museum Press, 1995), 83.

41. Renate Schlesier, "Sappho," in *Brill's New Pauly Supplements 2*, Vol. 7, *Figures of Antiquity and their Reception in Art, Literature and Music*, English ed. Chad M. Schroeder (2016), 359. Originally published as *Historische Gestalten der Antike: Rezeption in Literatur, Kunst und Musik*, ed. Peter von Möllendorf, Annette Simonis, and Linda Simonis (Stuttgart: J. B. Metzlersche Verlagsbuchhandlung und Carl Ernst Poeschel Verlag GmbH, 2013).

42. The work of Anne Carson has been instrumental in reviving interest in Sappho. Her translation into the English of almost all of the fragments of Sappho contains facing ancient Greek of that poetic discourse. Sappho, *If Not, Winter: Fragments of Sappho*, trans. Anne Carson (New York: Alfred A. Knopf, 2002). Appearing almost simultaneously was the translation by Stanley Lombardo. Sappho, *Sappho: Poems and Fragments*, trans. Stanley Lombardo (Indianapolis: Hackett Publishing Company, 2002). Other recent translations include that of the British poet, Robert Chandler, in 1998. Sappho, *Sappho*, trans. Robert Chandler (London, J. M. Dent, 1998); Sappho, *Sappho: A New Translation*, trans, Mary Barnard (Berkeley: University of California, 1958; reprinted 1986). Margaret Reynolds's edited volume, *The Sappho Companion* (2002), is also a promising piece of scholarship that collects writing on Sappho from Pope, Rossetti and Swinburne, Baudelaire, H.D., and Jeanette Winterson, for example. Margaret Reynolds, ed., *The Sappho Companion* (New York: Palgrave for St. Martin's Press, 2002).

43. Even ancient references to Sappho are partial and unsatisfactory accounts. One poet may talk about the beauty of her meter or the richness of her lyric but not one ancient document has given an account of Sappho that is a full rendering of her life and works such as of Alcaeus of Mytilene, the lyric poet from lesbos and perhaps lover of Sappho or Dionysius of Halicarnassus, the Greek historian.

44. In the German tradition, there are several works that treat Sappho: Franz von Kleist's *Sappho: Ein dramatisches Gedicht* (1793); Friedrich Wilhelm Gubitz's *Sappho: Monodrama* (1816); and Friedrich Gottlieb Welcker's *Sappho, von einem herrschenden Borurtheil befreyr* (1816).

45. Schlesier, "Sappho," 363.

46. Schlesier, "Sappho," 365.

47. Euripides, *The Medea*, trans. Rex Warner, in *Euripides I: Alcestis, The Medea, The Heracleidae, Hippolytus*, vol. 3 of *The Complete Greek Tragedies*, ed. David Grene and Richmond Lattimore (Chicago: University of Press, 1955), 65–108.

48. Marianne McDonald, "Medea as Politician and Diva: Riding the Dragon into the Future," in *Medea: Essays on Medea in Myth, Literature, Philosophy, and Art*, ed. James J. Clauss and Sarah Iles Johnston (Princeton, NJ: Princeton University Press, 1997), 301.

49. McDonald, "Medea as Politician and Diva," 303.

50. *Medea* is the final drama in Grillparzer's trilogy, *The Golden Fleece*. While I do devote some time to a discussion of the first two plays (*The Guest* and *The Argonauts*), this chapter is focused on the *Medea* drama.

51. Christian Rogowski, "Erstickte Schreie. Geschlechtliche Differenz und koloniales Denken in Grillparzers Medea-Trilogie *Das goldene Vließ*," *Jahrbuch der Grillparzer Gesellschaft* 21, no. 3 (2003–2006): 32–50.

52. Julia Kristeva's *Powers of Horror: An Essay on Abjection* (1982) is useful for an analysis of the figure of Medea since she disrupts the proper social functioning of the community and is thus excluded from the broader society. Kristeva writes that what causes abjection "disturbs identity, system, order. What does not respect borders, positions, rules. The in-between, the ambiguous, the composite." Julia Kristeva, *Powers of Horror: An Essay on Abjection* (New York: Columbia University Press, 1982), 4. This is Medea's role across the trilogy as someone who has been cast off, vilified, and banned. Medea experiences dispossession and dislocation; she is marginalized and alienated.

53. Sara Ahmed, "Whose Counting?" *Feminist Theory* 1, no. 1 (April 2000): 97.

54. Ahmed, "Whose Counting," 101.

Chapter 1

Sappho

The Gender of Belonging

You came, and I was longing for you; you cooled
my heart which was burning with desire.

—Sappho, Fragment 48

MAKING SAPPHO SPEAK

Franz Grillparzer organized *Sappho* around the categories of inclusion and exclusion, modes that quickly move into larger questions about tragic discourse and its intimate ties to questions centered on the role of the artist and her place in the world. Sappho, as a female artist, is out of place, an anachronism that is tolerated as long as her exceptional status is recognized as an error. She cannot be both female and poet. How do we encounter certain figures as being inimical to the proper articulation of conventional paradigms? Sara Ahmed notes that "[w]hen you try to fit a norm that is not shaped to fit your body, you create an incongruity. You become an incongruity."[1] Sappho *is* her poetic voice but that voice also marks her as unsuitable. Her fleeting gesture towards a self-representation which would allow her to inhabit multiple categories fails. This is, in part, due to her sense that she lacks a harmonious relationship with her environment within the discursive norms of the ancient world. Sappho, as heroine-protagonist, exists in a marked category whereby she is already an exception—an incompatibility.

The drama, *Sappho* attempts to reconstruct itself as "text" even if the original version (what has been lost) is never fully knowable. Grillparzer's *Sappho* is constituted in order to suggest the constructive and reconstructive work of gender, one which must contend with a dispossessed female presence. This presence is the disconcerting ways in which the voice of the female protagonist upsets cultural tropes—a narrative strategy in which gender troubles. In what way does discourse become marked or intensified in this drama? How does Grillparzer amplify language practices in *Sappho*? What are the emancipatory capacities of this drama? I suggest that the ventriloquial movement in *Sappho* allows Grillparzer to make a strong albeit negative assessment about Sappho's role in society, one which is further complicated by the constraints on her identity as poetess and the fragmentary knowledge that we have of her story. Any conversation about ventriloquism or even how Grillparzer processes his female characters thus takes on an ethical dimension addressing questions of action and agency as gendered categories.

Grillparzer's reworking must contend with language that is not meant to contain female subjects. How does Sappho initially defy and refuse the curtailment of her activity as lyric poetess? If Grillparzer imagined the voice as an event or as a situation, could we read *Sappho* as both a ventriloquy—a way of bringing the speaker's voice into being—and as a conversation between Sappho and Grillparzer: A passionate conversation about the role of the artist and "real life," one that takes place in the dislocated space of drama as both a presence and an absence.

Grillparzer's *Sappho*, while functioning as a revision of Sappho, is also by necessity a false reading, or, at best, an imperfect reading which can only reassert its own inability to access the poetess through an incomplete restoration of wholeness. The text is stretched to its interpretative limits in its assignment of meaning and, as readers, we are faced with a number of problems which compel us to think about the point of entry into the text, the function of impersonation, and the consumption of identity. If language, which is already only a representation of an idea, is the only way in which meaning can be presented, then how does one create a substantial edifice on which to construct meaning? Language cannot tell anything with certainty since it only means what we decide it should mean. This is where *Sappho* becomes distinctive and where I locate the feminism of this drama.

Feminism must be built in order to mean something. It is not a readymade singular structure that one simply fills out with female presence but rather it is a site out of which questions are asked that create and articulate forms of feminism. This provocation may be preliminary and perhaps will be incomplete but it does offer a vision for thinking how female life might be performed differently. Throughout the drama, Sappho asks questions about how a life can be led, how it can be made hospitable, and what the requirements are to sustain it. These are not merely general questions about any life but they are also feminist inquiries that seek to formulate not only knowledge but a truth about the conditions of female life and how the nontraditional has no place in that schema.

Because he positions himself as speaking for or in the name of these female figures, Grillparzer is also moved or animated by the characters that he is representing. That is, he is embodying something about them, their aspirations, and their principles. Grillparzer's authority as author is dislocated if he himself is implicated in these representations as a desiring subject as well. If his interaction with the text and, by extension, Sappho, is one that is about embodying or incarnating, what can one say about the production of the figure of Sappho? In making things speak, Grillparzer is giving voice to ideas about the role of the artist in society through the figure of the female but also saying something about his regard for the fragmentary past of Sappho. What Sappho as an artist has to say about her role in society in the drama forces us to think about Grillparzer as being/embodying two selves—the one that is conscious of the self and the other that is outside of the self. This necessitates that we look at ventriloquism in *Sappho* as a two-way interaction—Sappho talks back to Grillparzer using the same words that were part of his performance of her. Does this mean that Grillparzer and Sappho share some form of human agency and that the ventriloquism might itself be dialogic? That Sappho is somehow speaking on behalf of Grillparzer? This is perhaps unlikely although not unreasonable given that the point of ventriloquism is that Sappho is voiced in a way that suggests that she is speaking for herself. This proposition reverses the logic of ventriloquism and makes claims about the kind of interaction that is taking place. However, is there a certain kind of reciprocity implied between Grillparzer and Sappho? I hesitate to name the subject here—is it Sappho, the figure or is it *Sappho*, the drama. This interpretation of Grillparzer's intervention marks a moment of undecidability or hesitation where discourse becomes amplified to include Sappho's unnatural voice.

As I wrote earlier, the interpretation of the ventriloquial experience is again a moment of making something speak and the staging of two voices instead of one. What are the different valences under which we can understand impersonation and ventriloquism? Anything that Grillparzer does is both a representation and an interpretation in *Sappho*. Once the ventriloquism has begun, it cannot be interrupted. There is an obligation to continue the impersonation which creates layers of meaning. One layer is the subtext of the interaction between the ventriloquist and his dummy and the other is the actual text, *Sappho*, which is made to voice a condition. Each moment of speech in the drama does something beyond what is explicitly spoken. Sappho is positioned in the drama as driven by or animated by certain situations, interests, and beliefs to perform certain behaviors, actions, and gestures. But there are others in the text that are made to speak—Phaon, the young lover and Melitta, the slave—are invoked as foils to Sappho as the tragedy moves forward. Grillparzer is responsible for all three voices and therefore represents multiple interests with differing ontologies. Moments in which time and its contemplation are activated are a necessary aspect of thinking *Sappho*. If ventriloquism accesses a space in which temporality plays a role in its execution, then is the impersonation of a female figure from the ancient world also one that is historically embodied?

Sappho appears to conform to the features of ancient drama. The six elements around which Grillparzer organized his *Sappho* signal a commitment, at least a structural one, to the roots of Western drama theory based on a causal understanding of the world that finds its primary subject in the interconnections and limitations of character and action through the tragic drama.[2] But it is a commitment saturated with textual codes that produce a multiplicity of discursive practices which function as organizational and thematic networks in Grillparzer's body of work. Additionally, *Sappho* is embedded in seventeenth- and eighteenth-century Neo-Classical definitions of drama. The unities of character, plot, and time and the organizational categories of the French playwrights such as Racine, Corneille, and Molière are perhaps the most prominent features of *Sappho* for a modern reader. These categories align Grillparzer's work more formally with Goethe's *Iphigenie auf Tauris* (1779;1781;1786) and *Torquato Tasso* (1790) than with other possible dramatic subjects such as Heinrich von Kleist's drama, *Penthesilea* (1808),[3] a text that Grillparzer greatly admired.

I want to suggest here that Grillparzer's dramas are layered and convey a dual "aboutness." A strange word for a challenging idea. One could imagine that this is the need for a certain form of sacrifice that his texts demand: a double sacrifice that demonstrates how suicide (*Sappho*), murder (*Medea*), and the *Liebestod* (*The Waves of Sea and Love*) are images of each other; they are about each other. In *Sappho*, this is realized as the *only* death in the drama. Her suicide. There is a happy end in the drama but not for Sappho but rather for Melitta, her servant, who, along with Phaon, Sappho's lover, have grown into their roles as a normative pairing that is gendered in the "ordinary" way. This duality is one that confirms the life of the now perfect woman, Melitta, while demanding the suicide of the once ideal poetic figure, Sappho. What might this mean for *Sappho* and other dramas where the female figure *is* the tragedy? Yet even as these female figures leave our lines of sight or even life, they become increasingly visible through Grillparzer's work on classical themes as a cultural transfer. Thus, the reciprocal effects of myth, tragedy, and the inheritance of foundational tropes from the ancients become a rewriting of that very tradition in order to expose the themes that are central to such a cultural transfer: exclusion, incompatibility, and coercion.

It is quite possible that Grillparzer's *Sappho* reforms a tradition by embedding doubt into its very existence. Tragedy is perhaps a site of threshold experience rather than the practice of social life. It orients Sappho in a particular direction—one that is alienating and that removes her from the life that has taken shape around her. As I wrote at the outset of this chapter, this experience is also about the constructive and reconstructive work of gender as a performative act. Perhaps Judith Butler would see Sappho as a person who lives on the cultural edges of the social world—precisely at that moment when she returns home in triumph with Phaon by her side. In the 1999 preface to *Gender Trouble*, Butler formulates an anticipatory idea that could be applied to Grillparzer's *Sappho*:

> What continues to concern me most is the following kinds of questions: what will and will not constitute an intelligible life, and how do presumptions about normative gender and sexuality determine in advance what will qualify as the "human" and the "livable"? In other words, how do normative gender presumptions work to delimit the very field of description that we have for the human? What is the means by which we come to see this delimiting power, and what are the means by which we transform it?[4]

This is a question about precarity and ethics. While Sappho's life may seem secure and certain to her in the public culture, it is undeniably filled with a very real danger due to its non-normative depiction of gender relations. This inarticulability of gender leads to a failure to announce what a human—a gendered one—is and also what a livable life—one that is vulnerable but in need of care—could be. While some lives are deemed more worthy of attention and grief, others are disposable and distasteful. One could even say that for Butler, gender is the fulcrum around which what is human and livable rotates.

Sappho's decision to retreat from the lofty heights of poesy is the dream of integration, the alleviation of isolation, and the transformation of lyric prowess into domestic desire—the exchange of the laurel wreath of fame (the public sphere) for the myrtle (the domestic sphere). But Sappho, the historical and literary figure, is indecipherable. The details of her life and her death along with a body of lyric with which to "read" Sappho might dispel what is a tendency to overinterpret. The illusion of self-awareness and confidence that dissolves under the tension of failed yearning animates Grillparzer's *Sappho* wherein the expansion of her discourse becomes increasingly discordant. The poetess is a hieroglyph, a symbol representing a concept in Grillparzer's dramatic narrative. Throughout the drama, Sappho remains an "idea" which can only replicate itself as "idea." And, as such, Sappho's anxiety and desire exist only in impressions that Grillparzer also understands as anxiety and desire. If it appears that Sappho is a hieroglyph (there is a part of this statement that wants to call Sappho an ideogram: a picture or symbol that depicts an idea or thing rather than a word), then one is still actually under the influence of those fragments as we read Grillparzer's words and the references to her by other ancient poets and historians. Yet Grillparzer does indeed make the narrative attempt to decipher her. In the drama, Sappho is lifted from the papyrus in order to become a shape, a figure, a story in Grillparzer's deft hands. Sappho's ability to understand herself or to be understood outside of the artifice of representation is a mere impression of a life. The violence in the drama is directed toward herself and her inability to accurately represent and be represented—to have a livable life.

In scholarly studies of the drama, it seems as if Sappho has a mobile literary voice. That is, Sappho can serve a host of critical apparatuses for the scholar. Taking a moment to refresh our understanding of the criticism might get us nearer to expanding our exploration of *Sappho*. Attitudes about Grillparzer's works were diverse and complicated. Renny Keelin Harrigan's essay, "Woman and Artist: Grillparzer's *Sappho* Revisited," is particularly striking for its review of the literature. Harrigan makes a clear articulation of the *false* dichotomy between woman and artist: "In contrast to previous studies, Sappho is viewed here as a multifaceted person who lives but one level of existence and who neither ascends nor descends in any real existential or psychological sense. Her art is public and lived, and it ceases to find an outlet at the end of the play."[5] Dagmar Lorenz's *Grillparzer, Dichter des sozialen Konflikt* is a thoughtful treatment of the dramatist with a rich comprehension of the previous scholarship on Grillparzer. The chapter, "Geschlecht und Gesellschaft," with a section on *Sappho*[6] and *The Waves of Sea and Love* among others, is one of the strongest presentations of Grillparzer criticism.[7] Lorenz's reading of Sappho's place in society acknowledges the exceptional status of the poetess: "In einer Gesellschaft, die Frauen als Bürger nicht einplant, hat Sappho Bürgerrechte erlangt. Sie irrt, glaubt sie, daß sie nun wirklich gleichgestellt sei."[8]

Keeping Lorenz's work in mind, it might be useful to consider a small sampling of mid- to late-century studies of Grillparzer's *Sappho*. "The Concept of 'Sammlung' in Grillparzer's Works" (1949)[9] or Naumann's "Grillparzer: Der Dichter und die Sprache" (1953)[10] both address symbolic concepts in the dramas to the exclusion of broader structures around narrative activity, literary history, and the ancient sources. These critics embedded the work in conversations around such immediate topics as coterminous literary movements, Austrian theater traditions, Catholicism, and the influence of Spanish Baroque drama on Grillparzer. Such narrowly defined investigations neglected to engage the "difference" embedded in Grillparzer's writing. Rather than an active grappling with the dramatic material in order to pursue a literary framework that would shape our understanding of Grillparzer's strategy and process, these scholars have read the dramas as the expression of the agonized personality of the author. The two articles noted above are earlier examples of how scholars are often distracted by the details of

Grillparzer's personal life as if these details were the unequivocal source and signpost for the same kinds of struggles that are portrayed in the dramas. They may well be but should we attend to them with greater felicity than we grant the texts themselves?

OUT OF TUNE

What kind of gender do we have in *Sappho*? How does it appear and how do we recognize it when it does appear? What are the possibilities for a whole life in a world that is circumscribed by gender, sex, and desire? Butler suggests, and I agree, that gender may be descriptive or normative:

> We may be tempted to make the following distinction: a *descriptive* account of gender that includes considerations of what makes gender intelligible, an inquiry into its conditions of possibility, whereas a *normative* account seeks to answer the question of which expressions of gender are acceptable, and which are not, supplying persuasive reasons to distinguish between such expressions in this way.[11]

But how does Sappho live her gender, or is the question rather how does she live in her gender? The normative is the prescriptive and established while the descriptive may be read as much more subversive since it allows for variance and multiplicity. Sappho attempts to work out a middle point between the two ways of doing gender—the normative and descriptive—but the attempt fails as the options for gender have already been demarcated. Sappho is "misattuned" to the normative construction of gender, and this, as Ahmed stated earlier, is experienced as the violence of that which is clearly in tune. The descriptive is perhaps not a site in which the reality of the world can be experienced for our protagonist.

Sappho appears to have considerable autonomy as the drama opens. She embodies the term *agon*—she has achieved the most coveted prize for her lyric.[12] However, that initial sense of immense choice and freedom in her life disappears as the plot develops and the tragic situation unfolds. The possibility of achieving satisfactory fulfillment of her desires diminishes until Sappho is left with an untenable alternative. She recognizes the incompatibility of her very real human desires with the world as ones that emerge from her status as a female artist. This role offers her a single and rigid form of freedom that impedes the possibility of any other form of self-actualization. She must be either artist or woman; one precludes the other. At the end of it all, the independence, authority, and freedom of movement that Sappho as artist enjoys as the drama opens cannot be integrated with this other Sappho, the woman, who comes increasingly to the fore. One obliterates the other, or, rather, the reality of the world forces the excision of one as if the fact of femaleness leads to the natural exclusion of all other possible identities. Thus, femininity is constructed as singular and undifferentiated; overwhelmed with social meaning, the figure of the female is burdened with responsibility within the domestic realm and prohibited from action in the public realm. Sappho becomes an alienated being as the drama progresses. She is what Sara Ahmed would term "out of tune": "To be misattuned is to be out of step with a world. Not only that: it is to experience what is in tune as violence."[13] "Violence" might seem too severe a word to use for *Sappho* but if we think about what the poetess endures as an estranged female figure, then might not violence work as an abuse, a discord, a rupture? What is in tune, the ordinary way of doing gender, goes against the grain of what Sappho's lived experience is. There are moments of abuse, discord, and rupture in *Sappho* that come to the surface when she is most vulnerable. Instances when her determination to be in the world—to touch it—are rebuffed.

Gender, specifically, the female gender as a cultural phenomenon, is regulated in order to fortify and endlessly reproduce a particular idea of social order. Femininity is meant to understand itself as flat, unchanging, and prone, a status that undermines what it means to be an artist—generative and creative. This simplification of femaleness into one half of an either/or binary denies the possibility of both/and, a restriction that is played out on both physical and cognitive levels in *Sappho*. The inability to imagine the possibility of a seamless and harmonious incorporation of multiple roles, desires, or identities for the female figure is as unthinkable to Sappho at the close of the play as it is to anyone else in the tragedy.

The drama opens *en plein air* in an idyllic landscape; it appears untended. The flora and fauna have grown wild and are excessive. An altar to Aphrodite, the goddess of love, stands in a prominent position. Sappho's dwelling is located in a mixed space—between the sea and the mountains. The scene of her return to Mytilene on Lesbos is one which is formed by intersecting processes whose distinctive and multiple topographies frame the events of the drama which follow:

> Freie Gegend. Im Hintergrunde das Meer, dessen flaches Ufer sich gegen die linke Seite zu in felsichten Abstufungen emporhebt. Hart am Ufer ein Altar der Aphrodite. Rechts im Vorgrunde der Eingang einer Grotte mit Gesträuch und Eppich umwachsen; weiter zurück das Ende eines Säulenganges mit Stufen, zu Sapphos Wohnung führend. Auf der linken Seite des Vorgrundes ein hohes Rosengebüsch mit einer Rasenbank davor.[14]

Sappho's home is thrown into confusion at her triumphant return from Olympia. Rhamnes, once the tutor to Sappho and a slave, oversees the household and the slaves who serve Sappho. He tends to the routine matters of the home, activities that are largely inside and hidden from view. Cymbals and flutes, the music of revelry, interrupt this busy domesticity led by Rhamnes. This is a home in which the conventional gender roles have been reversed. Not only is Sappho an artist, she is also the head of the household and of Mytilene. And Rhamnes, a man, is subordinate to her. However, a simple reversal of roles is not quite the case. Her poetic talent was cultivated by Rhamnes, a male figure who has been narratively feminized in these first moments of the drama. Rhamnes equipped Sappho with the tools for competing in a world dominated by the masculine by introducing her to the lyric. She has won a place for herself among poets and simultaneously joined the ranks of men. Sappho engaged in a "noble strife" in order to win immortal prestige as a poet, but in so doing has upset the understanding of what it means to be a poet and what it means to be a man in the Greek world. Ahmed writes, "If environments are built to enable some bodies to do what they can, environments can be what stops bodies from doing: a *cannot* is how some bodies meet an environment."[15] Ahmed's analysis reveals to us how Sappho has disrupted categories and spaces that were never created to contain her. She is misattuned and her world is telling her that she is a cultural outsider and that she ought not to insist on engaging her environment as a full participant in any kind of doing. What is most clearly absent in this opening scene is any discussion of her actual achievement as a woman among men. The androcentric environment of Olympia was clearly not designed to accommodate her. The language of classification permeates the first scene and indicates that rank is a significant constituent of meaning in this drama. Sappho has won first place for poetry and song at Olympia, a victory which only increases her renown. Rhamnes announces:

Sie kehret von Olympia, hat den Kranz,
Den Kranz des Sieges hat sie sich errungen;
Im Angesicht des ganzen Griechenlands,
Als Zeugen edlen Wettkampfs dort versammelt,
Ward ihr der Dichtkunst, des Gesanges Preis.
Drum eilt das Volk ihr jauchzend nun entgegen,
Schickt auf des Jubels breiten Fittigen
Den Namen der Beglückten zu den Wolken.
Und diese Hand war's, ach, und dieser Mund,
Der sie zuerst der Leier Sprach' entlocken
Und des Gesanges regellose Freiheit
Mit süßem Band des Wohllauts binden lehrte. (*Sappho*, 1.1.11–22)[16]

Her presence at the games, one can only assume, was itself an anomaly, her participation unexpected, and her victory unprecedented. Her performance increases her fame in all of Greece but also singles her out as transgressive, a woman out of bounds, one who is bumping up against the cannot of her environment.

Rhamnes positions Sappho as the master by his word choice and the grammatical form of the word. "Bereitet lieber alles drin im Hause, / Nur dienend ehrt der Diener seinen Herrn" (*Sappho*, 1.1.28–29).[17] There is no distinct word for a female leader which indicates that the concept can only gain meaning through the masculine incarnation. In addition, Rhamnes increases the masculinity of Sappho's status by maintaining the form, "Herr," instead of replacing it with "Herrin." By refusing to feminize Sappho's leadership and power, Rhamnes linguistically affirms the power of the masculine form even as he carves out a space for the feminine within that structure. However, the space that Rhamnes creates for Sappho as artist and leader is invisible. The gender of her body is hidden beneath the gender of the language. It is only at the close of this first scene, after a male figure is detected in the distance, that Rhamnes then refers to Sappho as "Herrin:" "Ihr solltet wissen, daß die Herrin naht" (*Sappho*, 1.1.35).[18] Initially, Sappho is explicitly narrated as sexless, which, in this instance, means male. The detection of an indistinct figure at her side changes her from master to mistress. What forces gender to emerge as an identifying marker of Sappho is the approach of the "Herr," an introduction that recasts her as "Herrin."

The representation of Sappho rests on the tropes of Greek heroic striving and mastery. The chariot, the horses, the richness of her wardrobe, the lyre, and the laurel wreath document her achievement in Olympia as a poet but also testify to her elevated position in this society. Her entrance and the crowd that assembles to greet her are significant because they both isolate and accentuate Sappho's exceptional status. Sappho's speech frames her connection to the crowd but it also suspends and impedes that connection to the throng because of her exalted status even if she positions herself as both a member and leader of the islanders. Additionally, she delivers this speech with the mute Phaon (the shadowy figure of the first scene) by her side:

Dank Freunde, Landsgenossen Dank.
Um euretwillen freut mich dieser Kranz
Der nur den Bürger ziert, den Dichter drückt,
In eurer Mitte nenn ich ihn erst mein. (*Sappho*, 1.2.44–47)[19]

Sappho addresses the waiting crowd as friends, as countrymen and finally, indirectly, as citizens, even though she, as a woman, can herself never be a "citizen." While the wreath is a boon to the victor-as-citizen, a way of bringing prestige to the victor's homeland, it oppresses the victor-as-woman.

Sappho understands the reciprocal nature of the relationship with the people of Lesbos and praises them for their support of the "Bürger/Dichter." Whether convention of speech or error, Sappho speaks of herself in the third person, but does not use the feminine form of either citizen or poet. Is it possible that at this moment in her life, Sappho does not recognize that there is a difference? She may either refuse to understand herself in terms of gendered language, she may refuse to think of citizen or poet as gendered terms, or she may not have learned that a distinction exists in culture, law, politics, and language in an androcentric world. She uses a form of language which excludes her from its own meaning. The logic of citizen and poet is gathered up within itself—the meaning of which is singular, inflexible, and male. Her use of these words to represent herself to the people displays a lack of consciousness about her anomalous status. She is a woman and thus can neither be citizen nor poet. The speech that she delivers is as unseemly as is her participation in a competition so far from home, a speech that she loudly delivers surrounded by an eager throng that hangs on every word:

Hier, wo der Jugend träumende Entwürfe,
Wo des Beginnens schwankendes Bestreben,
Wo des Vollbringens wahnsinn-glühnde Lust
Mit eins vor meine trunkne Seele treten,
Hier, wo Zypressen von der Eltern Grab
Mir leisen Geistergruß herüberlispeln,
Hier, wo so mancher Frühverblichne ruht
Der meines Strebens, meines Wirkens sich erfreut,
In eurem Kreis, in meiner Lieben Mitte,
Hier dünkt mir dieser Kranz erst kein Verbrechen,
Hier wird die frevle Zier mir erst zum Schmuck. (*Sappho*, 1.2.48–58)[20]

The syntax and diction of Sappho's speech is noble—pitched at a level of lyrical intensity that is redolent of the classical dramas and poetry of Goethe and Schiller. She speaks of "schwankendes Bestreben," "Vollbringens wahnsinn-glühnde Lust," and a "trunkne Seele." These imitative phrases are aimed at the achievement of a poetic stature in which a humbly triumphant Sappho is through her discursive practices reintegrated into her social world.

Sappho has introduced Phaon to the people as the newest citizen. She grants him membership into this society by naming him "Bürger" and herself as his feminine counterpart, "Bürgerin," which reassigns her gender identity from her first words in the scene where she had designated herself as a masculine citizen, Bürger. Her words of praise embarrass her consort, which prompts him to say:

Du spottest Sappho eines armen Jünglings!
Wodurch hätt' ich so reiches Lob verdient?
Wer glaubt so Hohes von dem Unversuchten? (*Sappho*, 1.2.80–82)[21]

Phaon's bashful questioning of Sappho betrays his insecurity in his new surroundings, but also reveals much about the power dynamic in the relationship between the two. His statement gives the impression of a youth with an uncertain sense of self, one that is "unversucht [untested]" and unworthy of such lavish praise. Admitting his youth, Sappho insists upon Phaon's natural talents and his fitness for the noble life of a man. Through word and deed, she claims, Phaon has proven himself to be a stalwart friend in possession of innate aptitudes. Sappho's testimony on his behalf endows his character with multiple dimensions that point to the wisdom of her choice of him as citizen and to his status as a man:

Von den Besten stammt er
Und mag auch kühn sich stellen zu den Besten!
Obschon die Jahre ihn noch Jüngling nennen,
Hat ihn als Mann so Wort als Tat erwiesen.
Wo ihr des Kriegers Schwert bedürft,
Des Redners Lippe und des Dichters Mund,
Des Freundes Rat, des Helfers starken Arm,
Dann ruft nach ihm und suchet länger nicht. (*Sappho*, 1.2.72–79)[22]

Sappho depicts Phaon as a warrior, an orator, a poet, a friend, and a helpmate. His is a body that can carry out multiple roles which function at the level of speech and action. His is a talent so rich and encompassing that one need not seek any other. But why has Sappho chosen to introduce him thusly? Her speech provides a script for Phaon; she gives him an identity which is the most pleasing in her mind; one that might well have been fully hers if she were a "Jüngling" and not a woman. Why has she chosen to name him poet and orator when, in fact, he is a simple ferryman? What is at stake for Sappho in assigning these traits to one who is, by his own admission, untested? Phaon is a callow youth in contrast to Sappho, who has been tested and emerged successful. Her attempts to lend him credibility are transparent because she wishes to extend to him the same stature that she holds. Sappho desires a formal authentication of Phaon, the plunder of her poetic conquest, and perhaps, the greatest proof of her victory in Olympia—perhaps even more compelling than the laurel wreath.

Sappho's presentation of Phaon reproduces and reverses a marital convention in which the man introduces the woman to his household and demands its loyalty to her. Phaon plays the part well—he is humble, blushing, and subdued—as any new bride would be. Sappho has chosen him—"auf ihn fiel meine Wahl"—in an act that is subversive on several levels. By claiming Phaon, Sappho destabilizes social conventions about the conduct of gender relations. Her selection of Phaon also indicates that she understands herself as autonomous. Sappho does not recognize that the ability to choose or rather the belief that one has a choice is extraordinary. Slaves and servants do not have options. Stating that she has chosen Phaon indicates that Sappho does not know that women are also in the same category as slaves and servants: they are not endowed with the ability to have preferences. Sappho behaves in a way that suggests that her status as artist outperforms her status as woman. She does this by juxtaposing the selection of Phaon with the practice of poetry, as Sappho narrates it—"Er war bestimmt, in seiner Gaben Fülle, / Mich von der Dichtkunst wolkennahen Gipfeln / In dieses Lebens heitre Blütentäler / Mit sanft bezwingender Gewalt herabzuziehn" (*Sappho*, 1.2.89–92).[23] Her confession, voiced as poesy, reveals the essential opposition between artistic accomplishment and an ordinary life. It also shows that Phaon, too, has power of another sort. Additionally, it is Phaon, her erotic interest, who pulls her down, with delicate force, from the otherworldly heights of the lyric into the considerable depths of domesticity, an act which intensifies the incompatibility of the artistic vision with that of the private realm. The ironies of this new predicament are lost on Sappho, who, in this speech, is fully immersed in "Dichtkunst" [poetry] and is as blind to the gravity of her words as she is to the gravity that draws her down to Phaon.

Sappho, as poetess, understands and takes delight in the metaphorical significance of her words that marks a descent into the blossomed valleys of desire; it is the meaning behind the reverie which remains unexamined. Her vision is a fiction—a fancy of her poetic imagination whose meaning, on some level, she has internalized as ideal. Sappho's choice, expressed in the symbolic language of poesy, tumbles earthbound from the peaks of art into what is, in effect, a hole. This valley which she calls life is reclusive; it is a hollow space inside of another structure. If music and poetry are dispersive activities, which expand and elevate, then the art of love signals a retreat inward. Sappho's intent to exchange one form of life for another is a linguistic decision that has ramifications in the material world. By declaring the either/or status of her life heretofore, Sappho denies herself simultaneous occupancy of the both/and. By selecting Phaon and the trappings of domesticity, Sappho severs herself from poetry and imperils her identity as an artist and is precluded from making any other choices. "Phaon" has replaced "Wahl [choice]." More precisely, choice is no longer an option once she has made the choice for conventional domesticity.

Although conceived as a dialogue, the exchanges between Sappho and Phaon do little to enhance their understanding of each other. The third scene, the first in which they are alone, is constructed as a series of long stanzas in which Sappho and Phaon alternately talk past each other. The dialogue as a form of communication in which disagreements and discord may be articulated and resolved is pushed to the perimeter of this encounter. This profusion of language impedes direct access to true communion between Phaon and Sappho. Rather they are personal musings that indulge in individual fantasies about their uncommon situations. Sappho recounts the conditions of her life, her relationships, her emotional fragility, and her desperate love for Phaon in an unbroken verse of twenty-four lines. This dramatic testimony is then followed by a series of revelations by Phaon interspersed by one-to-two-line exclamatory responses by Sappho. The scene closes with Sappho's delivery of two long poetic ripostes to Phaon's confessions. What is perhaps the most striking aspect of Sappho's opening speech to Phaon is that it is not simply composed as dramatic verse but it is acutely aware of its function as poetry. Phaon responds to Sappho's outpouring of love by narrating his bemusement, his star-struck innocence, and his fantasy with respect to Sappho while utilizing diction that competes with Sappho's own. Her versification of disappointment is met by his imitative versification of inexperience. Caught up in his reverie, Phaon plays with the lyrical possibilities of his new position. In four long speeches, he reconstructs his life and the events that transported him to Lesbos as a melodrama of social mobility. Phaon's lines are the clearest evidence of the disconnect that exists between the imagination and reality. In his language, Sappho exists as a symbol overflowing with meaning for her young lover. She is desired for what she represents rather than for who she is. However, that statement might not accurately get at the obstacle because the suspicion grows that Sappho also understands herself as a symbol, a visible sign, or a token.

Sappho's lengthy versification of love and loss is answered by Phaon with "Erhabne Frau [sublime woman]." Phaon's first response to Sappho's lyrical formulation remains within the realm of an elevated and lofty mode of address, which is both formal and impersonal. This *Erhabenheit* suggests that though Phaon is transformed by Sappho's speech, the effect on him was as poetry to a rapt listener rather than words of devotion to the sublimity of a lover. He recognizes this sublimity on a purely academic level: her method is a sophisticated one that employs several poetic techniques that moves the listener to extremes of emotion. Sappho has brought Phaon to the threshold of love without transporting him to the critical state of being in love, a condition that is all too clear to Sappho who asks, "Sagt dir dein Herz denn keinen süßern Namen?" (*Sappho*, 1.3.131).[24] Phaon can only respond to these tender words and entreaties as one would to an exalted but still distant figure's compliments. His response to her urging to love is to narrate his journey from obscurity to prominence. The exchanges between the two hesitate between the exploration of reputation and fame and that of obscurity and anonymity, or perhaps, even more precisely, personal identity. Phaon, as the man "without a name" is measured against Sappho, a woman of reputation, who is nothing but name. In three sentences, Phaon tells of himself and his dream-like exodus to Sappho. He has suddenly become vocal after declaring his deficit in this area:

Weiß ich doch kaum was ich beginne, was ich sage
Aus meines Lebens stiller Niedrigkeit
Hervorgezogen—an den Strahl des Lichts,
Auf einen luftigen Gipfel hingestellt
Nach dem der Besten Wünsche fruchtlos zielen,
Erliege ich der unverhofften Wonne,
Kann ich mich selbst in all dem Glück nicht finden. (*Sappho*, 1.3.132–38)[25]

Phaon does know what to say and how to begin. His account of his rather prosaic life rivals the poetic diction that earned Sappho the laurel wreath in Olympia and which she had practiced earlier in the scene. However, Phaon approaches a level of stylistic sophistication that is unexpected in a young man who had claimed obscurity for himself. Although he has no lyre and therefore cannot accompany his words with music, his testimony is redolent of lyric.

Phaon's dreamlike experience of Sappho undercuts the intensity of her feelings for him. The reader senses the disproportion of emotion between the lovers. He is caught up in his own artless infatuation with the poetess who gives him a "name"; Sappho is smitten with the inexperienced youth who flatters her ego and banishes her loneliness. With Phaon as her companion, Sappho hopes to blend life and art:

Laß uns denn trachten, mein geliebter Freund,
Uns beider Kränze um die Stirn zu flechten,
Das Leben aus der Künste Taumelkelch,
Die Kunst zu schlürfen aus der Hand des Lebens. (*Sappho*, 3.3.280–83)[26]

Convinced of the suitability of the two, Sappho believes that she will be able to combine the heady pleasures of an erotic life with Phaon with the still headier gratification to be found in music and song. Recalling her youth when the world was still unknown, full of promise, and magical, Sappho dwells in the bitter lessons that life and love have taught her, schooling which she fears may have ruined her for a life of love:

Da steh ich an dem Rand der weiten Kluft,
Die zwischen ihm und mir verschlingend gähnt;
Ich seh das goldne Land herüberwinken.
Mein Aug' erreicht es, aber nicht mein Fuß. (*Sappho*, 1.5.394–97)[27]

Although she can conceive of happiness and pleasure, Sappho cannot complete this picture without the presence of a chasm to threaten the achievement of this life she so ardently desires, an image that is a prefiguration of the site of her suicide.

REREADING THE SELF

Grillparzer further expands the narrative in *Sappho* by giving space to the expression of the inner worlds of both Phaon and Melitta, already identified in multiple incarnations.[28] They serve as the counterweight to Sappho and the power that she wielded unopposed. The opening of Act 2 is constructed around the figure of Phaon who retreats to the scene of his initiation as adjunct to the poetess as an escape from the extended celebration of Sappho that now takes place inside her home. Phaon can no longer tolerate this continued acclamation of Sappho and desires a more tranquil setting for reflection. Phaon takes control of the space and positions his narrative as one of value, an act which substitutes the poetic observation of Act 1 for meditation of the mundane sort in this act:

Wohl mir, hier ist es still. Des Gastmahls Jubel,
Der Zimbelspieler Lärm, der Flöten Töne,
Der losgelaßnen Freude lautes Regen,
Es tönt nicht bis hier unter diese Bäume,
Die leise flüsternd, wie besorgt zu stören,
Zu einsamer Betrachtung freundlich laden. (*Sappho*, 2.1.456–61)[29]

Phaon takes this hard-won opportunity to install himself as the new dramatic center by opening the act with a lengthy monologue of dismay and disaffection. His escape from the interior space with its continued fêting of the poetess allows him to usurp Sappho as main character and rewrite the central theme of the drama as his own story. He withdraws and undoes the version of reality or the perspective that is presented in Act 1 where Sappho is the principal.

Here in this monologue, Phaon extends the analysis of hesitancy and nostalgia that he had begun in dialogue with Sappho as they arrived on Lesbos: "I hardly know what I am doing, saying . . ." (*Sappho*, 1.3.132).[30] By claiming the physical and narrative space earlier framed by Sappho's triumphant return for his own purposes, Phaon redefines this location to both express his alienation from the public spectacle and centralize his own life story as an idyllic one whose loss frames his dispossession. He narrates a life whose details are precisely the opposite of Sappho's biography and whose leave-taking has altered his concept of perspective, reality, and desire: "Wie hat sich alles denn in mir verändert, / Seit ich der Eltern stilles Haus verließ / Und meine Renner gen Olympia lenkte?" (*Sappho*, 2.1.462–64).[31] The language that Phaon has at his disposal to portray the change revolves around a revaluation of his own ability to construct meaning out of a general confusion.[32]

Phaon rereads himself and, by necessity, Sappho as well, interpretative acts which undercut the confidence that he has done the right thing by establishing a relationship with the poetess. In this instance, Sappho is not merely Grillparzer's main protagonist but also functions at the level of metaphor within the drama, now subject to Phaon's reading:

Sonst konnt' ich wohl in heiterer Besinnung
Verworrener Empfindung leise Fäden
Mit scharfem Aug' verfolgen und entwirren
Bis klar es als Erkennen vor mir lag.
Doch jetzt, wie eine schwüle Sommernacht
Liegt brütend, süß und peinigend zugleich
Ein schwerer Nebel über meinen Sinnen,
Den der Gedanken fernes Wetterleuchten,
Jetzt hier, jetzt dort, und jetzt schon nicht mehr da,
In quälender Verwirrung rasch durchzuckt.
Ein Schleier deckt mir die Vergangenheit,
Kaum kann ich heut des Gestern mich erinnern,
Kaum in der jetzigen Stund' der erst geschiednen. (*Sappho*, 2.1.465–77)[33]

Thus, Sappho, earlier in Act 1, and Phaon in Act 2 have set as thematically important the issue of reading and interpretation. Phaon's words play heavily with the senses: Besinnung [reflection], Empfindung [perception], Erkennen [knowledge], Sinnen [meditation], and Verwirrung [confusion]. Phaon relate a gradual reduction of the certainty that was once embedded in a practice of deliberation, disentanglement, and recognition. The change in Phaon appears to reach much deeper than his new geographical position. He experiences a diminishment in sensation, appreciation, and awareness of this new social existence. The overwhelming nature of his sudden relationship with Sappho has occluded his perceptual faculties and changed his response to external stimuli. After describing the prior clarity of his senses and ability to discern, Phaon suddenly chooses language that suggests weight and suffocation.

The change in tone is introduced by "doch jetzt," followed by a succession of adjectives, nouns, and verbs (schwül, brütend, schwer, Nebel, quälend, Schleier, decken) that indicate the state of confusion in which Phaon finds himself. This condition reveals the problem of the drama from the perspective of Phaon and reasserts the failure of perception. However, he extends this to a general and pervasive disengagement with his surroundings which renders the "kaum" that opens the final couplet of the first segment of the long speech, a second turning point, a parallel construction to the "doch jetzt," which marked a first emotional shift in Phaon's monologue. This structure within Phaon's speech reveals the contradictions of his relationship to Sappho.

Unable to cement the memory, Phaon ponders how it is he came to Sappho by thinking through the pairing of his and Sappho's names by the cheering Olympian audience: "War es dein Name, den des Volkes Jubel / Vermischt mit ihrem in die Lüfte rief?" (*Sappho*, 2.1.481–82).[34] Asking himself a series of questions, he tries to evaluate the reality of his relationship by returning to the scene of his first meeting with the poetess. However, Phaon observes how the fulfillment of desires dulled his senses instead of heightening or even maintaining that level of awareness. "Was für ein ärmlich Wesen ist der Mensch, / Wenn, was als Hoffnung seine Sinne weckte, / Ihm als Erfüllung sie in Schlaf versenkt" (*Sappho*, 2.1.484–86).[35] Continuing his self-analysis, Phaon considers the nebulous quality of the idea of Sappho that he believed in before he ever beheld her. The fantasy and his expectation collide with the reality of the woman. When Sappho existed as merely a poetess, her aura as artist was unshakeable and unassailable, but as Phaon here admits, it was also indefinite and misty:

Als ich sie noch nicht sah und kannte, nur
Die Phantasie ihr schlechtgetroffnes Bild
In graue Nebel noch verfließend malte,
Da schien mir's leicht für einen Blick von ihr,
Ein güt'ges Wort, das Leben hinzuwerfen. (*Sappho*, 2.1.487–91)[36]

The idea of Sappho served a self-sufficient fantasy that proved to be enough to compel his acclamation and the binding of his life with hers. But here Phaon quickly calls the reality "schlechtgetroffenes [poorly made]," which signals the failure of the image to match the reality. His acknowledgment of the ease with which he allowed fantasy to take hold of his actual decision-making process, an extreme alteration of his life, becomes evident in this speech. He has given over the direction of his life to the idea of a woman, an image based on her identity as a poetess. One could claim that Phaon was seized by poesy and the lofty claims of verse rather than by a deep love for the Sappho. In the final lines of this long rhetorical speech, he again returns to a language of development and change—the larval stage of desire transformed into the mature stage of actualization. This transformation offers him no satisfaction: "Jetzt frag ich noch und steh und sinn und zaudre!" (*Sappho*, 2.1.495).[37] Instead of emerging secure and fully formed from the initial encounter with Sappho, Phaon is thrown into despair—steeped in deliberation and hesitation.

Melitta's monologue in Act 2 is the final segment of this triangular construction, a structure in which she and Phaon are more akin to each other than to Sappho. The difference lies in their narrative formulation of kinship and belonging. While Sappho had spoken of estrangement from her family, both Phaon and Melitta mourn the loss of those ties. In Melitta's case, the memory of that loss is recognized, but largely absent in detail. Melitta's "Es geht nicht! [It's impossible!]" expresses her frustration with the circumstances of her life as servant and slave. Sharing an emotional introspection, Melitta also delivers a monologue which is patterned very much after those of Sappho and Phaon:

Da muß ich sitzen einsam und verlassen,
Fern von der Eltern Herd im fremden Land,
Und Sklavenketten drücken diese Hände,
Die ich hinüberstrecke nach den Meinen.
Weh mir, da sitz ich einsam und verlassen,
Und niemand höret mich und achtet mein! (*Sappho*, 2.3.554–59)[38]

The repetition of "einsam und verlassen [alone and forsaken]" reflects a discerning awareness of Melitta's banishment and exclusion from a community in which she can be a full participant (as completely as any woman could ever be). As an outcast, Melitta feels acutely this lack of affiliation, which pushes her emotionally and physically outside of any organic domestic structure:

Mir schlägt kein Busen hier in diesem Lande,
Und meine Freunde wohnen weit von hier.
Ich sehe Kinder um den Vater hüpfen,
Die fromme Stirn, die heil'gen Locken küssen,
Mein Vater lebt getrennt durch ferne Meere,
Wo ihn nicht Gruß und Kuß des Kinds erreicht! (*Sappho*, 2.3.562–67)[39]

Defining the security and function of the family through the paternal realm, Melitta effectively reorganizes the domestic constellation of Sappho's control of Mytilene. She asserts the power of the father to define or fix the viability of the family, an affirmation that renders Sappho's place as head of this small society illegitimate. This praise-song for the family directed by the father troubles the position of Sappho, a woman and a poetess, and renders her lifestyle illicit and misbegotten.

In the same space, the precarity of her situation not lost on her, Melitta knows that she is at the whim of her benefactress. Sitting in the grotto where she has set aside the wreath that she had been braiding, Melitta rejects Sappho's form of life in favor of the bonds of kinship:

Führt gütig mich zurücke zu den Meinen,
Daß ich an des Vertrauens weiche Brust,
Die kummerheiße Stirne kühlend presse.
Führt zu den Meinen mich, ach, oder nehmt mich
Hinauf zu euch, zu euch!—zu euch! (*Sappho*, 2.3.585–89)[40]

The desire to unearth her lineage and reconnect with her blood relations is constructed as a flight into the romance of the family, a line of escape that obliterates Sappho's patchwork ménage in favor of familial origins.[41]

Melitta also understands her role that is bound up with the identity of the poetess. Just as Sappho has multiple identities with which to serve her public, Melitta's identity keeps her inextricably tied to the fortunes of Sappho. Like Phaon, Melitta is also "stumm [mute]" and "schüchtern [timid]" in the face of Sappho, but she injects a level of critique into this observation which condemns the passivity that she must observe:

Sie dürfen lieben, hassen, was sie wollen,
Und was das Herz empfindet, spricht die Lippe aus (*Sappho*, 2.3.574–75)
...
Der Sklavin Platz ist an dem niedern Herde,
Da trifft kein Blick sie, ach und keine Frage,
Kein Auge, kein Gedanke und kein Wunsch!" (*Sappho*, 2.3.578–80)[42]

Melitta's ability to express her desires is constrained by her status as a slave and a woman. What is permissible for others is denied her in these social, legal, and gendered spaces. The option to love and to hate, to offer an opinion, to have her feelings considered, or to know the regard of the people is unavailable to Melitta in Sappho's world, one that is also hostile to Sappho's participation in it. Not everyone's experience of gender is the same and it is clear in the case of Melitta and Sappho that neither woman understands how her gender impacts her individual life. For Melitta, it is her status as slave that intersects with her gender thinking. While for Sappho, it is her role as poet that temporarily conceals her gender thinking since it does not always cohere in the same way across different situations. It then becomes difficult to parse how gender is used in political, personal, and cultural ways for future deployment in a heterosexual or heteronormative environment as a discursive strategy.

Phaon overhears Melitta's monologue, a listening-in that marks the creation of his love for her and ends with them in an embrace that signals their growing attraction.[43] Melitta's developing self-knowledge and a language with which to voice her frustrations gives Phaon the imagination to defy Sappho's claims to his love. Phaon develops a voice with which to refute the legitimacy of Sappho's fame, a renown which had been the basis of his love. He gains a forceful and censorious voice which is no longer that of consort, but of someone who is fully in control of himself—as a man, a lover, and a social insider.

This amplification of discourse between Phaon and Melitta signals that Sappho's way of life is being narratively overturned by a normative configuration that is found in the younger pair. While Sappho commands language use in Act 1, it is in Act 2 where her role as poetess and woman is questioned. Neither Phaon nor Melitta actively condemn Sappho but their own self-narrativizing prompts the reader to perceive the change in how each understands his and her place in Sappho's world. The pattern of Melitta's life and how she assesses those deprivations signal a plot shift that repositions Sappho and Phaon by escalating Melitta's role as a reader of society—someone who can articulate a discursive reality despite regulation and containment. Although unrealized and perhaps not fully understood, Melitta is filled with the desire for a voice that is as expressive as Sappho's voice appears to be as the drama opens. Their aspirations are for the conventional life of the family, which Sappho does not necessarily scorn, but with which she has had no success. Sappho's desire to retreat from the loftier public realm of poetry to the more mundane domestic sphere with Phaon is a concession, a decline in which she finds value. Her construction of and claims to a simple life are imperiled in the face of the considerable and, in a manner of speaking, much more realistic yearnings for the family on the part of Phaon and Melitta. The regularity and intimacy of such a life appeals to Sappho as an imaginary yet potent symbol of acceptance and love. Yet, it is this desire to belong that will dislodge her most completely and effectively from the human community and from the world of art. It is this dispossession—a state of wretchedness—that causes a discursive blurring of all of the ways in which she tries to speak. Now living an exposed life in ways that she never envisioned due to the new relationship between Phaon and Melitta, Sappho must soon contend with the catastrophe—the overturning—of all that she understood about her life. It is this moment when a feminist impulse might want to emerge—not a fully developed sensation but one that understands difference and grief. As if she were speaking directly about Sappho, early in *Living a Feminist Life* Ahmed writes:

The arrival of suffering from the edges teaches us about the difficulty of becoming conscious of suffering. It is hard labor to recognize sadness and disappointment when you are living a life that is meant to be happy but is not happy, which is meant to be full but feels empty. It is difficult to give up an idea of one's life when one has lived one's life according to that idea.[44]

Here, Ahmed is writing directly about feminism as an "unhappy archive" but we must now consider Sappho. She is the one that held a belief about the kind of life she wanted based upon the unhappiness of the life that she had previously lived. By giving up one identity bounded by gender for another, Sappho now encounters the harsh reality that what she thought she had found in Phaon is unachievable. Gender had become the center around which she managed her sense of self since arriving home and now that very condition has destroyed the possibility of happiness. And in its place, the two new lovers have developed agency in part because Sappho's discursive power has given them examples of how to speak themselves. Neither her constative nor performative speech acts serve her here.[45] Unable to separate worldly reality from linguistic utterance, she is bereft. Instead what she commands is a kind of emergency, an immediacy in her dissident voice.

AN IDEA OF LIFE

The final three acts of Grillparzer's drama depict the rapid unraveling of Sappho's world embodied in the rejection by Melitta and Phaon and the loss of belief in her identity as both poetess and woman. Sappho cannot maintain control over the personal story-world that she has advanced and the people who inhabit it because of the arrival of a "suffering from the edges" that Ahmed so carefully voiced. This exposes her vulnerability to the ever-increasing demands of a world defined by a compulsory heteronormative ideology. It is this belief system in which gender hierarchies determine and police who ought to be admitted to certain spaces and allowed to speak in specific ways.

Sappho's narrative is not only that of the failure of love, it is also the failure of the performance of the self, a self that is gendered and thus limited in what it can perform. Sappho's attempt to complicate herself—to be both woman and poet—defines the problem of performativity in the drama. In the Preface to *Gender Trouble*, Butler writes that ". . . performativity is not a singular act, but a repetition and a ritual, which achieves its effects through its naturalization in the context of a body, understood, in part, as a culturally sustained temporal duration."[46] Sappho's desire to write and then rewrite herself—she is both the composer and the subject of composition—further complicates the drama due to her shifting and plural identities that, as Butler writes, are desirous of a naturalization of her own body. How does a reader (we as the external readers and Sappho as the internal one) know if this is the story of the oppression of its female protagonist or if it is the tale of a misunderstood and alienated artist? The ambiguity of this question and the difficulty of proposing an answer is an achievement of Grillparzer's text. Is Grillparzer making a gesture at the limitations of gender roles or that of the limitations and marginalization of the artist? If this is a displacement of the role of the artist through use of the female as oppressed subject, is the dramatist undermining or "misreading" Sappho by creating a self-referential text in the service of an Austrian upper middle-class man?

Sappho's agitation intensifies as she laments the freedom and fickleness of men and the vulnerability of women. Sappho recognizes that:

Frei tritt er in des Daseins offne Bahn,
Vom Morgenrot der Hoffnung rings umflossen,
Mit Mut und Stärke wie mit Schild und Schwert
Zum ruhmbekränzten Kampfe ausgerüstet.
Zu eng dünkt ihm des Innern stille Welt,
Nach außen geht sein rastlos wildes Streben . . . (*Sappho*, 3.1.815–20)[47]

Although she is disturbed by what she had earlier witnessed, Sappho's words do not resemble those of a spurned lover. What troubles her in these lines is the difference and inequity between the genders. Her use of words such as "frei," "offne Bahn," "Hoffnung," "Mut und Stärke," and "nach außen" speak to the freedom that men have to change their situation while "eng," "das Innere" and "stille Welt" reflect what remains for women. Men are in possession of seemingly endless possibilities that outfit them with the tools to satisfy their needs—even in love. Sappho's voice is decidedly gendered but not directly towards the jealousy of erotic love, but rather towards a critique of the unfettered freedoms of men and the silence that inflects the figure of the female.

It is a challenge to relinquish an idea of a life when everything thus far has pointed in that direction. The perplexing and sudden change of circumstances forces the poetess to question her own existence as well as the certainty in the judgment of the self: "Bin ich denn noch, und ist denn etwas noch? / Dies weite All, es stürzte nicht zusammen / In jenem fürchterlichen Augenblick?" (*Sappho*, 4.1.1189–91).[48] Similar to Kleist's *Penthesilea*, Sappho suffers a crushing loss of coherence after the failure of the erotic relationship. Penthesilea, the leader of a warrior society, and Sappho, the famed poet who leads a small community, falter in their self-understanding in the face of personal rejection that had at its core a sense of power and eminence. Their experience of themselves as whole and dynamic is imperiled when the boundaries between the public and private self are exposed as aberrations. This revelation is the direct consequence of the attempt to connect erotically while managing social and civic duties. Phaon's narrative assault on Sappho's sense of wholeness, a coherent state that had sustained her as the leader of Mytilene and as the famous poetess, exhausts her ability to keep knowledge of herself secure and vertical. She can no longer rely on her identity as poetess—a crisis which unravels all that had been previously undeniable. Thus, the rhetorical questions she poses about reality further confound the notion of personal identity and suggest the unknowability or, even more dreadful, the absence, of a verifiable self.

Even as Sappho stumbles in her self-concept—her inclination for lyric—the transformation of reality into poesy, asserts itself:

Still ist es um mich her, die Lüfte schweigen,
Des Lebens muntre Töne sind verstummt,
Kein Laut schallt aus den unbewegten Blättern
Und einsam wie ein spätverirrter Fremdling
Geht meines Weinens Stimme durch die Nacht.
Wer auch so schlafen könnte, wie die Vögel,
Doch lang und länger, ohne zu erwachen;
im Schoße eines festern, süßern Schlummers
Wo alles, alles, selbst die Pulse schlafen,
Kein Morgenstrahl zu neuen Qualen weckt,
Kein Undankbarer—Halt!—Tritt nicht die Schlange! (*Sappho*, 4.1.1196–206)[49]

The versification of her distress is poignant and absurd; her style is elevated and whimsical, a creative choice which undercuts the scope of her confusion and dismay. Although she self-censors before composing further stanzas of distress, Sappho cannot refrain from translating even the most anguishing events into a verse-story, a strategy, or compulsion which undermines the gravity of her situation and the depth of her emotions. Her vocation as poet and, thus, her predisposition towards beautiful formulations, reminds us that it is poetry that has thwarted her domestic desires. Or perhaps the cause of her defeat in love was her coupling of artistic aptitude with that of the quotidian. In an apostrophe to Phaon, Sappho further reveals her refusal to descend from, even if briefly, the realm of the poetic and her status in that space in order to think through, in complex ways, the failure of her relationship with him:

Phaon, Phaon! Was hab' ich dir getan?
Ich stand so ruhig in der Dichtung Auen,
Mit meinem goldnen Saitenspiel allein,
Hernieder sah ich auf der Erde Freuden,
Und ihre Leiden reichten nicht zu mir. (*Sappho*, 4.2.1271–75)[50]

Having forsaken the eternal fame granted her by the gift of song and music for a commonplace and domestic life with Phaon, Sappho has been refused return. Ejected from that privileged sphere where she once wore the laurel wreath and was favored by the gods, she must now live unprotected from the menacing abyss. "Und jetzt, da er der einz'ge Gegenstand / Der in der Leere mir entgegenstrahlt, / Entzieht er mir die Hand, ach und entflieht!" (*Sappho*, 4.2.1285–87).[51] Phaon has abandoned Sappho for the love of Melitta and now Sappho must grieve that loss. Having declined the applause of the crowd who lauded her poetic prowess, Sappho has staked her life on the love of Phaon which he has now withdrawn from her. In Sappho's mind, Phaon's flight from her love and devotion forces her to confront what she terms "die Leere," an emptiness or void which acknowledges neither the authority of the poet, the creative power of her song, nor her desire for love.

Eucharis, a devoted servant of Sappho, frames the falling action of the drama: "Verwirrend scheint ein böser Geist zu walten / Seit Sapphos Rückkehr über ihrem Haus" (*Sappho*, 4.6.1473–74).[52] Sappho's desperate attempt to contain and regulate love and friendship is the result of a dearth of such love and friendship earlier in her life. Her decision to follow the artistic vocation with its laurels and public adulation contributed to an apartness impossible to bridge such that her whispered but distinct words to her servant, Eucharis, appear portentous: "O laß mich sinken! Warum hältst du mich?" (*Sappho*, 4.8.1542).[53] Still enmeshed in the language of artistic creation, Sappho does not see Melitta as an autonomous being imbued with a reality of her own. The younger woman is, instead, her construction, and as a fabrication of Sappho's imagination, she can be destroyed at will. Sappho treats Melitta the way one would handle an unruly poem—discard the inadequate stanzas and start anew. Sappho's refusal to acknowledge Melitta as a fully formed person—her view of the young girl is as a product of her own handiwork—drives the poetess to increasingly risky and self-destructive deeds and complicates how she understands gender. The preservation of herself as "maker," a label which is devoid of any biological considerations, shapes Sappho's language and behavior. She is the architect, the sculptress, the poetess and as such is specially endowed with the powers of those offices to build, shape, and author the world around her.

THE FAILURE OF (RE)CONSTRUCTION

The tragedy's final act opens with an unconscious Sappho surrounded by her loyal servants, anxious about her emotional state. When Sappho awakens from her faint, she is exhausted and confused about the details of the most recent events. Hiding from Phaon and Melitta, the stage directions show

Sappho's retreat from the center of the action to the altar of the goddess Aphrodite, surrounded by her maids: "Sie eilt dem Hintergrunde zu und umklammert den Altar, ihre Dienerinnen stehen rings um sie her."[54] When Phaon and Melitta reappear after their failed attempt to flee Lesbos and away from the poetess, Sappho remains in the background and does not yet enter into dialogue with either. Phaon acts as protector of Melitta and unleashes a verbal torrent which promises retribution if Melitta were to be harmed.

Appearing at the opening of the drama as an untested youth, Phaon is now in possession of a set of rhetorical skills to combat the vengeance of those loyal to Sappho. "Nicht wehrlos bin ich, wenn auch gleich entwaffnet! / Zu ihrem Schutz wird diese Faust zur Keule, / Und jedes meiner Glieder wird ein Arm!" (*Sappho*, 5.3.1595–97).[55] Equipped with the language to both envelop Melitta in his embrace and reject Sappho, Phaon again tells of his release from the illusory love for the poetess while still a callow youth. Armed with a newly elevated sense of self and his own power, he calls for Sappho to appear and exercises a new gendered sense of himself as a man. Additionally, he invokes the law in these brief words. The juridical nature of this surprising outburst reminds the reader that gender is a legal matter that circumscribes the life of a willful woman: "Bin ich nicht ein freier Mann? / Wer gab das Recht ihr meinen Schritt zu hemmen? / Noch Richterstühle gibt's in Griechenland, / Mit Schrecken soll die Stolze das erfahren" (*Sappho*, 5.3.1621–24).[56]

Phaon is now emphatically conventional in his self-assessment (free and a man) in contrast to Sappho's nontraditional resistance to normative gender roles. This declaration raises the issue of civic authority, legislative force, and the repression of the female. Phaon, becoming more at ease with his identity, contends that Sappho will be judged for her defiance of the rules of propriety as he repudiates her as a leader and as a woman. He asks of Sappho's countrymen, "Seid ihr so zahm, daß eines Weibes Rache / Geduldig ihr die Männerhände leiht, / Und dienstbar seid der Liebe Wechsellaunen? / Mir stehet bei, denn Unrecht widerfährt mir!" (*Sappho*, 5.3.1633–36).[57] Her poetic gifts and victory at Olympia have been erased from the discourse; all accusations revolve around Sappho's transgression of gendered boundaries. "Wer ist denn Sappho, daß du ihre Zunge / Für jene achtest an des Rechtes Waage? / Ist sie Gebieterin hier im Land?" (*Sappho*, 5.3.1639–41).[58] Phaon's language reveals his biases: any man who would attend to the petty wishes of a woman in this way is nothing more than a slave. He questions her authority; Phaon has now reframed the battle with Sappho as a fight for male liberation from haughty and arrogant women. The reference to tongue also points the reader to Sappho's refusal to remove herself from language as both poetess and willful woman. Sara Ahmed describes a woman such as Sappho in *Willful Subjects* as someone who is "reaching for something":

Willfulness can be a trace left behind, a reopening of what might have been closed down, a modification of what seems reachable, and a revitalization of the question of what it is to be for. Reaching for something, reaching for will, is thus an opening up of the body to what came before, reaching as going back in time. Willful action can create the possibility of not being willing by not giving will up or giving up on will.[59]

Ahmed's definition of willfulness takes us deep into the inner workings of Sappho's life choices. She does not fit, she fails to inhabit a norm, and she wants what she should not. She is reaching for will. Yet, I would argue that Sappho is also a feminist killjoy—someone who gets in the way of happiness. In her article, "A Willfulness Archive," Ahmed presents the disturbing traits and behaviors of some women.[60] She writes:

Feminist killjoys: those who refuse to laugh at the right points; those who are unwilling to be seated at the table of happiness. I became interested in how those who get in the way of happiness, and we call these those killjoys, are also and often attributed as willful. In witnessing the unruly trouble making of feminist killjoys, I caught a glimpse of how willfulness can fall, like a judgment on the fallen.[61]

Sappho is deeply rooted in both identities—the willful subject and the feminist killjoy—for she refuses to assimilate and take on the virtues of quietude and acceptance. The idea of a trace left behind is significant when thinking about Sappho as a remnant of a life rife with turmoil and grief. Her identity as a feminist killjoy turns on a number of factors: a frustrating family life, her own poetic genius, the leadership of Lesbos, her love for Phaon, a rejection of meeting the expectation of normative gender and sex roles, and the repudiation of the politics of social reckoning. She is both obstinate and perverse. Sappho renews the case for willful women but in the same gesture reopens the assertion of male power once she introduces Phaon into her once closed world on Lesbos. It is this double bind that leaves Sappho in a constraining space that emerges in juridical and personal ways in Phaon's language acts. This linguistic circumscription that he imposes on her does not allow Sappho the latitude to trace a new path for herself. Phaon's complete disavowal of Sappho centers on legitimacy—what is permissible.

Indeed, Phaon has enjoyed a successful transformation by discarding what is no longer needful and fortifying his emergence as a man. The relationship with Sappho, based as it was in a fantasy, becomes the root of his disgust with the poetess but which also positively contributed to his understanding of himself as a man repelled by the imposing claims of a woman. Phaon's words increase in vitriol when he directly addresses the exhausted Sappho on the steps of the altar of Aphrodite. His language strips away her identity by denying the legitimacy of her reality. Sappho's fragile notion of what constitutes a self cannot withstand Phaon's persistent attacks on her already fragmented and wounded identity:

Entweichst du mir? du mußt mir Rede stehn!
Ha, bebe nur! Es ist jetzt Zeit zu beben!
Weißt du was du getan? Mit welchem Recht
Wagst du es mich, mich einen freien Mann,
Der niemand eignet als sich selber, hier
In frevelhaften Banden festzuhalten?
Hier diese da in ungewohnten Waffen,
Hast du sie ausgesandt? Hast du sie? Sprich!—
So stumm? der Dichtrin süße Lippe stumm? (*Sappho*, 5.3.1653–61)[62]

Phaon attacks Sappho on terms which play with female impropriety and silence and male autonomy and desire for the ethics of an androcentric culture. Sappho is unable to counter his accusations for she is thrust into a space of nonlanguage by what Phaon calls the unseemliness of her weapon, the lyric. Phaon's belligerent rhetoric takes aim at Sappho's construction of herself as an authority figure, an artist, and a woman. His speech seeks to suppress and reorder Sappho's construction of herself in ways which increase his mastery of the situation. The control that he desires is anchored in shaming Sappho into silence and discrediting her leadership by substituting his own values into a new social existence. Sappho's retreat to a voiceless state provides Phaon with the opportunity to fill the silence with his male voice as an assertion of the gendered shape of the public and private spheres.

The violence of Phaon's rhetoric in Act 5 relegates Sappho to a position where she is unable to speak in any substantial or meaningful way. Phaon achieves the final obliteration of Sappho when he tempers his hostility with a credible assessment of the impossibility of Sappho as both woman in love and laurel-wreathed poetess:

Wenn ich dir Liebe schwur, es war nicht Täuschung,
Ich liebte dich, so wie man Götter wohl
Wie man das Gute liebet und das Schöne.
Mit Höhern, Sappho, halte du Gemeinschaft,
Man steigt nicht ungestraft vom Göttermahle
Herunter in den Kreis der Sterblichen.
Der Arm, in dem die goldne Leier ruhte,
Er ist geweiht, er fasse Niedres nicht! (*Sappho*, 5.3.1722–30)[63]

and

Ich taumelte in dumpfer Trunkenheit,
Mit mir und mit der Welt im düstern Streite;
Vergebens rief ich die Gefühle auf,
Die ich in Schlummer glaubt' und die nicht waren,
Du standst vor mir ein unbegreiflich Bild
Zu dem's mich hin, von dem's mich fort,
Mit unsichtbaren Banden mächtig zog. (*Sappho*, 5.3.1733–39)[64]

Having absorbed the lessons of loss and deprivation early in life, Sappho has placed all of her dreams and desires in this man. His final indifference further devastates Sappho's rapidly dissolving sense of self and is the ultimate humiliation that pushes her past the limits of her endurance and into suicide. Phaon's perception of Sappho as unfathomable, incongruous, and illusory is consistent with the irregularity of her role in society. If Phaon cannot comprehend her and has insufficient vision to accommodate the complexity of her identity, then it matters little to Sappho if she is adorned with laurel wreaths and celebrated in the wider society for her artistic prowess. Phaon's words undeniably refute Sappho by narratively excluding her from membership in the larger community.

Sappho's participation in the drama becomes progressively marginal as the other characters narrate the rapidly occurring events which transpired after Phaon's final rejection of the poetess. Sappho silently leaves the altar to wander the cliffs. Wearing the victory wreath won at Olympia and cloaked in her purple mantle, a repetition of the grand entrance which opened the drama, Sappho is now alone and lost in thought. Eucharis watches Sappho from a distance and describes her with a radiance that alarms Rhamnes and cause all to hasten to her side:

Wer sie jetzt sah, zum erstenmale sah,
Auf des Altares hohen Stufen stehend,
Die Leier in der Hand, den Blick gehoben,
Gehoben ihre ganze Lichtgestalt,
Verklärungsschimmer über sie gegossen,
Als Überird'sche hätt' er sie begrüßt,
Und zum Gebet gebeugt die schwanken Kniee.
Doch regungslos und stumm so wie sie war,
Fühlt' ich von Schauder mich und Graun ergriffen,
Ihr lebend toter Blick entsetzte mich ... (*Sappho*, 5.5.1937–46)[65]

Eucharis interprets Sappho as both serene and somber; she is a solitary figure contemplating an act which will recommit her to her artistic vocation. When the now contrite Melitta wishes to return to Sappho's service, the newly resolute poetess tells the girl: "Du faßtest nicht mein Herz, so fahre hin! / Auf festern Grund muß meine Hoffnung fußen!" (*Sappho*, 5.6.1961–62).[66] Sappho is steadfast in her understanding of herself; she has arrived at a place of reconciliation and feels free to pledge her life to that purpose. Sappho has a new realization of the struggle in constructing a life around a strict identity—either the gendered one of the domestic sphere or the artistic one of acclamation and fame in the public arena. Melitta asks Sappho if she now hates her and Sappho's answer is the clearest critical formulation of the both/and model which would have been able to assemble all of the claims that Sappho made on this life: "Lieben! Hassen! / Gibt es kein Drittes mehr?" (*Sappho*, 5.6.1963–64).[67] This third way would draw together all that was isolated and indistinct in order to fashion an alternate way of being, a compromise that would make room for the composite nature of the self and gather up what had been previously unincorporated. She gives her thanks to the gods for the gift of song and music in language that brims with an unadorned simple genius and shimmers with the numinous:

Erhabne, heil'ge Götter!
Ihr habt mit reichem Segen mich geschmückt!
In meine Hand gabt ihr des Sanges Bogen,
Der Dichtung vollen Köcher gabt ihr mir;
Ein Herz zu fühlen, einen Geist zu denken
Und Kraft zu bilden was ich mir gedacht!
Ihr habt mit reichem Segen mich geschmückt,
Ich dank euch! (*Sappho*, 5.6.1981–88)[68]

Her praise-song becomes her eulogy. Sappho throws herself from the Leucadian rock into the sea as Rhamnes announces her transfiguration: "verklärt ist all ihr Wesen, / Glanz der Unsterblichen umleuchtet sie!" (*Sappho*, 5.6.2023–24).[69] Although Sappho had discovered that there was perhaps an alternative, a way to live an integrated and full life, the decision that she ultimately made to end her own life was fixed in the knowledge that the choice for such a life was not hers to make. Sappho's death can thus be conceived as a defiance or perhaps a way to further communicate her truth—one that goes against the grain. In *Willful Subjects*, Ahmed writes:

> This perception of feminist subjects as having too much will, or too much subjectivity, or just as being too much, has profound effects on how we experience ourselves as well as the worlds we come up against. If to be a killjoy is to be the

one who gets in the way of happiness, then living a feminist life requires being willing to get in the way.[70]

Sappho is a drama that demonstrates an abundance of subjectivity that is both disobedient and desiring. Sappho was willing to thwart the performance of a conventional life. Her behavior throughout the drama upset the proper functioning of a traditional androcentric world. In Sappho's styling, gender, sex, and desire come together as a project that cannot as yet be fulfilled but remains an ethical struggle whose promises remain somber and unattainable.

In this drama, Sappho's story is formed from composite elements and diagrams. Her fragmentary status forces Grillparzer, as it did writers before and after him, to create an image of Sappho that could move, act, and react in a facsimile of a real person, or rather, a lyrical "voice," that seems to be a woman, embedded in a historical reproduction of known geographic and temporal spaces—the city of Mytilene on Lesbos in the seventh and sixth centuries BC. However, the drama, *Sappho*, is imagery, symbol, and grammar and yet it still is a true figuration of Sappho, the poetess. Here, Sappho is a caesura that has lasted several millennia; Grillparzer's *Sappho* is a pause in the telling which relinquishes itself to the real in the fragmentary rhythms of the sounds and syllables that Grillparzer constructed in his ventriloquy, a product of a nineteenth-century imagination.

As a contrast to the fragments of Sappho's verse, Grillparzer in *Sappho* has fashioned layers of worlds in the spaces between literature and imagination. His emphasis on contradiction, irony, and paradox is elemental to a recovery of Sappho as something a bit more than a symbol and a mark on a piece of stone by the end of the drama. The impression of a life—a process of theorization and analysis (and even archive)—suggests that Grillparzer's work in *Sappho* and Sappho's fragments—shards of lyric—are outside of life. They are therefore in need of extraction from the sediment of a forced burial so that Sappho can return to us as a radical figure of the real. As readers we must accept that Grillparzer's *Sappho* is not a drama of regeneration but rather of a distraught poetic idiom, one that is deeply skeptical of its schema, agitated by its task—which is to dramatize its own destruction, the wreckage of an entire existence on the cliffs of Lesbos.

Sappho's otherness and disjointedness inflect her character from the outset as we observe the burden of difference and the exclusion from life that hinge on gender and language. Might she be the fragment extraordinaire despite Grillparzer's narrative efforts to make her whole and connected? Could her suicide indicate that Sappho understands herself already as partial and chiseled away? Is the shattering of a poetic genius the true originality of this drama? Sappho was a voice of disruption and defiance. However, forms of action—literary or personal—do not always create a livable relationality or one that can contain a feminist impulse that might endure. The question that must be asked is whether or not *Sappho* can be read as a text that has the beginnings of a feminist impulse as a knowledge project. I would rather ask if it was necessary for this drama to do all of the heavy lifting of a feminist text? Sappho grappled with all three dynamics that I outlined in the Introduction: the work of gender; inclusion and exclusion; and the extension of discourse into otherwise unknown spaces or unfamiliar narratives. As an unstable object, *Sappho* offered a way to process this triangulation even as it remained a partial contribution to the narratives of Medea and Sappho, women who are also unwilling to be seated at the table of happiness.

NOTES

1. Ahmed, *Living a Feminist Life*, 125.
2. In his *Poetics*, Aristotle delineated a structure for tragedy that consists of six parts that were described in the introduction—plot, characters, diction, thought, melody and spectacle (the stage appearance of the actors). According to the text, the most important of these six is the combination of the incidents in the story. For tragedy to be successful, the protagonist must possess a tragic flaw (*hamartia*) that drives the plot forward. This leads to the *peripeteia* (the turning point or reversal) and the *anagnorisis* (the moment of recognition).
3. Kleist's *Penthesilea* focuses on masculinity and genre as vulnerable schemes for organizing the world. Kleist forces an encounter between the epic world and tragic drama. Each has a narrative concern and generic convention that have no role for the other. Thus, Achilles and Penthesilea are not only engaged in a battle for sexual and political dominance but also one which will determine whose story-world prevails. Crisis is the locus of action. Misreading causes and extends the crisis to the point of collapse of all knowledge and all bodies. The structure of the erotic, similar to the structure of perception, cannot be sustained under the ambiguities of language in *Penthesilea*. See Heinrich von Kleist, *Penthesilea: A Tragic Drama*, trans. Joel Agee (New York: Harper Collins, 1998).
4. Butler, *Gender Trouble*, xxiii.
5. Renny Keelin Harrigan, "Woman and Artist: Grillparzer's *Sappho* Revisited," *German Quarterly* 53, no. 3 (May 1980): 299.
6. See "Sappho," in Dagmar C. G. Lorenz, *Grillparzer: Dichter des sozialen Konflikts* (Vienna: Böhlau, 1986), 43–51.
7. For example, in the chapter, "Humanität, Nationalität, Bestialität," Lorenz offers a reading of *The Golden Fleece* where she asks provocative questions about race, racism, minority status, and ethnicity in the trilogy, 68–87.
8. Lorenz, *Grillparzer*, 45.
9. Paul K. Whitaker, "The Concept of 'Sammlung' in Grillparzer's Works," *Monatshefte* 41, no. 2 (February 1949): 93–103.

10. Walter Naumann, "Grillparzer: Der Dichter und die Sprache," *Monatshefte* 45, no. 6 (November 1953): 337–54.

11. Butler, *Gender Trouble*, xxii.

12. As we will see later, *agon* takes on its much more formal but arcane usage. Sappho and Phaon become antagonists rather than lovers and their interactions become formal debates between adversaries.

13. Ahmed, *Living a Feminist Life*, 41.

14. Grillparzer, *Sappho*, act 1, stage directions. "The curtain opens on a landscape. In the background is the sea, whose flat shore rises on the left to rocky heights. An altar of Aphrodite stands just by the shore. On the right foreground is seen the entrance to a grotto overgrown with bushes and ivy; further back is the end of a pillared passage with steps leading to Sappho's dwelling. On the left side of the foreground a tall rosebush stands behind a grassy bank." Franz Grillparzer, *Franz Grillparzer: Plays on Classic Themes*, trans. Samuel Solomon (New York: Random House, 1969), 29. See note 1 in the introduction regarding the German and English texts.

15. Ahmed, *Living a Feminist Life*, 124–25.

16. "She's come home from Olympia with the wreath, / Decked with the laurel wreath of victory. / Before the whole of Greece assembled there, / In eager witness of the noble strife, / She won the prize for poetry and song. / For this the people rush to her, rejoicing, / Dispatching to the clouds her happy name / On the broad wings of their triumphant shouts! / To think *this* hand it was and *this* my mouth / That taught her first the lyre's enchanting speech, / And how to fetter songs' unruly flow / With the sweet discipline of harmony." Grillparzer, *Sappho*, 1.1.11–22. The shortened references (separated by periods) in the text and notes correspond to act, scene, and line of Grillparzer, *Sappho* (hereafter cited as *Sappho*), respectively.

17. "Rather make sure all's ready in the house. / A servant's service honors best his master." *Sappho*, 1.1.28–29.

18. "You were to know the mistress was approaching." *Sappho*, 1.1.35.

19. "Thanks, friends, dear countrymen, my thanks! / For your sakes I take pleasure in this wreath / That crowns the *citizen* but irks the *poet*; / Only in your midst do I call it mine." *Sappho*, 1.2.44–47.

20. "Here, where the earliest plans and dreams of youth, / Where the beginners' hesitations, strivings, / And where accomplishment's ecstatic frenzy / Confronted suddenly my reeling soul; / Here, where the cypresses breathe out to me / Soft, ghostly greetings from my parents' graves, / Here, where so many, cut off young, repose, / Who once took pleasure in my tries, my triumphs, / Here in the midst of you who know and love me, / I feel at last this wreath is without taint / And I may deem its arrogance adornment." *Sappho*, 1.2.48–58.

21. "Sappho, you're mocking me, a simple youth! / How could I possibly have earned such praise? / Who thinks so highly of one so untested?" *Sappho*, 1.2.80–82.

22. "From the noblest stock he springs, / And proudly may take place among the noblest. / Although the years may call him still a youth, / By word and deed he's proved himself a man. / If ever you should need the warrior's sword, / The orator's bold lips, the poet's mouth, / A friend's wise counsel, or a strong right arm, / Then call to him and you need seek not further!" *Sappho*, 1.2.72–79.

23. "With his superb endowments he was destined / To draw me down with sweet compulsive force / From the high cloudy peaks of poetry / Into the fair and flowery vales of life." *Sappho*, 1.2.89–92.

24. "Cannot your heart urge you to sweeter names?" *Sappho*, 1.3.131.

25. "I hardly know what I am doing, saying. / Plucked from my quiet life's obscurity / And drawn magnetic to the ray of light, / Set high aloft upon an airy peak / To which the noblest vainly strive to attain, / My spirit faints with unexpected joy; / And in this bliss I cannot find myself." *Sappho*, 1.3.132–38.

26. "Let us endeavor then, my dearest friend, / To wind both garlands around our eager brows, / To quaff life from the dizzy cup of art / And art from out the gentle hand of life" *Sappho*, 3.3.280–83.

27. "There stand I on the brink of the abyss / That yawns devouring between him and me; / I see the golden land that beckons me. / My eye may reach it, ah, but not my foot!" *Sappho*, 1.5.394–97.

28. Renny Keelin Harrigan offers an excellent analysis of the mother-daughter relationship between Sappho and Melitta as one that is potentially erotic and much more multi-faceted than has been treated. See Harrigan, "Woman and Artist: Grillparzer's *Sappho* Revisited."

29. "How pleasant! Here it's quiet. / No loud feasting, / Nor clash of cymbals, nor the sound of flutes, / Nor noisy movement of unbridled joy / Reaches me here beneath the gracious trees, / That whispering softly, as though loath to jar, / Invite me now to solitary reflection." *Sappho*, 2.1.456–61.

30. "Weiß ich doch kaum was ich beginne, was ich sage." *Sappho*, 1.3.132.

31. "How everything within my soul has changed / Since I forsook my parents' quiet roof / And turned my horses toward Olympia?" *Sappho*, 2.1.462–64.

32. Similar to Hero's brother in *The Waves of Sea and Love*, Phaon is able to leave the home for adventures, a path reserved only for men.

33. "In calm deliberation I was able / To follow with keen eyes and to untangle / The subtle threads of complicated feelings, / Till, clearly recognized, each lay apart; / But now, like an oppressive summer night / That sweetly suffocates, there brooding lies / A heavy cloud over my sleeping senses, / Through which the distant lightning of my thoughts / Flashes, now here, now there and now / Not anywhere, in torturing confusion— / The past is hidden from me by a veil; / I hardly now remember yesterday, / Or in my present moment that just past." *Sappho*, 2.1.465–77.

34. "Was it *your* name that the delirious throng, / Coupled with her, shouted aloud to heaven?" *Sappho*, 2.1.481–82.

35. "What sort of wretched creature then is man, / When what, as hope, awakened all his senses, / Plunges them, in fulfillment, to sound sleep." *Sappho*, 2.1.484–86.

36. "When I had not yet seen nor known her, only/ Fancy had drawn her ill-resembling picture, / Seen through gray mist and still indefinite, / Then it seemed easy for her single glance, / For one kind word, to offer up my life. . ." *Sappho*, 2.1.487–91.

37. "I still stand asking, thinking, hesitating!" *Sappho*, 2.1.495.

38. "Here I must sit, forlorn and all forsaken, / Far from my parents' hearth in a foreign land, / With slavish fetters pressing on my hands/ That I stretch longingly

toward my kin. / Alas! I sit forlorn and all forsaken / And no one cares to hear or notice me!" *Sappho*, 2.3.554–59.

39. "Here no heart beats in sympathy with me, / And all my relatives live far from here. / I gaze at the children romping round their father, / Kissing his grave brow, his beloved locks; / My father lives beyond the distant seas, / Where nor his daughter's kiss nor voice can reach!" *Sappho*, 2.3.562–67.

40. "Ah, lead me gently back to my own kindred, / That I might cool my sorrow-fevered brow / Upon a soft sympathetic breast, / Ah, lead me to my kindred, or else bear me / Aloft to you! . . .to you!...to you!" *Sappho*, 2.3.585–89.

41. As we will see in *The Waves of Sea and Love*, Hero is desperate to escape the shackle of the family on multiple levels.

42. "And they may love and hate, do what they will, / And what the heart feels, may the lips express. . .The slave girl's place is by the humblest hearth, / No eye regards her there, and no tongue questions; / For her no glance, no thought and no desire!" *Sappho*, 2.3.574–75, 2.3.578–80.

43. Melitta and Phaon inhabit a common space which longs for the conventional, the bands of kinship and the comfort of home. This is where Phaon's love for Melitta develops—in their shared desire for home but also in their discontent with the conditions of their lives. Melitta's attempt to leave the grotto with the roses that she has collected for the celebration is the point where Phaon places a rose on Melitta's breast as a reminder of their encounter: "Sie sei Erinn'rung dir an diese Stunde, / Erinnerung, da nicht bloß in der Heimat / Daß auch in fernem Land es—Freunde gibt." ("Let it remind you of this hallowed hour, / Remind you that not only in your homeland, / But also in remote lands you have—friends.") *Sappho*, 2.4.690–92.

44. Ahmed, *Living a Feminist Life*, 60.

45. Butler was inspired by John Searle's formulation of speech acts ('language acts or linguistic acts') in John Searle, "What Is a Speech Act?" in *Philosophy in America*, ed. Max Black (Ithaca, NY: Cornell University Press, 1965), 221–39. For more on speech acts and performative language, see J. L. Austin's *How to Do Things with Words* (Oxford: Clarendon Press, 1962).

46. Butler, *Gender Trouble*, xv.

47. "He free bestrides the broad way of existence / Encompassed by the rosy dawn of hope, / With strength and courage, as with shield and sword, / Accounted for the laureled fields of fame. / He deems the spirit's quiet world too narrow, / The external draws his wild and restless strivings." *Sappho*, 3.1.815–20.

48. "Am I still here? Is anything still here? / Did not this widespread universe crash, crumbling / In that dread, dire, devastating moment?" *Sappho*, 4.1.1189–91.

49. "All round me quiet reigns, the breeze is silent, / And muted are the merry notes of life; / The leaves, all motionless, emit no sound, / And lonely, as a stranger straying late, / My weeping voice goes wandering through the night. / Whoever like the birds might fall asleep, / Only much longer, never to awaken, / Forever wrapped in deeper, sweeter slumber, / Where everything—the very pulse beat—sleeps, / No ray of dawn awakes to fresh despairs, / No thankless man—Stop! Do not stir the snake!" *Sappho*, 4.1.1196–206.

50. "Phaon! Phaon! What have I done to you? / Serene I stood in my poetic pastures, / Playing alone upon my golden lyre; I gazed down on the little joys of earth, / And all her sufferings did not reach me." *Sappho*, 4.2.1271–75.

51. "And now when he's the one and only thing / Shining before me in the wilderness, / He draws his hand from me, ah, and escapes!" *Sappho*, 4.2.1285–87.

52. "An evil spirit seems to reign, embroiling, / Throughout her house, since Sappho's come back home." *Sappho*, 4.6.1473–74.

53. "O, let me fall! Why are you holding me?" *Sappho*, 4.8.1542.

54. "She hastens to the background and embraces the altar; her maids stand in a circle around her." *Sappho*, act 5, stage directions.

55. "Defenseless I am not, although disarmed. / My fist will be a club for her protection, / And each one of my limbs become an arm!" *Sappho*, 5.3.1595–97.

56. "Am I not a free man? / Who gave her the right to bar my steps? / Thank heaven, in Greece there are still courts of justice! / With terror shall the haughty woman learn this." *Sappho*, 5.3.1621–24.

57. "Are you so tame, that you should lend your men's hands / So docilely to serve a woman's vengeance, / With slave obedience to the whims of love? / Then stand by me, I'm victim of injustice!" *Sappho*, 5.3.1633–36.

58. "Who then is Sappho, that you heed her tongue / As the determinant in the scale of right? / Is she the ruler in this land?" *Sappho*, 5.3.1639–41.

59. Sara Ahmed, *Willful Subjects* (Durham, NC: Duke University Press, 2014), 140.

60. Sara Ahmed, *The Promise of Happiness* (Durham, NC: Duke University Press, 2010), as cited in Sara Ahmed, "A Willfulness Archive," *Theory & Event* 15, no. 3 (2012).

61. Sara Ahmed, "A Willfulness Archive," *Theory & Event* 15, no. 3 (2012).

62. "Would you escape me? You must account to me! / You may well tremble, it's high time to tremble! Are you aware of what you've done? With what right / Dare you detain me here, in scandalous bondage, / Me, a free man, whom none owns but himself? / Look at these here! Did you not send them forth / With most improper weapons? Did you not? Speak! / So dumb! The poetess's sweet lips dumb?" *Sappho*, 5.3.1653–61.

63. "When I swore love to you, it was no sham; / I love you as one may, perhaps, love gods, / As one loves what is good and beautiful. / Let Sappho consort with the lofty one; / One may not with impunity descend / From the gods' feast to moral company. The arm, in which the golden lyre rested, / Is dedicated, may not touch what's earthly." *Sappho*, 5.3.1722–30.

64. "I staggered, in a dull intoxication, / At sharp offs with myself and with the world; / It was in vain I conjured up the feelings, / That I believed asleep, but where not there; / You stood before my gaze a baffling vision / To which and from which unseen forces drove me." *Sappho*, 5.3.1733–39.

65. "Whoever for the first time saw her now, / Standing upon the altar's lofty steps, / Her lyre in hand, her heavenward gaze, / And all her radiant form, of heaven breathing, / Transfiguration beaming all around her, / Would have saluted her as some great goddess / And bent in prayer his supplicating knee. / Yet motionless and silent as she

was, / I felt myself a prey to dread and terror, / Her death-in-life gaze filled my heart with horror. . ." *Sappho*, 5.5.1937–46.

66. "You could not grasp my heart, so go your way! / On firmer ground I now must base my hope." *Sappho*, 5.6.1961–62.

67. "To love, to hate! / Is there no third between?" *Sappho*, 5.6.1963–64.

68. "Sublime and holy Gods! / You have adorned me with your bounteous blessings! / In my hand you bestowed your bow of song, / Bestowed your quiverful of poesy, / A heart to feel, a mind to comprehend, / And power to fashion what I have conceived. / You have adorned me with your bounteous blessings! / I give you thanks!" *Sappho*, 5.6.1981–88.

69. "Her being is transfigured, / The radiance of the immortals shines round her!" *Sappho*, 5.6.2023–24.

70. Ahmed, *Willful Subjects*, 66.

Chapter 2

Medea
The Construction of the Other

Give me my robe. Put on my crown. I have
Immortal longings in me.

—Cleopatra, *The Tragedy of*
Antony and Cleopatra

THE DISSONANT VOICE

How does *Medea* speak back to *Sappho* in ways that articulate a way forward that is also decentered? This decentering is about how a story can be told from the perspective of the outsider or the other. It supports alternative forms of narrative development through persistence and resistance. Refusing the terms of negation and dispossession marks Medea as fugitive in this unstable narrative rendering. This chapter thinks through the ways that Medea is read as a figure of willfulness and difference, an alterity that evinces how gender and its conservative social and political mechanisms create a theoretical feminism located in trauma and exclusion.

How can we understand Grillparzer's liberation of Medea from the ways in which she had been portrayed in other contexts and offer another way of thinking Medea? Gender and ethnic difference are the sites where speech enacts the representation of the female figure, Medea. Her positioning between the center and the margin allows her to regard the world with different eyes, ones that observe and call out the inequities that govern her life. Although she recognizes how her life has taken shape around her, she is estranged from that existence. In a world that will not accommodate her through its exclusionary practices that rely on the rejection of gender difference and ethnic otherness, Medea must find a way to speak and refuse dismissal from the structures that will not make room for her. Unlike Sappho, Medea does not unswervingly belong to the center—fragile as it is. Even as a princess of Colchis, Medea existed on the periphery as a barbarian witch disobedient to the sovereignty of her father, the king. Thus, Medea's story is one that is already at a remove from *Sappho*. Although Sappho, the poetess, becomes increasingly marginalized as the drama progresses, she is initially a figure of value and consequence. It is Medea who has always had to navigate the relationships between the center and the periphery, those spaces between the interior and the margin.

As a victim of gender oppression, Medea destabilizes and undermines social and symbolic gender norms. The feminist impulse in this drama is much more coherent and well-articulated than what we had seen in *Sappho*. Sara Ahmed writes that "Feminism helps you to make sense that something is wrong; to recognize a wrong is to realize that you are not in the wrong."[1] The recognition of this "wrongness" of things is fundamental to this reading of Grillparzer's *Medea*. Medea (along with Sappho and Hero) begins to notice things and asks questions about the world around her and, in the process, exposes its wrongness. Ahmed writes about feminism that "it seems (though perhaps it is not sudden) what you tried so hard not to notice is all you can hear. A sensation that begins at the back of your mind, an uneasy sense of something amiss, gradually comes forward, as things come up; then receding, as you try to get on with things; as you try to get on despite things."[2] Medea is a woman who tried to live—to get on with things—but began to perceive that something was awry.

If we read Grillparzer's *Medea* alongside the feminist work of Sara Ahmed, we can secure a rich way of thinking about how gender can often be regarded as a regulation of possibility. What is it that women are allowed to do and be? This restriction of possibility is a way of imagining the ways in which feminist thinking, despite this constraint, can develop and come to the fore in a text or in a character. We saw how this functioned in *Sappho* and the ways in which Sappho navigated her world within the constraints of gendered norms although, in the end, she was limited in what she could become. Medea uses language in order to understand what is happening to her and how the world moves around her. She is focused on how we know the things that limit.

Central to the discursive framing of Grillparzer's *Medea* is the constructive and deconstructive work of gender and the competing gestures of inclusion and exclusion to which Medea is subject. By the constructive work of gender, I am thinking about how femaleness is connected, arranged, and articulated in the drama around the use of language that has gender as its central motivation. Ideas about femininity, what it looks like, and how it behaves are part of this constructive work that Medea destabilizes. This is closely tied to the ways in which practices of exclusion are linked to the female presence and used punitively as ways to disallow the figure of the female from naming and then negotiating the terms of her life even when granted a measure of autonomy in other areas. As an outsider, Medea is subject to various forms of marginalizing and censorious language from a series of men for whom she does not perform as desired. Cast as a wretched being and contemptible, Medea defies that affiliation through her defiant language use.

When asked to account for herself across all three dramas of the trilogy, *Das goldene Vließ,* Medea is essentially asked to justify her existence, the possibility of her humanity:

> To be questioned, to be questionable, sometimes can feel like a residence: a question becomes something you reside in. To reside in a question can feel like not being where you are at. Not from here, not? Or maybe to become *not* is to be wrapped up by an assertion. To be asked "Where are you from?" is a way of being told you are not from here.[3]

This questioning considers what it means to live life as if it were an unceasing crisis situation. To be asked to give an account of oneself over and over becomes an impasse or an emergency condition. By emergency, I mean circumstances in which a person can go no further, where there is no escape— neither backward nor forward or even out. Medea's plight is one in which she must always give answer and explain herself to those who will never receive her even if she gives the proper reply. Alienated from life, Medea dwells in the question of her humanness through the persistence of crisis situations. Ahmed discussing the idea of crisis writes:

> When we say we have reached a breaking point, we often evoke a crisis . . . when what you come up against threatens to be too much, threatens a life, or a dream, or a hope. A crisis can also be an opening, a new way of proceeding, depending on how we do or do not resolve that crisis; depending on whether we think of a crisis as something that needs to be resolved.[4]

Medea causes crisis by living in her body and embracing her genealogy as a witch while speaking her truth from those origins. Yet, her performances throughout the trilogy offer us a reading of the periphery as a site where trauma is voiced as both a knowing and a not knowing. This knowing hinges on Medea's knowledge of her marginal status as a Colchian, a witch, and a woman. However, the not knowing is where Grillparzer's ventriloquism of Medea becomes the way in which she can articulate her refusal and defiance of the social experience of the Greek world. Both (knowing and not knowing) function at the level of comprehension and repetition in this space where

Medea must live inside of a life that consistently refuses to accept her. The ventriloquial moment in *Medea* is about how Grillparzer infuses her testimony about her life with a critique of what the creation of alterity does and how it performs its exclusionary function.

While Medea may occupy the center of the dramatic discourse of the drama, she is also marginalized as the witch, the foreigner, the other.[5] But throughout this familiar strangeness, Medea is also a textual riddle that stands on the periphery and makes incursions (or, perhaps raids) into the center. She is both central to and at the edges of social experience which makes her language use a form of political labor and trespass. Her determined efforts to become known are rebuffed and she is represented as both the familiar and the foreign. Although identified as the dangerous stranger, Medea is also recognized as "something" that is somehow *known* by the community (both Colchian and Greek) to be wrong—unseemly and incongruous. This marginalization is also about her gender—her assignment as woman is also part of her outsider status—as a social and political entity. Medea causes problems. She willfully disturbs and interrupts. Yet she is also the victim of socially inscribed structures that push her to the outside and construct her as a danger. As a female figure, she should be silent and compliant. Yet, Medea demands more for herself and insists that space be made for her needs. She asks questions which disrupt the proper functioning of the male world in Colchis and in Corinth. She makes claims that are exceptional coming from a woman by questioning power and its use. The manner in which she speaks is contemptuous yet still yearns for social belonging.

We have seen how Medea's difference is depicted as multiple: she is a barbarian, an identity which suggests signs of ethnic (and racial) difference, she is a witch, and she does not perform her gendered female role as she should.[6] Sara Ahmed writes: "A gender system is not at work simply in how you do or do not express gender: it is also about how you perform within a wider system that matches meaning and value to persons and things."[7] Medea's refusal to be conditioned to a gender system is what marks her as the wrong sort. Her performance is out of step with the requirements for the system. Medea, the tragic heroine, makes little effort to become attuned to the values and norms of the space she now inhabits as a stranger and as a female subject.

Medea willfully resides in spaces that were not made for her. Thus, she becomes an unresolved problem because she refuses to leave those unwelcoming spaces. As readers, we become invested with her right to belong: "Think of this; how we learn about worlds when they do not accommodate us. Think of the kinds of experiences you have when you are not expected to be here."[8] Going forward, I wonder if this isn't an important way to understand Medea—as someone who is unwelcome, a figure that is unassimilable?

How does this drama turn? How does it move over time? Grillparzer's *Medea* is descriptive: The work is not tidy and it shows its own struggle, our struggle, with thinking with this Medea. Her story is not an unfamiliar one. We know her well. Perhaps too much so. Our knowledge of Medea leaves little room for her to be alive in a new way. Thus, Grillparzer's step back into the ventriloquial space gives her language in which to tell a story, one that is tightly woven, sharp, and tense. Dirk Weissmann writes that, "It is a story of migration, exile, asylum, and more generally of contact between cultures, which Grillparzer's adaptation emphasizes by being the first in theatre history to retrace the origins of the Golden Fleece."[9]

We have a rich idea of the figure of Medea—a legacy of the many revisions and adaptations of her story.[10] This abundance allows Grillparzer to transform the story of Medea into a trilogy, *The Golden Fleece*, one that explores situations and behaviors that disrupt and challenge conventional social structures. This trilogy also poses questions about what literature, specifically, Attic tragedy, says about human life and its cultural and ritual representation. Indeed, Grillparzer has transgressed by creating a trilogy. His is a subversion of the narrative that we have come to expect of *Medea*—this elongation confronts the closing off of the legend of Medea by insisting that there was more to this myth that remained unarticulated or understated. And Grillparzer's version provides a more holistic and potentially transformative version of *Medea*. That is, he changes the social and textual meaning of the word "Medea" in *The Golden Fleece*.

Since Grillparzer wrote the story of Medea across three dramas, he was able to be expansive about the details of the text that were briefer narrative acts in Euripides' text. Grillparzer's decision allowed him to offer the reader a much richer articulation of who Medea was, what her motivations were, how she lived, and under what conditions. While all versions of the Medea myth offer incredible detail about the nature of her crimes, they still remained condensed—locked in a narrative time that had no recourse to the past or to the site of the alleged crimes. By choosing the trilogy as his form and layering time and space, Grillparzer is already at play with the narrative of Medea made famous by Euripides.

Grillparzer recasts the conflict in *Medea* to include problems of internal dissonance in order to dramatize the collapse of the external and ornamental against that of the internal and unadorned. Medea struggles to communicate the conflict that is internally generated when external circumstances threaten the status of the self. Grillparzer takes great efforts to present Medea as cognizant of the multiplicity of impulses that organize her behavior through speech-acts. This is about the need to uncover and force into language the silences that regulate the social world and thus explore problems of genealogy, civic duty, and power within a gendered system. Thus, *Medea* revolves around language and representation, or, more specifically, what language can accomplish from attempts at representation.

Grillparzer's rendering of Euripides' *Medea* initiates a discourse between Grillparzer's present and the Euripidean past.[11] The fascination with representing women in Greek tragedy, which was written and performed by men and primarily directed at a male audience, appears contradictory to what we understand of the classical world. However, the dramatization of identity, kinship, and authority as the central activities of ancient tragedies renders the representation—perhaps over representation—of the female in drama an intelligible choice given the socially and politically marginal position occupied by women in antiquity.[12] Margaret Williamson wrote that the distinction between the public and private spheres in the study of Athens of the fifth century BC gained currency as a historical and sociological interest in "the construction of the idea of the private and [that] tragedy is an important source for our understanding of it."[13] The private in *Medea* is made fully public in Grillparzer's account of the challenges that she must confront.

Because Grillparzer effectively uses the female heroine to explore conflicts that are located in genealogy and power—sites of masculinity—it is a creative strategy that undercuts the firmly established concept of what is allowed to be depicted in a culture dominated by the male. Grillparzer's frequent utilization of the female as lead protagonist had compound and perhaps unexpected rewards. He produced works which, by design or otherwise, generated a discourse about the problem of social cohesion and compliance, a dialogue which coalesced around the concepts of the family, inheritance, and duty (a discussion reserved for the final chapter on *The Waves of Sea and Love*). What emerges from this socially embedded preoccupation with behavior and propriety is a critical formulation of a shift in how language functions as a "teller" of people. Representation and language are central to *Medea* as are the ways in which gender and ethnicity are critical modes that underwrite representation and language in the drama.

CRISIS AND KINSHIP

The Golden Fleece is the title that guides our understanding of the trilogy. In the very titles of the first two dramas, Grillparzer delays the declaration of the name Medea and one must imagine how the first two dramas, *Der Gastfreund* [*The Guest*] and *Die Argonauten* [*The Argonauts*], might lead us to *Medea*. Grillparzer's manner of assembling the trilogy and locating *Medea* as the final drama suggests that the real story begins much earlier and with a different crime than the one we have come to know from the ancient literature.

The first drama of the trilogy perhaps better called a prologue, *The Guest*, is a one-act tragedy that dramatizes the origins of the Golden Fleece: the dream in Apollo's Temple in Delphi that causes Phryxus, a minor Greek figure,[14] to bring the fleece to Colchis and his eventual murder by the King of Colchis. The fleece, a ram's pelt, is also here represented as intimately tied with concepts of kinship and legitimacy. The slaying of the foreigner, the guest, is thematized as an insult to laws about hospitality and the moral obligation by the host to extend *Gastfreundschaft*, a theme that announces the importance of the stranger as a feature of society—something that is prominent in *Medea* but which does not benefit her otherwise.

Medea is figured in this drama as a willful and independent woman outraged by her father's actions that portend the fall of their house. She condemns her father for the murder of the foreigner and decries his actions as they will call down the wrath and curse of the gods. What is most interesting about this brief drama is that it is Grillparzer's addition to the story of Medea in the trilogy. It was not a particularly popular tale in the many mythic treatments or even in Euripides' *Medea,* but rather this lesser-known story in the Greek pantheon is a unique feature of the trilogy that demonstrates how Grillparzer pieces narratives together to depict the stranger and how he or she is always in a position of danger.

The Guest begins with a sacrifice of a deer to the Colchian goddess, Darimba (the virgin goddess of the hunt similar to Artemis or Diana), by Medea who stands with bow in hand. While triumphant at her success, she is intractable in her distaste when it comes to one of her loyal servants, Peritta, who has done the unforgivable and fallen in love with a man. As a faithful devotee of Medea, Peritta belonged to her: "Versprachst du nicht du wolltest mein sein, mein / Und keines Manns? Sag' an, versprachst du's?" (Grillparzer, *Guest*, 53–54).[15] Medea is unyielding in her disgust for what she sees as Peritta's disgrace. She displays no sympathy for Peritta, and Medea's self-righteousness leads her to overly dramatic and damning words. When Peritta says that she was swept away with no free will, Medea is both cruel and unforgiving in her response to the girl: "Sie wollte nicht und tat's! Geh du sprichst Unsinn. /Wie konnt' es den geschehn / Wenn du nicht wolltest. Was ich tu' das will ich / Und was ich will—je nu das tu' ich manchmal nicht" (*Guest*, 64–67).[16] There is already some sense that Medea's words will come back to haunt her in the second drama. She is contemptuous of Peritta but will also fall prey to the same speechless and senseless feelings of love for Jason in *The Argonauts*. One could say that Medea is the unwitting victim of her own language in this moment.

With the arrival of the stranger, Phryxus, the Colchians, on guard, are prepared to do battle. The king of Colchis enters the scene for the first time and asks that Medea stay and advise him. It is apparent that they have a strained relationship when Aietes tells his "good child" to help him and Medea responds:

Bin ich dein gutes Kind!
Sonst achtest du meiner wenig.
Wenn ich will, willst du nicht
Und schiltst mich und schlägt nach mir;
Aber wenn du mein bedarfst
Lockst du ich mit Schmeichelworten
Und nennst mich Medea, dein liebes Kind. (*Guest*, 121–27)[17]

Grillparzer immediately creates tension between father and daughter that centers on obedience, duty, and love: Aietes calls on Medea's skills as a witch, an inheritance from her mother, while Medea condemns her father's unpredictable need for her powers. The designation of her as "good child" is rejected by Medea in the face of her father's manipulation of her for his needs in monitoring the arrival of the strangers and overseeing their movements. There is a past between the father and daughter that is unknown, but one can only imagine that it is connected to Medea's intransigence in matters related to her family duties. Calling her a clever girl, Aietes now positions himself as the doting father. Unfortunately for Medea, her life has been reduced to her use-value. Her tumultuous relationship with her father leads to this charged and hostile exchange of words between the two but also tells the reader that Medea is a woman who can use language to evaluate and assess situations: Aietes needs her help in order to defend himself and his people against the stranger who has certainly come, Aietes believes, to destroy the Colchians and take Aietes's crown and his life. Phryxus enters the scene with the golden ram's pelt in the shape of a banner on his lance and plants it in the ground. When Phryxus sees Medea for the first time, he greets her as a ". . . gute Vorbedeutung / Für eine Zukunft, die uns noch verhüllt" (*Guest*, 254–55).[18] Phryxus's omen of this unknown future challenges the reader to think about ideas not simply kindred to Medea as the future consort of Jason but also to those that center around the status of the guest, the stranger. Phryxus's own story of his journey to Colchis is one that Medea will also contend with as she makes her way with Jason to the Greek world at the close of the second drama. At the end of *The Guest*, after a short battle, Aietes stabs Phryxus whose dying words signal the ways in which the murder of the guest is an affront to the gods, how ruin will come to Aietes's house, and how revenge will be meted out. In opposition to her father's demands that she remain, Medea slowly dismantles the structures that were not meant to accommodate her, refusing to participate, and thus becomes a category of difficulty as she flees the scene of the murder to her tower in the wilderness.

The second text, the four-act drama *The Argonauts*, is fully in the Colchian world with the arrival of Jason and his Argonauts. Taking place years after the murder of Phryxus, it is essentially a revenge drama. However, the problem of the stranger, the foreigner, and the potential criminal remains central to the discourse. It has as its core motivations Medea's family loyalty, her alienation from that family, her vocation as a witch, and her sudden and inexplicable love for Jason. It also focuses on Jason and his quest to become the king of his land, Jolkos, if he retrieves the well-guarded fleece, an impossible task set to him by his uncle Pelias who has seized Jason's rightful throne. With the help of Medea, Jason does retrieve the fleece which is guarded by a terrifying dragon in a cave. The drama concludes with the death of Medea's brother, Absyrtus,[19] and the pronouncement of a generational blood curse on Medea by her father. Medea, who has reluctantly fallen in love with Jason, leaves Colchis with him as a disgraced and now homeless woman.[20]

Medea's role in *The Argonauts* is invested with a performative function which cannot be represented but whose insistence on self-presentation—as a woman who speaks—is already in defiance of procedural authority. Her father, Aietes, king of the Colchians, commands Medea:

Jetzt komm!—Doch erst sag' an wer dir erlaubt,
Zu fliehn des väterlichen Hauses Hut
Und hier, in der Gesellschaft nur der Wildnis
Und deines wilden Sinns, Gehorsam weigernd
Zu trotzen meinem Worte, meinem Wink? (*Argonauts*, 1.87–91)[21]

As a woman, the daughter of a royal house, and a subject of sovereign power, the constraints on her are multiple and tether her to a set of expectations located around the sovereign, the father, and the man—all identities of authority that demand compliance. Aietes, as both sovereign and patriarch, is invested with a dual power which should restrict Medea in all ways—domestic, civic, and psychological. Her presence should be acquiescent and unreadable. Since custom has already prescribed her function as a witch, Aietes's attempt to rein in her unruly behavior by regulating where her body is permitted to be—the physical parameters of her obedience—indicates that the figure of Medea is already directed elsewhere: to a site beyond custom and duty where language rather than actions structure her life and where the form of address operates in the wilderness, a place without constraints.

Medea could be said to open up two critical modes of rupture (rather than difference)—the linguistic defiance of sovereign and patriarchal (gendered) power and the unintelligibility of her own representation: She imperils the social mechanisms of male dominance and female subordination by speaking:

So höre wenn du kannst und zürne wenn du darfst.
O könnt' ich schweigen, ewig schweigen!
Verhaßt ist mir dein Haus
Mit Schauder erfüllt mich deine Nähe.
Als du den Fremden erschlugst,
Den Götterbeschützten, den Gastfreund
Und raubtest sein Gut,
Da trugst du einen Funken in dein Haus,
Der glimmt und glimmt und nicht verlöschen wird,
Gössest du auch darüber aus
Was an Wasser die heil'ge Quelle hat,
Der Ströme und Flüsse unnennbare Zahl
Und das ohne Grenzen gewaltige Meer.
Ein törichter Schütze ist der Mord,
Schießt seinen Pfeil ab ins dunkle Dickicht,
Gewinnsüchtig, beutegierig,
Und was er für ein Wild gehalten,
Für frohen Jagdgewinn,
Es war sein Kind, sein eigen Blut,
Was in den Blättern rauschte, Beeren suchend.
Unglücksel'ger was hast du getan? (*Argonauts*, 1.94–113)[22]

Her linguistic intervention undermines firmly established arrangements of power—over life and death and over children and genealogy. Her condemnation of her father and his inhospitable behavior toward Phryxus has opened the floodgates of a language of (female) recrimination that is now impossible to close. Medea uses the verb "schweigen" to announce the impossibility of remaining "silent" in light of her father's murderous greed regarding the fleece.

   The struggle for Medea's powers in both dramas forces her to realize that she is already an outsider amidst the familiar. Although a Colchian and born of a royal family, she is still not entirely trusted by her father because of her gender and the magical powers that she wields. As a Colchian, she is deemed barbaric and lacking the civilization of the Greeks by Jason. Yet, both men need her, or, at least, need to appropriate her skills as a sorceress for their own purposes. Thus, female power has its place when it is brought under the strict control of male authority in order to serve men's needs. It might be useful to think about this rupture in Medea's self-concept—her enigmatic relationship to herself—as one engendered by the contradictory messages that she receives from the male figures in her life grounded in the cultural subordination of women as other.[23] She has use and value but she is not to be trusted; she is wanted and needed, but must be held at a distance; she is a potential foe but that danger can be beneficially exploited. In *The Guest* and *The Argonauts,* Grillparzer dramatizes themes that will become dominant in *Medea*. It is the fleece which connects all three dramas as it represents the extraction of wealth—material and existential—from the Colchians by the Greeks. Both plays rely heavily on issues related to the foreigner and stranger, power and will, and rejection and exile. What Grillparzer presents in these first two dramas of the trilogy are the primary problems, which will only be fully fulfilled, in the final drama, *Medea*.

Taking care not to oversimplify Medea, I want to look at points in the drama where her alienation from the structures around her speak directly to her gender and how this drama moves around those moments where Medea functions as the rogue female figure. Here, we might look briefly to Judith Butler's *Antigone's Claim*,[24] a theorization of the role of Antigone in Sophocles' drama.[25] Butler explores the legacy of the feminist impulse to confront and defy the state.[26] Using readings of *Antigone* that include Hegel, Lacan, and Irigaray reading Hegel, Butler's Antigone is one who, like Medea, will not be silent even though she is a figure in and of crisis. The crisis that Antigone evokes is the crime that violates the decree of the new king of Thebes, her uncle Creon, when she buries her brother Polyneices. Polyneices had raised an army against his brother, Eteocles in order to win his rightful place as King of Thebes. Both brothers die in battle and Creon, the brother of Jocasta and uncle to the dead brothers, deems Polyneices a criminal and illegitimate in his claims to the throne. Creon buries Eteocles with all due honors and reverence and denies Polyneices a proper funeral—in fact; he wants his corpse left exposed to the elements, where birds and dogs may savage him. Antigone believes the human law forbidding the burial of her brother Polyneices to be unjust and contrary to the laws of the gods. Therefore, she acts. Her deed is that she buries her brother not once, but twice. Each time placing a dusting of earth on his body and pouring libations to him. It is the second time that the guards discover her in the act and she is brought before Creon where her speech is also an act. She admits that it was she who did the deed.

Antigone, like Medea, has challenged kinship relations through her defiance of her uncle Creon and his authority as sovereign; she has caused a crisis of sovereignty through her insubordination. In her act of rebellion, she defies both gender and kinship norms by burying her brother, Polyneices. Here, my analysis is pulled into affinity with *Medea* and with Butler's attempt to understand Antigone as "a feminine figure who defies the state through a powerful set of physical and linguistic acts."[27] Contrary to this initial analytical inquiry, Butler found something else. In her readings of Hegel and Lacan on *Antigone* she discovered that Antigone was not taken up as political figure in their studies. Rather she had been read by the two as a defiant figure, whose speech "articulates a pre-political opposition to politics, representing kinship as the sphere that conditions the possibility of politics without ever entering into it."[28] This is where I want to stop to think about both propositions in the case of Grillparzer's *Medea*: the Medea who is mired in the political and the Medea who occupies a space that centers a pre-political opposition representing breaking points and moments of crisis. I would argue that Medea is a deeply political figure and her mode of resistance is entangled with kinship norms and rights. Kinship and the state cannot be divided in Grillparzer's rendering of the myth and appear to be unresolvable. Medea's actions have direct consequences for political life as well as civic life. Butler goes on to write that Antigone has already departed from kinship.[29] Here, Butler makes a sharp argument about Antigone's wielding of power as being about how kinship makes "its claim within the language of the state but with *the social deformation of both idealized kinship and political sovereignty that emerges as a consequence of her act.*"[30] In a similar manner, Medea participates in political life as defiant: a speaker and creator of crisis whose insistence on the validity of her claim resides in the discursive potential of her actions. Antigone enacts crisis in a similar fashion to Medea's own performance as disruptive of normative kinship relationships and their generative fulfillment. While Medea is both complicit in acts of state and defiant of that very statism, she remains a puzzling figure due to her dual roles as a political figure and one whose very figure is directed elsewhere. Thus, the possibility of contextualizing Medea is a slippery game whose actions on both sides articulate opposing ideas about the state, kinship, and ethics. She is the crisis.

Grillparzer's lengthy and heavily detailed composition extends and complicates Medea as an articulation of practices of inclusion and exclusion as well as the mechanisms of gender difference. His version of Medea is a representation that is both foreign and new. It might even be called dangerous. The ethical process and moral aspirations that we have witnessed in other works by Grillparzer remain ambiguous and the dramatist offers no moral principle with which to formulate answers about Medea and the events of her life, the decisions that she makes, the suffering that she endures, or the revenge that she takes. The energy that saturates the drama is anxious, ironic, and despairing. Yet, Grillparzer creates a sympathetic character in his interpretation of Medea. How does he manage such a feat when we, the reader, know her story? Her offenses, as they have come down to us as a murderess and an infanticide, are well-known and horrific.

Grillparzer's detailed adaptation is subjective, uncertain about the character of the dramatic world, and doubtful about the position of moral experience in such a world. The helplessness of Medea, her emotional breakdown, and the physical destruction that she organizes in the final drama all point back to her experience of guilt, rejection, and banishment on Corinth and from her ancestral home, Colchis. Like Jason, we wonder what will happen next in this drama but give in to the inevitability of an extreme outcome. For Phryxus, Aietes, and Jason, the fleece is a prized object which launched an insatiable and destructive desire for power.

EXILE IN THE KINGDOM

Grillparzer's revision commences with Medea on the shores of Corinth. In Euripides' *Medea*, the nurse, Gora, speaks a long descriptive monologue which narrates the stories that Grillparzer dramatizes in the first two dramas of the trilogy—this is a temporal and geographic omission that Grillparzer retrieves for the details of *Medea*. However, it is now Gora who becomes the voice that tortures Medea.[31] She retells the story of their endless wandering, their fugitive status, and their greeting as outcasts and barbarians by the inhabitants of Hellas. Gora is the choral voice that reminds Medea, who would forget, all that she has suffered as the banished princess of a faithless husband.

In her explication, the Euripidean nurse opens the text by giving the audience the motivation for her own resentment and what life has turned out to be since they left Medea's ancestral home. Three critical points that Euripides' nurse makes are about Medea's actions on behalf of Jason while in exile, the ways in which love is contaminated and destroyed, and what it means to be homeless, or, in Medea's case, "unhomed." The nurse speaks the opening lines of the tragedy and concludes with:[32]

She's a strange woman. I know it won't be easy
To make an enemy of her and come off best. (Euripides, *Medea* 44–45)

The nurse's opening monologue in Euripides' *Medea* provides the audience with all necessary information about the story up to the betrothal of Jason to the daughter of the king of Corinth. In the very first scene of the Euripidean *Medea*, the nurse does the linguistic and contextual work that Grillparzer had apportioned to the first two plays in the trilogy. For Grillparzer, these pre-stories exist in time, and they also exist in place. On the other hand, Euripides condensed those actions to a narrated testimonial past and focused only on the evidentiary now of the events in Corinth. Grillparzer's dramas take on the work of extending our understanding of the initiating stories. This is critical because it confirms that for Grillparzer the story of Medea was not only about her relationship with Jason and her rage over his betrayal of her for the daughter of the Corinthian king. That is, it was not just love and desire that were at stake for Medea. She was also looking for a way out of a life that left her with few possibilities for personhood and self-possession due to her precarious social and political situation as a figure without a home.

My usage of the term "unhomed" above originates from Homi Bhabha's formulation of this condition in the introduction to *The Location of Culture*.[33] For Bhabha, "unhomed" is "not to be homeless, nor can the 'unhomely' be easily accommodated in that familiar division of social life into private and public spheres. The unhomely moment creeps up on you stealthily as your own shadow."[34] It is not a problem of being homeless but rather one of being compelled to manage anew one's place in the world because of dislocation—geographic or cultural. Medea, like many postcolonial and migrant people is outside of "home" due to "extra-territorial and cross-cultural initiation."[35] Medea's "unhomed" identity changes the ways in which she intervenes in the social world of Corinth—she is active in both public and private provinces and upsets the balance that has long functioned in those areas. Medea no longer commands a space out of which she can identify—that has been lost to her. Thus, her unhomed self is a coming to light, a surfacing that intermingles with the private and the public. This causes a refocusing of her vision of the world, one which is no longer easily demarcated between public and private. The merger between the two spheres is, according to Bhabha, in service of feminism (Bhabha's formulations emerge from his discussion of Nadine Gordimer and Toni Morrison):

> By making visible the forgetting of the "unhomely" moment in civil society, feminism specifies the patriarchal, gendered nature of civil society and disturbs the symmetry of private and public which is now shadowed, or uncannily doubled, by the difference of genders which does not neatly map on to the private and the public, but becomes disturbingly supplementary to them. This results in redrawing the domestic space as the space of the normalizing, pastoralizing, and individuating techniques of modern power and police: the personal-is-the-political; the world-in-the-home.[36]

Although Bhabha's analysis takes us, in many ways, beyond Grillparzer's *Medea*, one can observe patterns in the drama that resonate with the ways in which Bhabha comes to identify the feminism of a text—through the gendered and patriarchal program of the society.

The uncanny doubling of the private and public is an important aspect of Medea's intervention into those spaces where she is least welcome. She is an adjacent figure that strains the proper operation of civic society by her necessary inclusion within it as a stranger. Sara Ahmed notes and this is important for the idea of the "unhomed" that "[r]ecognizing strangers becomes a moral and social injunction. Some bodies are in an instant judged as suspicious, or as dangerous, as objects to be feared, a judgment that is lethal. There can be nothing more dangerous to a body than the social agreement that that body is dangerous. We can simplify: it is dangerous to be perceived as dangerous."[37] For Medea, the restriction of her life resides not only in her gender and the way she expresses it but also in her position as the familiar stranger—someone who is alien but who can still be identified as a known entity—a danger to the proper functioning of life. Medea reveals this forgetting of the "unhomely" by becoming a transgressive site of knowing how dislocation and alienation come together to form a desire for home, a longing which is both political and personal. The composure that had long been the provenance of patriarchal structures is upset by the infiltration of a Medea. The visibility of this "unhomed" woman and her troublesome presence cannot be separated from established discourses about power and its operation as an essential feature of the public and the private.

In Act 1, Medea and Jason have landed on Corinth in search of safe haven from their years of wandering. The fleece has traveled with Medea from Colchis and served Jason whenever he has required it.[38] At this moment, Medea makes the conscious decision to renounce dark powers and conjuration in exchange for a life among the Greeks. This chest is filled with death and destruction; it holds the marks of unnatural powers and signs. It also carries within it all the shame that Medea has been unable to keep at a distance—the guilt caused by the destruction of her father and brother and the downfall of her house on Colchis. The journey to Corinth and the hope of a new life coupled with years of endless wandering have led the enchantress to this final decision. Medea wants to banish the supernatural from what she imagines to be the inauguration of a new life on Corinthian soil. As the drama opens just before daybreak, Medea has a slave bury the chest containing the fleece along with her other magical tools. "Die Zeit der Nacht, der Zauber ist vorbei / Und was geschieht, ob Schlimmes oder Gutes, / Es muß geschehn am offnen Strahl des Lichts" (*Medea*, 1.4–6).[39]

Gora appears to have a prophetic role in that her recounting of Medea's life since leaving Colchis pre-tells the coming betrayal by Jason. Gora's words in the first act of Grillparzer's

Medea prefigure the downfall of another house (that of the king of Corinth). Indeed, Gora, in her opening commentary, insistently and persistently admonishes Medea to recall the deprivations that she has endured for Jason. She chastises Medea for burying the chest containing the fleece, the veil, and the flaming goblet: "Vergraben willst du / Die Zeichen eines Dienstes, der Schutz dir gab / Und noch dir geben kann?" (*Medea*, 1.23–24).[40] [i] Gora understands the symbolic but also very tangible powers of those objects. These items represent Medea's authority and resourcefulness as a witch, but they also negatively link Medea to her Colchian heritage by reminding us of her presence at the original murderous act, the killing of Phryxus. Once these tools are interred, Medea has abandoned all of her defenses against the Hellenes, a condition which Gora perceptively diagnoses as perilous for Medea. Jason also understands the significance of Medea's powers in a different way and wants her to abjure all habits that are reminiscent of her previous life: "Ich aber sage dir, / Du tust sehr wohl, wenn du es unterläßt! / Brau nicht aus Kräutern Säfte, Schlummertrank. / Sprich nicht zum Mond, stör nicht die Toten, / Mann haßt das hier, und ich—ich haß es auch! / In Kolchis sind wir nicht, in Griechenland, / Nicht unter Ungeheuern, unter Menschen" (*Medea*, 1.178–83).[41] [ii] Jason wishes that she renounce her past life—a life that had given her power and a stake in Colchis' civic world. This is his way of announcing that there is a difference between what is deemed appropriate for life among the Greeks represented by Corinth, whom he endows with humanity, and that of the Colchian world, a barbarian one lacking civilization.

In Act 1, Jason reflects on what it feels like to be a stranger, a foreigner, and an asylum seeker. The king enters and asks: "Wo ist der Fremde?—Ahnend sagt mein Herz, / Er ist es, der Verbannte, der Vertriebne— / Der Schuldige vielleicht.—Wo ist der Fremde?" (*Medea*, 1.273–274). Jason responds to the king with these words:

Hier bin ich, und gebeugt tret ich vor dich;
Kein Fremder zwar, doch nur zu sehr entfremdet.
Ein Hilfesuchender, ein Flehender.
Von Haus und Herd vertrieben, ausgestoßen,
Fleh ich zum Gastfreund um ein schützend Dach (*Medea*, 1.276–80).[42]

The king's words are clear about who he expects to see on the shore—the stranger, the exiled, the expelled, the guilty one. This is a rich lexicon for describing that, which is disallowed within the confines of his world. Jason's vocabulary in his address to the king is remarkable for its multiple use of words that perform an outsider status, a state that repeats the king's own language about the stranger and that previously had only been applied to Medea. The syntax of Jason's short speech is suffused with language that has a lyrical momentum that turns him into an object of his own speech. He is not a stranger but still estranged. He seeks help; he is a supplicant. He has been expelled and driven out and now comes to the king seeking acceptance as a "Gastfreund." It is especially important to keep Jason's speech at the forefront of our thinking when it comes to Medea's status as one who is not at home. Jason may be able to name himself as an exile or stranger, but Medea has those same terms thrust upon her as identificatory words. It establishes how she will be treated in the drama and how she will respond to that treatment.

Act 1 is also the space in which one form of femininity meets another. Kreusa, the daughter of the Corinthian king, is the proper sort of woman and reproduces an acceptable form of femininity much like Melitta did in *Sappho*.[43] She is gentle and demure; she fades into the background; and she only speaks when directly addressed. Medea, also the daughter of a king, is the very antithesis of Kreusa. She fills out the space with her willful presence; she will not stop talking; and she refuses to allow others to deny her agency. At one point, Kreusa calls the children of Medea and Jason "homeless little orphans [heimatlosen Waisen]," a designation which angers Medea by suggesting that the boys are both homeless and motherless. However, it also implies that the children are fatherless, an interesting movement in the drama and one that triggers a sort of vigilance on the part of the reader to pay greater attention to the myriad ways in which parents are separated from their children. It also forces the reader to think of how Medea's children are also displaced in this social space where they will perhaps be treated with disdain due to their mother's origins. Although initially denied entrance to the city by Kreon, Medea is finally and with great reluctance allowed to enter Corinth at the close of Act 1—with the caveat that should she disturb the peace, she would be driven out.

There are moments in the drama when Kreusa and Medea appear to join in common cause: Kreusa defends Medea from allegations of savagery when she sees that Medea is able to weep. Yet Medea recognizes that her outsider status is due to her otherness: "Weil eine Fremd' bin ich, aus fernem Land / Und unbekannt mit dieses Bodens Bräuchen, / Verachten sie mich, sehen auf mich herab, / Und eine scheue Wilde bin ich ihnen, / Die Unterste, die Letzte aller Menschen" (*Medea*, 1.400–404).[44] Again, the language is unmistakably caught up in the idea of the foreigner who is depicted as the despised outcast. It is here in Act 2, that Medea makes her complaint against Jason in her strongest terms yet. Kreusa is the audience for this outpouring of recriminations:

Du kennst ihn nicht, ich aber kenn ihn ganz.
Nur er ist da, er in der weiten Welt,
Und alles andre nichts als Stoff zu Taten.
Voll Selbstheit, nicht des Nutzens, doch des Sinns,
Spielt er mit seinem und der andern Glück.
Lockt's ihn nach Ruhm, so schlägt er einen tot,
Will er ein Weib, so holt er eine sich,
Was auch darüber bricht, was kümmert's ihn!
Er tut nur recht, doch recht ist, was er will.
Du kennst ihn nicht, ich aber kenn ihn ganz,
Und denk ich an die Dinge, die geschehn,
Ich könnt' ihn sterben sehen und lachen drob. (*Medea*, 2.629–40).[45]

In this bold speech, Medea lays bare her complaints against Jason and shocks Kreusa with the depth of her animosity toward him. Medea is both enraged and also grieving for her life which has been handled carelessly by Jason. She has the deepest knowledge of Jason, his motivations, his selfishness, and his mercenary ways. He uses people to attain his goals without thought or remorse. Medea understands something about Jason that Kreusa does not. It is Medea's ability to interpret Jason that gives her the insight expressed with the severest of language.

At the close of Act 2, Medea has been ordered to be banished from Corinth. News has come that she was the one responsible for the death of Pelias, Jason's uncle. Grillparzer's version remains ambiguous about Medea's culpability in the death of Pelias and tacitly pardons her from that crime carried out in Jason's ancestral home. Jason, spared exile by Kreon, is deemed innocent in the matter. Kreon immediately takes Jason in as his new son-in-law, the betrothed of Kreusa. Medea must leave Corinth before daybreak or face death. However, she insists that Jason follow her and share the mutual guilt and the punishment (*Medea*, 2.1041–46). In one of the most foreboding exchanges between Medea and Jason, he tells her that she has robbed him of his life and happiness and demands that she give him back to himself. "Laß ab von mir, du meine Tage Fluch! / Die mir geraubt mein Leben und Glück.../ Gib Jason mir zurücke, Frevlerin" (*Medea*, 2.1047–48, 2.1054).[46] Medea's response is one that gets to the core of the problem between the two: "Zurück willst du den Jason?—Hier!—Hier nimm ihn! / Allein, wer gibt Medeen mir, wer mich?" (*Medea*, 2.1055–56).[47] Both insist that a crime has been committed and that crime is about the loss of a stable identity or the theft of the identifier for the self. Speaking in the imperative and as complainants, each accuses the other and pleads for the return of the self. This self that is wanted is both intangible and abstract and also substantial and material. It is both internal and external. In a linguistic move, Medea "gives" Jason back to himself but then in a moment that is about loss, she asks who will give Medea back to her. She understands that Jason cannot do that nor would he if he could. Medea is asking a question and asking it incessantly, trying to find an answer where none exists. Overflowing with anger and despondency, a deep sadness holds the power to make and break narrative in this exchange. Medea is immersed in the material of her life and there is no escaping that very thingness or actuality that exists between her and Jason. Acting in the name of language, Medea can fulfill Jason's demand. However, as a familiar stranger, Medea cannot act on her own behalf and reclaim herself due to her own precarity. This danger is based on her exclusion from all forms of sociality because of who she is and what she represents. While Jason can reclaim his identity as a sovereign being, Medea is unable to do so in her position as the gendered other.[48] This inability to recall herself is as much about her present circumstances as it is about her lack of kinship ties and social or political power.

Gora and Medea become the voices of female fugitivity in the third act. Gora reminds Medea of all that she has suffered and endured because of Jason. She goads Medea on to exact revenge: "So straf ihn, triff ihn, / Räche den Vater, den Bruder, / Unser Vaterland, unsre Götter, / Unsre Schmach, mich, dich!" (*Medea*, 3.1221–24).[49] The two plan ways to destroy Jason and his newly formed family. Gora's words give Medea momentum, and after a tense exchange with both Jason and Kreon, Medea loses the battle for her children who have chosen to stay in Corinth with Kreusa and Jason. In great distress, Medea throws herself to the ground where she cries out: "Ich bin besiegt, vernichtet, zertreten. / Sie fliehn mich, fliehn! / Meine Kinder fliehn!" (*Medea*, 3.1710–12).[50] With these three words [defeated, destroyed, and trampled] Medea has been forced into a position where she has no other options. She has been banished from Corinth. She is an exile from Colchis. No other city-state will accept her because of the nature of the crimes of which she has been accused. And now her children reject her in favor of Kreusa just as Jason did. Medea has been cast out and has lost all meaning and value in this gendered and imperialist system of male oppression.[51] However, Medea remains a willful woman who gets in the way of a smooth transition to the form of normalcy that the Greeks require:

> A history of willfulness is a history of violence. An experience of violence might lead us to a sense of things being wrong, and when we sense things being wrong we are punished by violence. A feminist history is thus also a history of disobedience, of how we risk violence because we sense something being wrong. This history seems to condense in a set of figures: from Eve to Antigone. These figures are not the whole history, but they have a history, a feminist history as a history of women who pulse with life before law.[52]

Sara Ahmed's language of injustice and violence are the very properties in which Medea and Antigone survive as defendants before the law in an archive of common experiences and a radical discursive figuration.

UNHOMED

The close of Act 4 is where I want to start a final reading of *Medea*. An odd place to begin—we know how it ends—it is a literary reality that is understood if we are versed in the dramatic world of the Greeks. Yet, Medea's difference embraces a socially unintelligible entity—the non-Greek. She is cast, as we know, as uncivilized, barbaric, and wretched. Her genealogy and defiance of the laws of kinship mark her as socially abhorrent to the Greeks. Her resistance to this ostracism emerges from her insistence on representation, a status that is multiply complicated and troublesome. Her social challenge tests the viability and vigor of the practice of power and social control, which regulate and abridge all segments of life, in particular, female life. These are usages based in patriarchal systems designed to limit female participation and standardize behavior.

Kreon has found the chest that had been buried at dawn by Medea and brings it back to confront her with it. Medea's chest is filled with her tools of magic including the fleece, an indication of the dark and fiery forces over which she still maintains control. Jason and Kreon want the fleece for themselves, which they imagine is a source of power.[53] The shifting significance of the fleece for the men in the drama alters how Medea perceives this gift from the gods. The magical nature of the objects in the chest is revealed and returns to Medea "confidence in the otherness of her identity."[54] The children have been sent by Kreusa to Medea for a final goodbye and Medea has decided to unleash the fury of the contents of the chest. After a short incantation once the two men leave the scene, the chest springs open and Medea says, "Noch bin ich machtlos nicht! / Da liegt's! Der Stab! Der Schleier! Mein! Ah, mein! / Ich fasse dich, Vermächtnis meiner Mutter, / Und Kraft durchströmt mein Herz und meinen Arm / Ich werfe dich ums Haupt, geliebter Schleier!" (*Medea*, 4.1985–89).[55] She has regained the power that she once wielded, and accepts that authority with a renewed energy and determination. In a deviation from Euripides, Medea does not have her children bring the fatal gift (a fiery vessel wrapped in the fleece) to Kreusa, rather she sends Gora, who, with great reluctance, obeys Medea. As Gora leaves, Medea's two sons appear and after a brief but ominous conversation she tells the tired children to sleep, first on a bench and then later, inside where she will kill them at the end of the act.

Gora is successful in carrying out Medea's wishes, and Kreusa dies a fiery death. Unlike the events of Euripidean Medea, Kreon is not immolated along with his daughter. He lives bereft of child and the ability to extend his line into the future. The grandchildren he hoped to gain from a union between his daughter and Jason will no longer be. Recalling the plaintive words of Aietes in *Die Argonauten* to restore to him his daughter, Kreon also must cry out in a similar fashion for Medea, "Wo ist sie, die mir mein Kind geraubt?" (*Medea*, 5.2223).[56] And to the new criminal, Jason, Kreon says:

Du aber geh, wohin dein Fuß dich trägt.
Befleckter Nähe, merk ich, ist gefährlich.
Hätt' ich dich nie gesehn, dich nie genommen
Mit Freundestreue in mein gastlich Haus.
Du hast die Tochter mir genommen! Geh
Daß du nicht auch der Klage Trost mir nimmst! (*Medea*, 5.2267–72)[57]

This plea for the return of the child and the body of the child in order to mourn has a literary tradition and is a strong symbol in all three dramas of *The Golden Fleece*.[58] Jason was the recipient of Aietes' plea that he return Medea to the father. A similar cry: "Du hast die Tochter mir genommen!" (*Argonauts*, 3.1283) now links the sovereigns, Aietes and Kreon.[59] Medea is the thief of kinship in that she has now robbed both Jason and Kreon of their progeny. Genealogy is destroyed in a series of linguistic moves, which commence with Phryxus in *The Guest*, Aietes in *The Argonauts*, and concludes with Kreon and Jason in *Medea*. The difference that once set Medea apart from Jason and made her a liability has disappeared. The collapse of that difference briefly equalizes the two. Both are pollutants that must be removed from the civilized world to a bleak domain reminiscent of the wilderness of Colchis. Jason's desire to consolidate his place in society by making a traditional marriage to Kreusa is destroyed. Medea has ensured that Jason is not just deprived of one family but of two, and in the end, he does not even have a corpse—from the old family or the new—to bury.[60]

Gora's ability to frame the drama and intensify the betrayal of Medea offers the reader knowledge of another motivation behind Medea's actions. When Jason and Kreon lament the death of their children, Gora pointedly reminds the two of their own crimes:

Habt ihr es nicht umstellt mit Jägernetzen
Des schändlichen Verrats, das edle Wild,
Bis ohne Ausweg, in Verzweiflungswut
Es, überspringend euer Garn, die Krone,
Des hohen Hauptes königlichen Schmuck
Mißbraucht zum Werkzeug ungewohnten Mords.
Ringt nur die Hände, ringt sie ob euch selbst! (*Medea*, 5.2245–51)[61]

Gora uses metaphorical language to depict the restriction of Medea and the extreme behavior that resulted from the feeling of entrapment and suffering. The hunter's net, the lack of an exit, and Medea's despair forced her to this aberrant act which is both defiant of the crown, male power, and maternity. Her command to them to "wring their hands" is one normally reserved for the woman in mourning. Gora's instruction to Jason and Kreon to perform a feminine act of lamentation reverses the conventional composition of bereavement. Gora then poses the question to Jason which Medea would also have put to him: "Was stahlst du sie, hast du sie nicht geliebt? / Und liebtest du sie, was verstößt du sie?" (*Medea*, 5.2253–54).[62] Thus, Gora links the act of lamentation with love and theft, Jason's crime against Medea.

Medea's need for revenge as retribution for Jason's misuse and disposal of her is detailed in her encounters with Gora who is then able to convey this information to Kreon and Jason. When Medea tells Gora of the pain she felt when her sons rejected her embrace to turn to Kreusa, she also recognizes the ambiguity of their fortune if left to the care of Jason and his new bride. "Bleiben sie hier beim Vater zurück, / Beim treulosen, schändlichen Vater, / Welches ist ihr Los?" (*Medea*, 5.1786–88).[63] Medea was fearful for their fate and would not have them shunned in favor of children born of Jason and Kreusa. This worry foreshadowed the lengths that she would go to secure a possible future for her children but also the fury that she felt when they rejected her for Kreusa and the Greek world. She understands that as half-Colchian, her sons will never be fully accepted into the folds of Greek life. Medea suspects, and perhaps rightly so, that the taint of her barbaric birth will follow them throughout their lives. They will be mocked, insulted, and eventually, consumed by anger and hurt, face exile from the household of Jason and Kreusa. In this speech, Medea utters the feeling that death would be preferable to a life of disgrace but also speaks about her origins and her thoughts on life and living:

Denn wenn das Unglück dem Verbrechen folgt,
Folgt öfter das Verbrechen noch dem Unglück.
Was ist's denn auch zu leben?
Ich wollt', mein Vater hätte mich getötet,
Da ich noch klein war,
Noch nichts, wie jetzt, geduldet,
Noch nichts gedacht—wie jetzt (*Medea* 4.1796–802).[64]

If her father had killed her as a child, she would have been spared the unmistakable desperation of her present situation as well as avoided the history that began with Phryxus and the Golden Fleece. In Medea's turbulent and distressed perception, very nuanced and in-depth interpretations emerge about the nature of blood, kinship, and the function of truth as verbal manifestations of actions. The limits and validity of Medea's perception are unclear. However, her complete certainties about the causal factors which have shaped her life are unambiguous. Her mind turns to thoughts of her home on Colchis and how her life could have been. Medea makes an important statement that tells a great deal about her perspective with respect to causality and her flexible and contingent grasp of its function. This essential causality turns chronology, continuity, and the defining act or process on its head, a movement which linguistically purifies Medea's misfortune and her crime.

The flames that consume Kreusa are also implicated in this causal relationship in which the origin of the violent force is set back in the past with the arrival of the guest, Phryxus. This is a force that is brought to a higher intensity by Jason who seeks the fleece. Is it Medea's fault then that such venomous flames reach out to consume Kreusa, the new bride of Jason, who has also played fast and loose with this heat? The flames that devour Kreusa in *Medea* are also reminiscent of the flames in the cave where the fleece had been kept and which signaled Medea's passion for Jason in *The Argonauts*. They have become a symbol of destructive love but also greed and revenge. Jason has destroyed Medea and she, in turn, destroys Kreusa using the same imagery of fire. Thus, Kreusa's off-stage death is a linguistic movement that uses the metaphor of the flame to replicate a physical destruction.

At the close of Act 5, Jason has been shunned by Kreon and is left to make his way in the wilderness. He is alone, with neither home nor friend; his reputation is sullied and he is childless. He is an outcast, and as such, his future is bleak. He asks Kreon what he should do, and then betrays his true weakness and inability to understand how far he has fallen by the content of his entreaty:

Wer leitet meinen Tritt? Wer unterstützt mich?
Mein Haupt ist wund, verletzt von Brandes Fall!
Wie, alles schweigt? Kein Führer, kein Geleitet?
Folgt niemand mir, dem einst so viele folgten?
Geht, Schatten meiner Kinder denn voran
Und leitet mich zum Grab, das meiner harrt. (*Medea*, 4.2275–80)[65]

Jason is unable to integrate the reality of what has transpired. He does not understand that he also played a decisive role in this catastrophe. Exhibiting palpable anxiety, Jason cannot internalize his loss of status and his ability to command allegiance. The reach of his authority has shrunk to what he can control within himself and he is left bewildered about his place in this new arrangement of life. Now that all structures have been razed and there is no ready formation into which he can install himself, Jason does not know how to orient himself or discover a new meaning for his life.

At dawn, Jason, still on Corinthian soil, emerges exhausted from the previous night's activities into a "Wilde, einsame Gegend von Wald und Felsen umschlossen, mit einer Hütte"[66] a description which mimics the opening description of *The Guest*.[67] He has no resources at his disposal other than his name, a word which no longer holds authority and, in fact, is now a slur rather than one that commands respect. He announces himself to a peasant at whose hut he asks for help with the expectation that he will be housed and cared for by the man. He relies on his old reputation without recognizing that he no longer has the luxury of falling back on the comfort of that previous fame. His is a name that is eternally tarnished by the series of events that ended with the death of his children and of his new bride. "Ich bin der Jason! / Des Wunder-Vlieses Held! Ein Fürst! Ein König! / Der Argonauten Führer Jason, ich!" (*Medea*, 5.2293–95).[68] Jason has a series of identities that he expects will protect him and ease his way through life. The countryman instantly repudiates Jason's insistence on an elevated identity and on naming himself in ways that no longer hold any positive value. He is not simply a man; his identity and self-concept depended on a list of titles, which, at this time, hold no truth or only contaminated ones. He inhabited a multitude of personas, which have all been destroyed, symbolically and materially.

But where are we as readers? Is our moral consciousness stunted by Grillparzer's literary inventions that the sympathy we hold resides with the murderess witch? Is our conflict of impulses as erratic as Medea's? If self-will is as tenuous as Grillparzer suggests, then is our lack of outrage at Medea's actions an indication of an awareness of the dependence on a universal order of being that is beyond our control? Does reading Medea permit us to reach out beyond our own subjectivity and observe our existence as part of her world order? Has Grillparzer made us an outsider to ourselves by transforming us into a function of the tragic action whereby we are responsive—in a positive manner—to Medea's extreme deeds? We have been led astray by Grillparzer's ambiguity about the ethical world of drama; our moral stance is no longer regular but attuned to the fragmentation of Medea, her fury, and her desolation.

Grillparzer's Medea does not escape to Athens as the Euripidean Medea did.[69] Wearing her red veil, she steps out from behind a crag where she encounters Jason, with the fleece flung over her shoulder as one would a cloak. What she buried at the start of the drama, she now carries with her in triumph. She has unearthed the identity that she had once hoped to destroy to align herself with Jason and his desire for a life in the Hellenic world. This is a symbolic show which informs Jason that she has renounced his world and will return to the symbols of her past. Medea's revenge was not about ameliorating her own suffering, but rather about pulling Jason into the depths of her own misery and outrage.[70] She returns to the reality that she once lived. Jason declares his desire to die and join his children. It is important that Medea appear at this moment when Jason wishes for death, for she will not allow him to seek refuge in death. She takes that decision away from him and forces him to confront his life. In a refrain reminiscent of her words to Gora that she wishes her father had killed her when she was still young ("Ich wollt', mein Vater hätte mich getötet, / Da ich noch klein war . . ."), Medea counsels Jason to temper his outrage and despair:

Dir scheint der Tod das Schlimmste
Ich kenn ein noch viel Ärgres: elend sein.
Hätt'st du das Leben höher nicht geachtet
Als es zu achten ist, uns wär' nun anders.
Drum tragen wir! Den Kindern ist's erspart! (*Medea* 5.2312–16).[71]

For Jason, death is the worst that could happen to him now that he no longer has his name and the privileges that this identity conferred upon him. Medea displays an insight into the nature of suffering that still eludes Jason. She understands that death would be less painful than a life of suffering. She has spared her children the misery of life as the offspring of a barbarian witch. To live with the knowledge of one's misdeeds (crimes and failures) is a much more horrible fate than the effortless escape into death. She empties his life of hope by depriving it of a future. Medea tells Jason, "Nicht traur' ich, daß die Kinder nicht mehr sind. / Ich traure, daß sie waren und daß wir sind" (*Medea*, 5.2324–25).[72] She cannot mourn the death of her children or despise her murder of them. Rather, Medea laments that they ever lived. Her position rests on what can only be termed a new clarity, an unambiguous although violent loss of self-deception. Here, at daybreak, where she confronts Jason, Medea has achieved the clarity that she sought throughout her life. In this undistorted reality, a bitter one that she likens to a desert, Medea's insights into violence and revenge are at their sharpest. Jason fails to understand his culpability in this story and cannot appreciate his crimes. The male principle to which Jason holds firm, based in greed, overweening ambition, and subjugation is no longer a viable way of life; it holds no honors or benefits. Medea has exposed it as hollow yet belligerent even as she acknowledges her role in the catastrophe.

The final path that Medea has chosen for herself is uncompromising and harsh. Jason must endure what fate may bring him: continued existence and endless sorrow. She will travel to Delphi to return the fleece to the oracle and meet her fate. "Nach Delphi geh' ich. An des Gottes Altar. Von wo das Vließ erst Phryxus weggenommen/ . . . Dort stelle' ich mich den Priestern dar, sie fragend, / Ob sie mein Haupt zum Opfer nehmen an, / Ob sie mich senden in die ferne Wüste / In längerm Leben findend längre Qual" (*Medea*, 5.2354–55, 5.2360–63).[73] Medea condemns Jason to endure and suffer for what he has done and takes her final leave of him. Returning to the fleece, the dark symbol of their story, Medea poses two rhetorical questions to Jason, which express her understanding of the night:

Was ist der Erde Glück?—Ein Schatten!
Was ist der Erde Ruhm?—Ein Traum!
Du Armer! der von Schatten du geträumt!
Der Traum ist aus, allein die Nacht noch nicht. (*Medea*, 5.2366–69).[74]

In his article, Edward McInnes astutely observes that Grillparzer repeatedly reveals the weakness and delusion of his male protagonists which acts as an "effective frame" to explore Medea's experience. "She appears throughout as a being who, in contrast to the male figures, is capable of confronting genuine moral crisis in herself and who ... is driven more and more to acknowledge a world which contradicts her deepest spiritual intuitions."[75] Medea denies Jason's version of life and success. She shuns his dreams as illusions.[76] Medea first declares Jason's life as mere shadow, a deceptive silhouette, and then further diminishes him by calling those shadows merely dreams, two escalating linguistic moves that nullify the very foundation of all that he had once sought. The dream is over and all that remains is bare life—without the mediation of either *polis* or family. Catharsis is unachievable in such a tortured world, one that is devoid of any normative moral imperative. The murder of Kreusa and then his own children is the ultimate evacuation of meaning for Jason. He is barren and powerless.

Medea is an insurrectionary power that remains central to the political and its satisfactory execution. She stands at the boundaries of the political, yet that sphere would be impossible and possibly unintelligible without the likes of a Medea. Does this unequivocally substantiate the need for the disenfranchised or the outsider in order to complete the state and solidify its power? Without Medea, the barbarian and the foreigner, would there be a need to form the outside or the foreign as interpretative categories?

DISASTER AND DISCOVERY

Medea is a text that is haunted by a series of traumatic events that are generated as a function of her marginal status in the two prefatory dramas of Grillparzer's trilogy. Medea is also a figure of trauma that allows us to think about how access to one's own history may not be immediately available as a self-understanding but that it might be reconstituted in a way that is ethically, politically, and emotionally responsive to that history. This is where we might want to locate Medea as a traumatized subject.[77] The trauma remains unabated in the final drama where Medea is constructed as the outsider and "unhomed," both of which can be considered sites of trauma. Her interactions with other characters are violent and combative. Her life is marked by a volatility that remains unabated across the three plays of the trilogy. Every encounter is one that sheds the semblance of stability in her life. There is almost a repetition across each drama wherein a crisis situation further estranges Medea from the thing that is her life. These situations recall trauma narratives, especially those of the dispossessed and the colonized.

The potentially disturbing eruption of defiant and unwanted female speech is the primary force in Grillparzer's adaptation of the story of Medea. As I wrote earlier, Grillparzer's dramas often display an agitated ambivalence about the values of the ancient Greek world and, in the case of Medea, ideas around civilization, barbarism, and belonging come to the forefront of a linguistic duel between competing voices. Medea must always give answer, defend and insist on her right to know, to be understood, and to decide. These are realities that overlap and occur repeatedly in Medea's life even though she can neither recognize nor assimilate the full effect of the damage in the immediate moment. For Medea, the truths of the traumas in her life remain inaccessible and unknowable—even as they haunt her—until the final moments of the eponymously named drama, *Medea*. They can only be accessed belatedly as ethical signifiers of a less than ideal world order whereby her strangeness is, in fact, a newness that is coming into being.

Medea's performances throughout the trilogy offer us a reading of the periphery as a site where trauma is voiced as both a knowing and a not knowing, spaces which invite crisis to enter—breaking points. Both function at the level of comprehension and repetition in this space. This is where the voice that cries out in pain is both criminal and victim. Might it be possible to argue that Medea is the architect of her own traumatic experiences and might not be able to claim the full extent of those incidents as both criminal and victim?

I want to cite this passage from *Living a Feminist Life* once more. Ahmed was referring to Woolf's *Mrs. Dalloway* but there is something here that inflects Medea's own life. There is a potent energy that can be applied to the ways in which she manages her world.

> We might sense how a life has a shape when it loses shape. . . .. Perhaps feminist consciousness also means becoming aware of one's life as a marvel or even marvelous. Being estranged from one's own life can be how a world reappears, becoming odd. You might become conscious of a possibility once it has receded.[78]

Medea has signaled to Jason and to herself that the choices that she makes about life are ones that are severe and persistent. However, the shape of that life is no longer something that contains meaning:

Was ist der Erde Glück?—Ein Schatten!
Was ist der Erde Ruhm?—Ein Traum! (*Medea*, 5.2366–67)[79]

Here, I read a feminist consciousness in Medea's words to Jason that resonate with Ahmed's "even marvelous." Repeating these earlier words to Jason, Medea calls into question the nature of earthly happiness and renown as shadow and dream. Fortune and fame have little meaning because they are ephemeral features of the imagination. They are human creations rather than solid objects that one may touch and know that they are real and have tangible meaning. The shape of her life is now vividly clear to Medea now that it is revealed to her that it was an illusion. That former life—the one with Jason—is now unmistakably deformed and distorted. Its destruction is how Medea comes to understand what it means to lose a life. But the destruction also causes other forms of life to develop that may not be ideal or be the best possible, but they are ones that hold some form of truth. Losing a life is astonishing and sensational. It is about discovering a new shape or even the reappearance of a world.

The revisioning of life around notions of kinship, belonging, duty, and authority is bound up with the status of Medea as compulsive, disruptive, and defiant. Grillparzer's *Medea* signals a shift, a transition in thinking about the management of crisis, and how to repudiate claims which systems of authority—formal and informal as well as domestic and political—make on the individual. Medea claims crisis; she will not abridge the tragedy—and that is her feminist consciousness. Her actions extend the tragic into a space that plays with the details of her deeds, embraces them as knowledge, and formulates that revision of action as a theory about living on even when life loses its shape. At the conclusion of the drama when Medea confronts Jason, this is a powerful moment of claiming crisis in a marvelous way. Her astonishing and intense intervention into a life that was damaging her gives her story a feminist momentum.

The incomprehensibility of the myth of Medea is one that compels Grillparzer to expand it at each moment of catastrophe where the uncontrollable and the unknowable are both activated and reinscribed. These are the stories that in earlier accounts were narrated retrospectively. Grillparzer's inclusion of *The Guest* and *The Argonauts* allows the reader to not only explore the story of these incidents but also provides a broader space for narratively understanding Medea as a casualty of the myth of "Jason and Medea." Here, Grillparzer takes the *muthos* and reimagines Medea as both victim and victimizer. She has been repeatedly wounded by the men in her life and this mistreatment, in private and public ways, brings her to an understanding of human action that embraces the pain and rage of her marginal status as a woman and an outsider. There are no aftershocks of remorse in Medea. Rather, she has absorbed the knowledge of her own apartness and uses her alterity to demonstrate that she also wields a power that can expel, curse, and lay waste.

Medea exists as one of the great texts of the traditional Western canon. Yet Grillparzer's encounter with the ancients is also an estranged one. His *Medea* delivers an opportunity, a history, a thing that is not a statement about what is already past but also a thing that says something to the present. Here, I suggest that Grillparzer's *Medea* is not only a telling of the past myth but also a foretelling of a new Medea. This is a figural perspective, an interpretation which reveals something else that is not symbolic but rather something that is real, a sign of something outside of and larger than itself.

The incomprehensibility of the myth of Medea is one that compels Grillparzer to expand it at each moment of catastrophe where the uncontrollable and the unknowable are both activated and reinscribed. Grillparzer's inclusion of *The Guest* and *The Argonauts* allows the reader to not only explore the story of these incidents but also provides a broader space for narratively understanding Medea. *Medea* presents a radical reality that advances a version of humanism in the articulation of trauma. Yet how does one reconcile tragic discourse—the language of tragedy—with that of the uncontrollable return of a trauma that remains inaccessible? Thus, the traumatic event resonates throughout all three dramas of the trilogy and shapes *Medea* as a drama that articulates what can be known and what is never known.

NOTES

1. Ahmed, *Living a Feminist Life*, 27.
2. Ahmed, *Living a Feminist Life*, 27.
3. Ahmed, *Living a Feminist Life*, 116.
4. Ahmed, *Living a Feminist Life*, 187.
5. In the introduction, "Stranger Fetishism and Post-coloniality," Sara Ahmed articulates the identity of the other, or the alien as someone who already recognizable: "The figure of the alien reminds us that what is "beyond the limit" is subject to representation; indeed, what is beyond representation is also, at the same, overrepresented." Ahmed, *Strange Encounters: Embodied Others in Post-Coloniality* (London: Routledge: 2000), 1.
6. For a deeper analysis of the racial and ethnic components that are a part of Grillparzer's adaptation but also feature heavily in later revisions such as Paul Heyse's novella *Medea* (1896; 1899), Hans Henny Jahnn's *Medea* (1924), or Max Zweig's *Medea in Prag* (1949), see Inge Stephan, "Rasse und Geschlecht: Medea als 'schwarze,' 'Jüdin' und 'Zigeunerin,'" in Inge Stephan, *Medea: Multimediale Karriere einer mythologischen Figur* (Köln: Böhlau, 2006), 48–69. McCarthy-Rechowicz devotes a chapter ("Grillparzer and Kyriarchy") in which he makes a sustained argument about *Medea* and Rahel from *Die Jüdin von Toledo* that centers ethnicity, imperialism, intersectionality, and feminism as ways in which these dramas are constituted. McCarthy-Rechowicz, *Dramatic Heroines*, 154–186. Further reading includes Markus Winkler's *Von Iphigenie zu Medea: Semantik und Dramaturgie des Barbarischen bei Goethe und Grillparzer* (2009) as a close reading of the two dramas against the backdrop of an ancient telos. Winkler explores the function of human sacrifice, racial and cultural exclusion, xenophobia in the Greek world and nostalgia for a Hellenic ideal through a close reading of Goethe and Grillparzer. This study is a well-articulated and sustained account of a social and political world using two very different dramas—one that insists on the ideal of the ancients and the other that casts a shadow over the very same group. This texts along with Brigitte Prutti's study which I will discuss in the following chapter have done much to re-establish the significance

of Grillparzer for the twenty-first century after he had been recuperated by twentieth-century philology. The careful research carried out by Prutti and Winkler redress the often reductive and half-committed work that had been done on Grillparzer's contribution to theatre studies, the reception of the ancient world, language and form as well as gender, ethnic categories, and nationalism. Markus Winkler, *Von Iphigenie zu Medea: Semantik und Dramaturgie des Barbarischen bei Goethe und Grillparzer* (Tübingen: Max Niemeyer Verlag, 2009).

7. Ahmed, *Living a Feminist Life*, 55.

8. Ahmed, *Living a Feminist Life*, 10.

9. Dirk Weissmann, "When Austrian Classical Tragedy Goes Intercultural: On the Metrical Simulation of Linguistic Otherness in Franz Grillparzer's *The Golden Fleece*," *Critical Multilingualism Studies* 5, no. 3 (2017): 54. Weissmann offers a compelling reading of the distance between the Greeks and Colchians: "The gap between Greeks and Colchians originates in a fundamentally xenophobic attitude, based on a categorical and structuring opposition between an 'us' and a 'them,' between self and Other, trimmed down to a difference between friend and foe" (55).

10. Apart from Euripides, the Medea myth has been treated many times in ancient Roman and Greek writing. An in-depth discussion of the multiple versions can be found in James Joseph Clauss and Sarah Iles Johnston, eds., *Medea: Essays on Medea in Myth, Literature, Philosophy, and Art* (Princeton, NJ: Princeton University Press, 1997) or Maria Luise Kaschnitz, *Medea: Dichtung und Wirklichkeit* (Frankfurt am Main: Verlag Ullstein, 1966). For a comprehensive anthology of Medea treatments, see Ludger Lütkehaus, ed., *Mythos Medea: Texte von Euripides bis Christa Wolf* (Stuttgart: Reclam, 2007).

For studies of the interaction between poetry and painting (text and image) using Timomachus' Medea and Euripides' play, see Kathryn Gutzwiller, "Seeing Thought: Timomachus' Medea and Ecphrastic Epigram," *American Journal of Philology* 125, no. 3 (Autumn 2004): 339–86. Gutzwiller treats the painting as case study in order "to be able to trace a tradition of thought, debate, and judgment about a famous dramatic protagonist through the Hellenistic and early imperial periods and to see the interaction of art and text in making and transmitting cultural meaning" (340). Gutzwiller asserts that Timomachus' painting depicts the moment in Euripides' *Medea* (Euripides, *Medea* 1019–1080) as one of indecision as Medea thinks about whether or not to kill her children (348). For further references to Timomachus and the play of painting and poetry, see Lessing's *Laokoon oder Über die Grenzen der Malerei und Poesie* (1766). See *'Laocoon': An Essay upon the Limits of Painting and Poetry, With Remarks Illustrative of Various Points in the History of Ancient Art*, trans. Ellen Frothingham (Boston: Roberts Brothers, 1887): "Among the old painters Timomachus seems to have been the one most fond of choosing extremes for his subject. His raving Ajax and infanticide Medea were famous. . .He did not paint Medea at the moment of her actually murdering her children, but just before, when motherly love is still struggling with jealousy" (18). For additional eighteenth-century scholarship which touches on Medea and an explication of Lessing's aesthetics of tragedy, subject formation, and abjection, see Susan Gustafson's chapter, "*Miss Sara Sampson*: The Mother Within and the Father Without," in Susan E. Gustafson, *Absent*

Mothers and Orphaned Fathers: Narcissism and Abjection in Lessing's Aesthetic and Dramatic Production (Detroit, MI: Wayne State University Press, 1995), 123–169. Also important in this 'bourgeois' or domestic tragedy is Lessing's demonization of Marwood, the former lover of Mellefont, in which she calls herself "a new Medea" [Sieh in mir eine neue Medea! (*Medea*, 2.7)]. Gustafson, *Absent Mothers and Orphaned Fathers*, 150–155.

For individual versions, see Apollonius of Rhodes, *Argonautica*, trans. R. C. Seaton (Cambridge: Harvard University Press, 1988), 431; Jeffrey S. Rusten, *Dionysius Scytobrachion* (Opladen: Westdeutscher Verlag, 1982), 183; Ovid, *Metamorphoses*, trans. Charles Martin (New York: W.W. Norton & Co., 2005), 624; and Herodotus, *Histories IV*, trans. Michael A. Flower and John Marincola (Cambridge: Cambridge University Press, 2002), 357. Additionally, the film productions of the Medea myth are multiple: Lars von Trier, Paolo Pasolini, and Michael Cacoyanis.

11. The importance and appeal of the Medea myth and the different versions of the same mythic episode, what he calls the 'vertical tradition' are addressed by Fritz Graf, "Medea, the Enchantress from Afar: Remarks on a Well-Known Myth," in Clauss and Johnston, eds., *Medea: Essays on Medea in Myth, Literature, Philosophy and Art*, 21–43.

12. For critiques of over-representation of the female as titular hero of several Attic tragedies of Aeschylus, Sophocles and Euripides see Helene P. Foley, *Female Acts in Greek Tragedy*. (Princeton, NJ: Princeton University Press, 2001), 410; Edith Hall, "The Sociology of Athenian Tragedy," in *The Cambridge Companion to Greek Tragedy*, ed. P. E. Easterling (Cambridge: Cambridge University Press, 1997), 93–126; Froma I. Zeitlin, "Playing the Other: Theater, Theatricality, and the Feminine in Greek Drama," *Representations* 11 (Summer 1985): 63–94; and Barbara Goff, *Citizen Bacchae: Women's Ritual Practice in Ancient Greece* (Berkeley: University of California Press, 2004), especially "Working Toward a Material Presence" (25–76). For an equally significant and thorough counterweight, see Mary R. Lefkowitz, *Women in Greek Myth*, 2nd ed. (Baltimore, MD: Johns Hopkins University Press: 2007).

13. Margaret Williamson, "A Woman's Place in Euripides' *Medea*," in *Euripides, Women, and Sexuality*, ed. Anton Powell (London: Routledge, 1990), 16.

14. For one such treatment of Phryxus and the Golden Fleece, see "The Fable of the Golden Fleece," *Ballou's Monthly Magazine*, October 1892, 297–98. "In very ancient times their lived in Thessaly, a king and queen, named Athamas and Nephele. They had two children, a boy and a girl. After a time Athamas grew indifferent to his wife, and put her away and took another. Nephele suspected danger to her children from the influence of the stepmother, and took measures to send them out of her reach. Mercury assisted her, and gave her a ram, with a golden fleece, on which she set the two children, trusting that the ram would convey them to a place of safety. The ram vaulted into the air with the children on his back, taking his course to the East, till when crossing the strait that divides Europe and Asia, the girl whose name was Helle (Phryxus's sister), fell from his back into the sea, which from her was called the Hellespont—now called the Dardanelles. The ram continued on till he reached

the kingdom of Colchis, on the eastern shore of the Black Sea, where he landed the boy Phryxus, who was hospitably received by Eetes [Aieties], the king of the country. Phryxus sacrificed the ram to Jupiter, and gave the golden fleece to Eetes, who placed it in a consecrated grove, under the care of a sleepless dragon" (297).

15. Did you not promise you would be mine, mine, / And no man's? Say, did you not promise this?" Grillparzer, *Guest*, 53–54. All references in the text and notes to Grillparzer's *Der Gastfreund* (hereafter shortened to *Guest*) correspond to lines in the one-act text. The numbering remains the same across the German and English versions. For more on the German and English texts of Grillparzer's dramas, see note 1 in the introduction.

16. "She did not will it, but did it! Off, what nonsense / How could it ever happen / If you did not *will*? What I do, I will, / and what I will—well, sometimes I *don't* do" (*Guest*, 64–67).

17. "Am I your dear child? / Usually you hardly heed me, / When I want something, you do *not* / And scold me and repulse me; / But when you need me, / You flatter me with smooth words, / Calling me, Medea, your dear child." (*Guest*, 121–27).

18. He greets her as a "shining augury / Of a future that is still veiled to us" (*Guest*, 254–55).

19. Unlike other versions of the Medea myth, Grillparzer does not have his Medea murder her brother. Instead, the despairing Absyrtus jumps from the cliffs into the sea and drowns.

20. Aietes tells the now forsaken Medea that she will be "disdained, despised, discarded and distraught." Grillparzer, *Argonauts*, 3.1371. This prefigures the very conditions under which Medea lives in the final drama but also harkens back to her angry words to Peritta who has fallen in love with a man. The shortened references (separated by periods) in the text and notes correspond to act and line of Grillparzer, *Die Argonauten* (hereafter cited as *Argonauts*). For more on the German and English texts of Grillparzer's dramas, see note 1 in the introduction.

21. "Come now; but first tell me who gave you leave / To flee the shelter of your father's house / And here, denying obedience, to defy / My orders and my summons, in the bosom / Of but this wilderness and your wild ways?" (*Argonauts*, 1.87–91).

22. "Then listen, if you can; take umbrage, if you dare. / Could I be dumb, forever dumb! / In find your house abhorrent, / Your presence makes me shudder. / When you destroyed the stranger, / The guest, the gods protected, / And robbed his estate, / You threw into your house a spark / That glows and glows and will not be extinguished. / Even should you pour on it forever / The entire water of the holy spring, / And all the mighty ocean measureless. / Murder is a foolish marksman / That shoots his arrow into a dark thicket, / Greedy for games and spoils; / And what he took to be his prey, / The joyous game of the chase, / He finds it was his child, his flesh and blood, / Doomed man! What have you done?" (*Argonauts*, 1.94–113).

23. It is critical to note that Kreusa, the daughter of the King of Corinth, is a representative of the right sort of femininity. One that understands itself as subordinate to the patriarchal system which is all that has ever been known. Its oppression is not apparent to Kreusa and, in fact, she is also abusive to Medea, an act which acknowledges that it is their ethnic and cultural difference which separates the two women.

There is no unity in gender here; Kreusa is the model woman—silent, obedient, and ornamental.

24. Judith Butler, *Antigone's Claim: Kinship Between Life and Death* (New York: Columbia University Press, 2000).

25. See Sophocles, *Antigone*, trans. Elizabeth Wyckoff, in *Sophocles I*, vol. 8, *Complete Greek Tragedies*, ed. David Grene and Richmond Lattimore (Chicago: University of Chicago Press, 1954), 158–203.

26. Butler, *Antigone's Claim*, 1.

27. Butler, *Antigone's Claim*, 2.

28. Butler, *Antigone's Claim*, 2.

29. Butler, *Antigone's Claim*, 6.

30. Butler, *Antigone's Claim*, 6, italics in the original.

31. Gora also serves a religious role throughout the three dramas. In *Der Gastfreund*, it is Gora who sings the praisesong to the virgin goddess, Darimba, after Medea has killed the sacrificial deer with her arrow: "Darimba, mächtige Göttin / Menschenerhaltenen, Menschentöterin" (Darimba, mighty goddess, / Preserver of morals, destroyer of mortals), *Guest*, 4–5; and "Gib, daß wir recht tun und siegen in Schlacht / Gib, daß wir lieben den Wohlwollenden / Und hassen den, der uns haßt. Mach' uns stark und reich, Darimba, / Mächtige Göttin!" (Make us do right and triumph in battle, / Make up love the well-disposed, / And hate him who hates us! / Make us strong and rich, Darimba; / Mighty Goddess!), *Guest*, 18–22.

32. The references in text here are to lines from Euripides' *Medea*. See Euripides, *The Medea*, trans. Rex Warner, in *Euripides I*, vol. 3 of 9, *The Complete Greek Tragedies*, ed. David Grene and Richmond Alexander Lattimore (Chicago: University of Chicago Press, 1955), 59–112.

33. Homi Bhabha, *The Location of Culture* (New York: Routledge, 1994), 1–27.

34. Bhabha, *Location of Culture*, 13.

35. Bhabha, *Location of Culture*, 13.

36. Bhabha, *Location of Culture*, 15.

37. Ahmed, *Living a Feminist Life*, 143.

38. The symbols of the trilogy are patterns, which work, like the wilds of Colchis, to enhance and frame the texture of the meaning. These symbols are both of the material sort and ones that originate in the natural world. Medea's chest, buried at the opening of the drama, is filled with her tools of magic including the fleece, an indication of the dark and fiery forces over which she cannot maintain control. The shifting significance of the fleece for the men in the drama changes how Medea perceives this gift from the gods. The symbolic power of the trilogy is undeniable. Grillparzer relies on these icons to propel the action but also to make links between texts. The statue of Peronto (similar to Zeus), the dark god, in *Der Gastfreund* where Phryxus dies, the dragon's cave in *Die Argonauten*, and in *Medea*, Kreusa's lyre, Medea's veil and Grecian dress, and the flaming jar are just some examples of the tangible symbols which Grillparzer employed. Additionally, fire, light, water and dark also pervade the imagery of the trilogy. For a thorough account of the symbols—linguistic and physical—in this trilogy see Christa Suttner Baker, "Unifying Imagery Patterns in Grillparzer's *das goldene*

Vließ," *MLN* 89, no. 3 (April 1974): 392–403, and T. C. Dunham, "Symbolism in Grillparzer's *das Goldene Vließ*," *PMLA* 75, no. 1 (March 1960): 75–82.

39. "The dark of night, of conjury is past; / And what will happen, whether good or evil, / Must happen in the open light of day." Grillparzer, *Medea*, 1.4–6. The shortened references (separated by periods) in the text and notes correspond to act and line of Grillparzer, *Medea* (hereafter cited as *Medea*). For more on the German and English texts of Grillparzer's dramas, see note 1 in the introduction.

40. "Do you intend to bury all these emblems / Of rarest service that protected you / And may protect still?" *Medea*, 1.23–24.

41. "I must, however, tell you: / You would do well to put that all aside! / Do not brew drugs from herbs, nor potent potions, / Do not address the moon, nor rouse the dead; / They hate that here, and I—I hate it too! / We are no more in Colchis but in Greece. / No more among monstrosities but men!" *Medea* 1.178–83.

42. "Here I am and respectful bow to you! / No stranger, true, estranged: / One seeking help, a suppliant for asylum; Expelled from hearth and home and quite thrust out, / I beg for my protectors friendly roof." *Medea*, 1.276–80.

43. In Act 2, Kreusa tries to teach Medea to play the lyre and sing a song for Jason that he once sung as boy. Jason refuses to listen to Medea even after she repeats three times, "Jason, ich weiß ein Lied" (Jason, I know a song). *Medea*, 2.876. After her attempts fail—Medea can neither play the lyre nor sing—she breaks the lyre in outrage after a brief back and forth with Jason. Her attempt to perform a gendered activity fails as does that moment of a possible cultural transfer.

44. "Because I'm foreign, from a far-off land / And unfamiliar with the manners here, / They all despise me and look down on me / And think I am a wild and barbarous woman, / The lowest and the last of all mankind." *Medea*, 1.400–404.

45. "You do not know him, but I know too well! / In all the wide world only he exists, / The rest to him are but his exploits' field. / Quite selfish, less of matter than of mind, / He juggles with his own and others' fate: / If glory beckons, why, he strikes one dead; / If it's a wife he wants, why then, he takes her; He does but right, yet right is what he wills. / The cost to other irks him not at all! / You do not know him, but I know too well! / And when I call to mind what has befallen, / I think I laughingly could see him die." *Medea*, 2.629–40.

46. Away from me, my life's abomination! / Who've robbed me of my days and happiness; . . . / Give Jason back to me, you criminal!" *Medea*, 2, 1047–48, 2.1054.

47. "So you want Jason back? Here! Take him, take him! / But who will give Medea back to me?" *Medea*, 2.1055–56.

48. See Clemens Ruthner's chapter, "Argonaut und Tourist: Repräsentationen der Fremde(n) bei Franz Grillparzer," for a deeper analysis of difference, alterity and otherness in *The Golden Fleece*. Clemens Ruthner, "Argonaut und Tourist: Repräsentationen der Fremd(e) bei Franz Grillparzer," in Henn, Ruthner, and Whitinger, eds., *Aneignungen, Entfremdungen*, 49–68.

49. "Then Punish him, strike him! / Avenge you father, your brother, / Our country, our gods, / Our shame, me, you!" *Medea*, 3.1221–24.

50. "I am defeated, destroyed, trodden to dust! / They flee me, flee, / My children flee me!" *Medea*, 3.1710–12.

51. In one of the most lapidary moments in *Living a Feminist Life*, Ahmed thinks about white male structures and I would cosign that Medea is absolutely caught up in such a structure, she writes: "When we talk of white men [white Greek men], we are describing something. We are describing an institution. An institution typically refers to a persistent structure or mechanism of social order governing the behavior of a set of individuals within a given community. So when I am saying that white men is an institution, I am referring not only to what has already been instituted or built but the mechanisms that ensure the persistence of that structure. A building is shaped by a series of regulative norms. White men refers also to conduct; it is not simply who is there, who is here, who is given a place at the table, but how bodies are occupied once they have arrived." Ahmed, *Living a Feminist Life*, 152–53.

52. Ahmed, *Living a Feminist Life*, 74.

53. The king tells Medea: "You think you'll cheat us with prevarication? / The earth has it! Well, now I understand. / Don't look away. Turn, look at me and listen! /Upon the seashore where you camped last night, / While working on the building of an altar / To Pelias' shade at my command, / They found—you pale?...fresh buried in the ground, / A casket, black, with strange mysterious signs." *Medea*, 4.1940–47.

54. McCarthy-Rechowicz, *Dramatic Heroines*, 168.

55. "Back has come my power! / All there. The wand! The veil! Mine! They are mine! / Once more I hold my mother's legacy, / And power wells in my heart and in my arm. / Beloved veil, I cast you around my head." *Medea*, 4.1985–89.

56. "Where is she who robbed me of my child?" *Medea*, 5.2223.

57. "And you, go forth, where'er your feet may lead. / Pollution all too near, I see, is dangerous. / Oh, had I never seen, ne'er welcomed you / With loyal friendship to my generous house. / You took my daughter from me! Therefore, go / Nor take with you the solace mourning brings!" *Medea*, 5.2267–72.

58. Priam's personal plea to Achilles in "Achilles and Priam," the final Book of the *Iliad* (trans. Robert Fagles) for the return of Hector's body: The gods agree that Achilles must return the desecrated corpse to the Trojans and Priam, guided by Hermes, journeys to the Greek camps for a conference with Achilles in which he wins the return of his son's body for proper burial. Homer, *Iliad*, Book 24, trans. Robert Fagles, ed. Bernard Knox (New York, NY: Penguin, 1990), 580–591.

59. In *The Argonauts*, Aietes orders Jason to give him his child back: "Verruchter Räuber, mein Kind gib mir zurück!" (*Die Argonauten*. 3.1283). "Mad robber, give me back my child!" (*Argonauts*, 3.1283).

60. See the section, "The Destruction of the Natural Order: *Medea*," in Richard Garner, *From Homer to Tragedy: The Art of Illusion in Greek Poetry* (New York: Routledge, 1990), 90–99.

61. "Did you not tight beset your noble game / With hunter's nets of shameless treachery, / Till no way out, in rage of desperation, / She sprang beyond your snare, the royal crown, / The ornament of lofty brows, brought low / As implement of unaccustomed murder? / Wring, wring your hands! Yes, wring them for yourselves!" *Medea*, 5.2245–51.

62. "Why did you steal her, if you did not love? / And if you loved her, why did you forsake?" *Medea*, 5.2253–54.

63. "If they are left here with their father, / With their faithless shameless father, / What lot is theirs?" *Medea*, 5.1786–88.

64. "If crime is sometimes father of misfortune, / Misfortune far more often fathers crime! / What matters living then? / I would my father had murdered me, / When I was little yet, / As now had nothing suffered, / Had nothing thought—as now!" *Medea*, 4.1796–802.

65. "Who guides my erring feet? Who will support me? / My head is bleeding, bruised, bruised by falling brands! / What, no one speaks? No leader, no companion? / None follows me whom once so many followed? / Come, shades of my two children, lead the way, / And take me to the grave that waits for me." *Medea*, 4.2275–80.

66. "Wild, lonely region, shut in by woods and rocks, with a hut." *Medea*, 5.2.

67. "Colchis. Wild landscape of rocks and trees, with the sea in the background." *Guest*.

68. "I am that Jason, / The Wonder-Fleece's hero, prince and king! / The leader of the Argonauts, I, Jason!" *Medea*, 5.2293–95.

69. In a reading of Grillparzer's *Medea*, Yixu Lü notes how the dramatist did not employ the endings that either Euripides or Seneca used. Grillparzer's Medea does not triumph over Jason rather the ordeal continues without catharsis. Yixu Lü, *Medea unter den Deutschen: Wandlungen einer literarischen Figur* (Freiburg im Breisgau: Rombach, 2009), 122.

70. Edward McInnes, "Psychological Insight and Moral Awareness in Grillparzer's *Das goldene Vliess*," *Modern Language Review* 75, no. 3 (July 1980): 579.

71. "To you death seems the worst; / Something far worse I know; stark misery. / Had you not put a higher store on life / Than it deserves, our fate were very different! / We must endure. The children now are free" (*Medea* 5.2312–16).

72. "I do not grieve the children are no more, / I only grieve they were and that we are." *Medea*, 5.2324–25.

73. "I go to Delphi. Upon Apollo's altar whence the fleece / In former days by Phrixus was removed [. . .]There I will place myself before the priests / And ask if they as sacrifice would take me, / Or banish me to some far wilderness, / To find in longer life a longer torment." *Medea*, 5.2354–55, 5.2360–63.

74. "What is earth's happiness? . . . A Shadow!/What is earth's laurel crown? . . . A dream! / Poor you, who have of shadows only dreamed! / The dream is spent, only the night not yet." *Medea*, 5.2366–69.

75. McInnes, "Psychological Insight and Moral Awareness," 577.

76. Pedro Calderón de la Barca's *Life is a Dream (La vida es sueño)*, originally published in 1635, had a decisive influence on Grillparzer's entire oeuvre, in particular the composition of Medea's final words to Jason. Pedro Calderón de la Barca, *Life is a Dream (La vida es sueño)*, trans. William E. Colford (Woodbury, NY: Barron's Educational Series, 1958). The work of Pedro Calderón de la Barca (1600–1681), the Spanish Baroque dramatist, was a major dramatic model for Grillparzer. These lines are direct reflections of the final scene of Calderón in which his protagonist, Segismundo, the son of the Polish king, is caught between free will and fate. Segismundo's monologue in act 2: "Quite so; then let us curb this temper and / This fury, this ambition, lest perchance / We are just dreaming, and indeed we will, / For

we are in a world so very strange / That life is but a dream; experience / Has taught me that each man who draws a breath / Dreams what he is until he wakes in death. / The king dreams he is king; believing this / Illusion, he lives ordering, ruling, / And governing; the borrowed plaudits he / Receives are writ upon the wind, and Death / (Sad fate!) converts them all to ashes" and "In short, all men are dreaming what they are, / Although nobody understands, by far. / I dream that I am here, encumbered with / These chains . . ." Calderón de la Barca, *Life is a Dream*, act 2, scene 18.

77. For a richer discussion of trauma, see Cathy Caruth, ed., *Unclaimed Experience: Trauma, Narrative, and History* (Baltimore, MD: Johns Hopkins University Press, 1996). In an edited volume, *Trauma: Explorations in Memory*, Caruth continues the conversation on trauma as "a response, sometimes delayed, to an overwhelming event or events." Cathy Caruth, ed. *Trauma: Explorations in Memory* (Baltimore, MD: Johns Hopkins University Press, 1995), 4. In that same anthology, Laura S. Brown's contribution, "Not Outside the Range: One Feminist Perspective on Psychic Trauma," offers a feminist analysis of trauma where she suggests that one look "to the private, secret experiences that women encounter in the interpersonal realm and at the hands of those we love and depend upon" (102). She goes on to explore what a traumatic event is, who decides what is or is not trauma, and "how some experiences have been excluded and turned inward upon their victims, who are then blamed for what has happened to them" (102). Laura S. Brown, "Not Outside the Range: One Feminist Perspective on Psychic Trauma," in Caruth, ed., *Trauma: Explorations in Memory*, 100–112.

78. Ahmed, *Living a Feminist Life*, 47.

79. "What is earth's happiness? . . . A Shadow! / What is earth's laurel crown? . . . A dream!" *Medea*, 5.2366–67.

Chapter 3

Hero

The Challenge of Virtue

> ... *they* stretch out, astonished, and one by one
> stride into their imaginary world. . . .
>
> —Rilke, "The Flamingos"

ORIGINS AND AFFILIATIONS

Des Meeres und der Liebe Wellen (*The Waves of Sea and Love*) (1831), the story of the doomed lovers, Hero and Leander, was Grillparzer's final antique drama framing the figure of the female as its central motivation.[1] Two significant versions of the myth of Hero and Leander are Ovid's *Heroides* (Ep. 18 and 19)[2] and Musaeus's short epic *Hero and Leander*[3] from the late fifth century AD. The medieval dissemination of the myth came via reception of Ovid's two letters between the lovers while Musaeus's piece has been the most important vehicle for dissemination of the story since the Renaissance. Both versions work with the same basic narrative material. The myth of Hero and Leander has its most lucid and multiple depictions in lyric, articulations that start with Ovid and Musaeus and continue to Christopher Marlowe's unfinished poem "Hero and Leander" (1598), Friedrich Hölderlin's "Hero" (1788), Schiller's ballad "Hero and Leander" (1801), Lord Byron's reference to Leander in the poem "Written After Swimming From Sestos To Abydos" (1810) to the postmodernism of visual artists such as Cy Twombly[4] and Anselm Kiefer.[5] However, Grillparzer's nineteenth-century adaptation is considered "the most important literary testimony to reception from this period, in particular because Grillparzer brought together several permutations of the myth."[6] Unlike the antique version and perhaps akin to his trilogy, *The*

Golden Fleece, Grillparzer's rendering complicates the story with the addition of new motifs, characters, and motivations.

Like many star-crossed lovers, the original legend of Hero and Leander is one that is easily recognizable—the love story with a tragic ending.[7] Hero, a priestess of Aphrodite, lives in a secluded tower in Sestos, the European side of the Hellespont and Leander in Abydos, the Asian side. During a feast to Aphrodite, Leander falls in love with Hero. Because they cannot marry, they decide to meet in secret. Each night Leander swims across the Hellespont guided by the light of her lamp in the tower, and at dawn he swims back to Abydos. On a stormy winter's night, the light is extinguished, and Leander drowns in the Hellespont trying to swim to Hero. When Hero sees the body of Leander washed ashore the next day at dawn, she throws herself from the tower in despair to join Leander in death.[8]

Although Grillparzer's adaptation of *The Waves of Sea and Love* received a lukewarm reception at its premiere at the *Burgtheater* in Vienna in 1831, it is now regarded as one of his finest and most popular dramas with its almost universal comparison to the ill-fated love between Romeo and Juliet.[9] With this narrative, Grillparzer presents a new kind of heroine into his body of work, one who behaves and understands differently than either his Medea or Sappho. While she is subject to the same kinds of pressures that are bound up with the claims of kinship as was Medea and the duties of the elevated as was Sappho, Grillparzer's Hero breaks the normative gender and family rules in ways that may appear to be less troublesome on the surface. Butler notes in her 1990 preface to *Gender Trouble* that, "trouble became a scandal with the sudden intrusion of, the unanticipated agency, of a female 'object' who inexplicably returns the glance, reverses the gaze, and contests the place and authority of the masculine position."[10] In a discourse located in her truth, Hero disturbs the workings of the customary by contesting conventional sites of authority. Her discursive practices cause conflict and discord, but they function as strategies that allow her to become trouble. Her story has its own interests and subtexts that do indeed return the gaze. Still, it is a drama that is somehow milder than the two earlier plays, even if Hero is fundamentally radical in her wants by disrupting traditional meanings located in the sacred structure of life and claiming autonomy and agency.

We might see that over the decade long period since the appearance of *Medea*, Grillparzer's work with discursive exclusion and the opportunities for language to advance understanding has changed, and a certain resignation prevails. This resignation is a sign that perhaps even his own considerable talents as a writer of female troublemakers is strained by the weight of social convention and slippery teleological goals. For in *The Waves of Sea and Love*, our main character is no magical Medea nor is she a gifted Sappho. She is essentially a good but naive young woman in a struggle with desire—a desire whose existence Grillparzer does not attempt to suppress. It is challenging to accurately and fully name the desire at this moment since it is both about integration into a system and separation from that same system, but it is undoubtedly about the laws of the family and of religion. I would even contend that this desire, or erotics, is how Grillparzer has his Hero move through her world—how she makes it different and "reverses the gaze." Thus, her feminist impulse is about the content of her speech and the relationship between desire and meaning. This discourse is about desire in all of its manifestations—a bodily desire and a longing to be free from the constraints of a life barely understood. Language creates these experiences and individual realities become more important than any other objective reality.

Hero has been subject to the ultimate inclusionary practice—that of the consecrated—and life outside of that space remains unknown and unwelcome to her. Hero has given up a possible life whose loss she cannot appreciate because she has been secluded in a radical practice of containment that does not allow her to think of herself as separate from her sacred role. However, Hero's desire to escape the conventional domestic role as wife and mother is also very much imbricated in Grillparzer's essentially negative portrayal of the role of life-long religious devotion and the coterminous loss of the erotic. While she is able to evade one obligation (marriage), she must enter into contract with another obligation (religion). In the opening of Act 1, Hero processes herself as an object but one endowed with autonomy due to the privilege of the sacred office. However, this independence is circumscribed by the nature of her duty—chastity. Here, sexuality is the power dynamic that is in play. Hero can avoid the sexual requirement of marriage by becoming a priestess but that means that she must also reject sexual desire when she becomes a priestess. However, it will become clear to the reader that Hero's flight into the sacred life is a form of urgent escape rather than a path that she takes with focused intentionality.

This title and the myth that it engages appear to provide us with a way out of the despair of Grillparzer's *Medea* and *Sappho* even if we quickly return to that bleakness by the end of *The Waves of Sea and Love*. The drama presents us with two people who have quickly fallen in love with each other. The animosity that overshadows the lives of Sappho and Medea is lacking in Hero's story even if the path that each woman takes is substantially the same. That is, Sappho, Medea, and Hero must all manage lives that have compulsory gender behavior and linguistic boundaries built into them. However, in the case of Hero, the consciousness of her linguistic utterances is largely hidden from her while Sappho and Medea are immediately knowing subjects. Hero might be called the most "human" figure out of the three women. Using the word human creates a problem because it supposes that there was something wrong with Sappho and Medea and that Hero's story is a recuperative one for the figure of the female or "woman."[11] If we consider these three dramas as a set of strategies, Sappho might be seen as one in which the amplification of discourse is one such strategy. Medea might be seen as a strategy of inclusion and exclusion. But how we do understand Hero in this strategic way and what does her drama have to tell us?

What may be lacking on the surface in the story of Hero is overabundant in *Sappho* and *Medea*. Or what Sappho and Medea signal to in their dramas is something that goes largely unrecognized and unstated in Hero's drama. While Medea and Sappho take self-consciously radical positions about the conditions of their lives as their stories progress, Hero *seems* to accept her future as a priestess without a conscious examination of the circumstances in which she has come to be held. Thus, *Des Meeres und der Liebe Wellen* could be said to function as an unreconstructed coda to *Medea* and *Sappho*. By unreconstructed, I mean that the drama takes a step back from the intensity of the earlier dramas. The heroine remains inside the language of her own oppressive social milieu even though she comes to act in ways that suggest refusal, thereby creating her own reality.

As an imaginative space, Grillparzer's story of Hero and Leander suggests that the myth is only a partial rendering of the meaning of the title. Thus, the title can only provide the impression of motion, or perhaps, gesture at something that is already in movement. Perhaps, the fluctuation of the waves already suggests something that is constant but almost always irregular in its intensity and flow. So much so that Grillparzer cannot name the woman in the title but can only reference her story metaphorically—*The Waves of Sea and Love*. The thinking backward that is useful in considerations of gender and its operation in the other classical plays also finds its place in this drama. Originally titled *Hero and Leander*, Grillparzer made the move to a much more suggestive but occlusive title. This could be the way that we "unthink" gender. Instead of exclusively dramatizing the pair of lovers much as he did in *Sappho* and *Medea* and making the names of the protagonists signal the theme, Grillparzer remakes the myth of Hero and Leander into a drama that has as its main impulse the desire to escape from a life rather than a desire to be included into a different form of life that is orderly and bound to social conventions. Medea and Sappho suffer from the dream of integration even as they are forced out of the lives in which they only have nominal membership while Hero's desire is flight. She has a sacred function to inhabit as the drama opens, one which is an escape from another role—that of wife and mother. She flees from the fate of the domestic realm where she would be subordinate to a man to what she imagines is the superior space of priestess for the virginal goddess, Aphrodite. Similar to Medea, Hero's development as a figure is bound up with kinship and her obligation to a role to which this affiliation ties her. In this case,

Hero is obligated to a sacred function that forestalls any alternative forms of figuration.

Hero's experience of her world is curtailed, and, in fact, one meets her in the opening scene as she is in the process of "becoming" something other than what she was. Hero is moving from the role of a young girl in training to a virginal priestess for life—essentially, a slight shift from one embodiment to another that indicates what sorts of roles women may inhabit out of a limited number. The sacred life is, however, empty and, in the end, offers no internal alternative structure with which Hero could use as a buttress against the overweening demands on her as a figure of sacred devotion. Hero seeks a complete but impossible liberation from structures of domestic power that would make her life an unlivable one. Power works from the inside out and does not reveal its own operations. There are spaces in which freedom can be imagined and even performed but even those moments of liberty are always bound to power. Hero attempts to flee from the operations of two types of power that are present in her reality. The first is the family (father, brother, and servile mother) with its domineering and demeaning authority. The second is the realm of religion with its own privations that generates a form of self-estrangement. In both instances of the performance of power, Hero refuses to accept established systems of subject formation that are conceived under the aegis of captive power by fleeing the possible forms of life that have been allotted her.

In *The Waves of Sea and Love*, Grillparzer demonstrates how precarity is almost always built into life—whether or not the danger is understood. Or was he interested in a presentation of how subject formation functions in violation of the law of the family and of religious practice? Hero's story is also about the riskiness of an emergent personhood for a woman. Yet this subjective personhood is also tied to her physical body. While much of feminist theory remained clearly uninterested in the body in thinking about subjectivity, I would argue that Grillparzer, in his time, intentionally made Hero's body (and that of Leander's) a central site of tension. In her introduction to *Volatile Bodies: Towards a Corporeal Feminism*,[12] Elizabeth Grosz writes:

> As a concept, sexuality is incapable of ready containment: it refuses to stay within its predesignated regions, for it seeps across boundaries into areas that are apparently not its own. As drive, it infests all sorts of other areas in the structures of desire. It renders even the desire not to desire, or the desire for celibacy, as sexual.[13]

Hero's longing for Leander is out of bounds. It knows no limits and cannot be subdued by the requirement for celibacy that her role as priestess demands. Her corporeality is entangled with her role as priestess to Aphrodite and her sexuality—her bodily acts. I am not abandoning the idea that Hero's interior world was foundational in her development in favor of an idea that too easily concentrates on her bodily desires. Rather, I want to combine the subjective (Hero's interiority) with the body such that sexuality and its effects influence the ways in which the story unravels. I'd like to return to this idea of the structure of desire for it informs my reading of the drama in differing ways. On the one hand, Hero's body has been designated as a site of virtue and chastity obligated to the family lineage through the goddess. On the other hand, Hero's body is a desiring one that takes Leander as her lover on the night that she is consecrated. Both situations focus on her body and how it has been prepared for certain practices. Her chaste body and her sexual body are part of a structure of desire—one where the absence of desire is the sole objective and the other where desire is realized and fulfilled. Without resorting to an approach to Hero's story where mind and body remain committed to a dualistic relationship, I do want to suggest that there is an interdependence wherein the inside and the outside stray into each other's spaces. This irrepressible movement from the inside to the outside and the outside to the inside is a current that allows the action in the drama to develop.

Concepts about power, its function, and that relationality are central to Grillparzer's thinking about how we are formed as subjects and the demands placed on us by formal governing bodies. In the case of Hero, this would be her uncle and the duties that are now hers to carry out. By questioning her role as priestess as she is becoming the priestess, Hero is already forming herself in opposition to that very position and its legitimacy. These demands are also about responsibility. What does Hero owe the goddess, the priest, or her mother and father? What kinds of interdependencies are created when one is born into a civic environment that immediately constitutes the figure of the female as subject to various forms of power?

By falling in love with Leander, Hero challenges conventional tropes of narrative understanding about the role of women and especially that of women who have been selected for excellence. That exemplary status does little to help Hero climb out of the fairly constricted world into which she has been placed. As I noted earlier, the female protagonists in Grillparzer's dramas narrate themselves and are the subject of narration. They evoke crises when they enter social or sacred spaces. While she acts and speaks, Hero is also concealing and revealing the truth of her own self. While Hero's story is instructive, it is because we have studied *Sappho* and *Medea*; Hero's story is only fully realizable because we have the counterweight of Medea and Sappho. Her meaning is located as an imaginative dislocation of the witch and the poetess.

Ideas about containment and seclusion are part of the framework of the narrative as it moves from one form of social and textual affiliation to another. In this final drama, Grillparzer has moved in a direction that feels very different from the stories of Medea and Sappho. One might instinctively believe that Hero's youth and innocence give shape to this very distinctive drama. Yet again, might it not be worthwhile to read this drama as the most human of Grillparzer's dramas? Here, we are presented with a young girl who appears to know nothing of herself other than as an object endowed with a religious value. The drama appears to move from one description to another—as a series of individual actions—without offering the reader the opportunity for a compositionally rich narrative experience. We are transported from one moment to another in this representation of actions and things—the lamp and light, the dove, the sea and the tower, the night, and so on—as if they were a single complete image. This lends an almost episodic quality to the drama that disrupts the flow of the text—there is an interruption of narrative sequence. The drama begins with Hero's consecration as priestess to Aphrodite. We know nothing of her back story. We are only given a partial family story later in the drama. Thus, our understanding of Hero doesn't suggest a forward progression but rather movement that is contingent on other information being revealed. Temporal stability is not present in this drama even though it appears to move smoothly through the narrative with the tone of linearity. Because she has dedicated herself to the service of the goddess under the urging of her family, the play opens already in a space of limited possibility.

DISTRACTION IN GRILLPARZER

Briefly exploring selected scholarship about the concept of "Sammlung" or composure (quiet contemplation or the happiness of quiet self-possession) in *The Waves of Sea and Love* offers the beginning of an analysis of the term that informs, in some part, how I approach a reading of the drama. The concepts of composure versus that of "Zerstreuung" or distraction are also located in Grillparzer's diaries and autobiography.[14] Paul K. Whitaker's article on Sammlung explores possible meanings behind the use of composure and distraction in Grillparzer's personal writings.[15] That study suggests that for Grillparzer composure was a necessary pursuit that could eliminate the danger of distraction. Whitaker writes, "It is not primarily an active dissipating of the energies so much as a failure of the individual to prevent outside influences from disturbing the inner harmony and unity of his being."[16] Composure was something that Grillparzer believed he failed to achieve in his own life. For him, distraction was the danger of life that stood diametrically opposed to composure.[17] The concept of composure allows a whole host of behaviors to become unwelcome and unappealing when held up against this idea of stability of character that is internally resolute and unhampered by the lability of life's events. E. E. Papst defines Sammlung as "a state of irreducible wholeness of being and recollected composure in which the self at once possesses, fulfills and transcends itself. Whereas the principle of composure was still only implicit and relatively undefined in Grillparzer's previous plays, in *The Waves of Sea and Love*, it now finds an articulate mouthpiece in a major protagonist and is placed at the heart of the tragic conflict as the explicit counter-pole of love."[18] Papst makes a convincing argument about the dichotomy between "Sammlung" and "Leben" or life in which a contrast between the spirit that has risen ". . . above the inner and outer chaos of passions and events" and the life that "drives man irresistibly into the ocean of uncontrollable events and passions" is apparent.[19] This contrast drives the drama and gives greater weight to the ways in which Hero understands herself in dialogue with Janthe, her servant, the priest, her mother, and later, Leander. Gisela Stein's *The Inspiration Motif in the Works of Franz Grillparzer* also seizes on the use of Sammlung and "Begeisterung" (enthusiasm) as concentration or inspiration: a dedication to higher ideals in the realm of art and creativity in order to gain and maintain an inner equilibrium untouched by the cares of the external world.[20]

The concept of composure in Grillparzer's drama is significant because it demonstrates how Grillparzer, ventriloquizing Hero, understands the ideal of internal composure in opposition to the distractions of the external world. The term is an opening into the conditions of Hero's new life: she should strive for the model of composure. It provides a context in which to think through how Hero moves in this new existence as priestess or rather how the priest understands how Hero should enact or perform her new role. It also stands in relationship with the terms "Wunsch" (wish) and "Neigung" (inclination) in Act 1 since both words arouse emotions and needs which Sammlung as a project rejects. I read this concept of composure and self-possession as the real opposing force to the desire and passion that is ignited in Hero as distraction. Thus, one could say that Sammlung or composure is the way in which Hero is meant to be organized: restraint, transcendence, and completeness. However, love and passion intervene and disrupt the quiet life that Hero is meant to live. It is my claim that Hero was never meant to achieve composure. From the onset of the drama, Grillparzer has Hero give voice to ideas that deny a fully realized commitment to the sacred office, principles which would signify this notion of concentration or composure. Instead, Hero is the embodiment of "zerstreut," a kind of dispersal of energy, discord, a failure to master the self.

My attentiveness to *The Waves of Sea and Love* is also shaped by Dagmar Lorenz's (1986) reading of the Hero-myth on desire and sexual emancipation and the equally significant unremarkable and ordinary status of Hero: "Hero ist weder durch ihre geistige und intellektuelle Begabung zur Ausnahmegestalt vorbestimmt."[21] Lorenz makes several important points about Hero's story that, in my opinion, are undertheorized in the earlier scholarship. First, Lorenz suggests that Hero's story functions as kind of countertext to Sappho's: "*Des Meeres und der Liebe Wellen* gehört thematisch zu der viel früheren Sappho. Dialektisch betrachtet ist es das Gegenstück. Grillparzer hatte die Hero-und-Leander Thematik bereits 1819 in Erwägung gezogen, also unmittelbar nach *Sappho*."[22] This brings the reader of Grillparzer's classical plays full-circle from the vexed brittleness of *Sappho* to the placid yet lethal experience of *The Waves of Sea and Love*. Yet both dramas are essentially unstable structures where the women believe that they possess something certain and that their worlds are secure and protected. Second, Lorenz contends that Hero has fled into the service of the goddess in order to avoid the predestined social fate of being mother to children and wife to a man: "Sie möchte dem Los der Frau entgehen, das sie in der Gestalt ihrer moralisch gebrochenen, gedemütigten und demoralisierten Mutter . . . vor Augen hat."[23] Third, her mother realizes that Hero is also trapped by the sacred—the freedom of the temple is only appearance and her decision to avoid men such as her brother and father to become a priestess is only one solution to a larger social problem: "Hero glaubt, mit der Priesterschaft Selbstbestimmung zu wählen. Da ihre Göttin "ihre Frau" ist, (I, 333) bildet sie sich ein, unter weiblichen Schutz zu stehen und übersieht den männlichen Priesterapparatus . . ."[24] In a similar spirit, Brigitte Prutti's study of several works by Grillparzer also recognizes the gender relationships in his dramas, and I would argue especially so in his three classical plays: "Das Geschlechterthema ist durchwegs zentral für Grillparzers Dramen und es betrifft das kulturelle Geschlecht der Protagonisten im doppelten Sinn von Gender und Genealogie und die Rolle von Sexualität und Erotik in unterschiedlichen dramatischen Beziehungs- und Problemkonstellationen."[25] Later, in her chapter on this drama, Prutti rightly states that Grillparzer:

> stellt ein junges Mädchen ins Zentrum seines Liebesdrama und entfaltet den Konflikt dieser Figur zwischen Autonomieverlangen und erotischen Verschmelzungswünschen. Die individualpsychologischen Voraussetzungen dieser widersprüchlichen Wünsche lokalisiert er in der repressiven Geschlechtsordnung der modernen Kernfamilie, der sich die Helden seines Stückes mit ihrer Entscheidung für das jungfräuliche Priesterinnentum entziehen will.[26]

This brief review of selected scholarship on Sammlung is central to understanding how Hero manages her special circumstances, or rather, is unable to do so.

REPRESENTATION AND OBLIGATION

The Waves of Sea and Love opens in a ritual space. We are immediately in the midst of a sanctified location—the temple of Aphrodite Urania, the celestial manifestation of the goddess (in contrast to that of Aphrodite Pandemos, the goddess of sensual pleasure). The ceremonial is the marker of this opening scene, and, indeed, the idea of the sacred informs this drama. This is the day in which Hero is initiated as priestess to Aphrodite Urania and is prepared for a new life devoted to the goddess. In the foreground of the courtyard of the temple of Aphrodite are statues of Hymen, the god of marriage, and Amor, the god of love. Hero enters the scene caught between these two statues. The abundance of the sacred and the divine receives Hero as she enters the narrative space of the drama. It contextualizes Hero's sense of self and the value attached to her self-concept, one that is marked by her relationship to the family tradition shaped by the civic and the sacred. Hero's entry into the setting creates a tension that she does not recognize. Surrounded by the sensual, Hero is on the brink of relinquishing that very aspect of her life. Yet, we can imagine that there will be a pull between Hero and the two gods. There is even a tension between what each god represents. Both are symbolic of a bond but there is a difference in how those unions are presented. Having mythical origins, Hymen presides over marriage ceremonies and Amor over erotic love. One is socially normative in wedlock while the other is about the loss of self-possession in desire. Both are forbidden Hero. Amor and Hymen immediately bring us into a space that is overdetermined by their figures, both of which represent the sensual in some way. As she addresses each god in turn, Hero is dismissive about their very potent roles in myth and her relationship to each.

Hero's long monologue about the new life that she is about to enter and the attendant responsibilities offer immediate insight into how she understands herself and the function that she assumes in the role of the virginal priestess. As she prepares the temple and its surroundings with myrtle, roses, and other flowers for the coming festival, Hero unwittingly presents herself as an object of the celebration rather than as an active participant in a ceremonial initiation. Before one has the opportunity to understand Hero as an individual, she has narrated herself out of any form of selfhood and now functions as an object. Thus, the baseline of this drama is already aimed at erasure of personhood and the foregrounding of the virtuous subject. There is the suggestion of moral excellence that is appended to the status of Hero's new life as well as the imperative for a chaste existence of abnegation.

Indeed, Hero can only understand herself as a thing that is outside of time; both indulged and locked in an oath with the goddess (and with her uncle, the high priest):

Mir wird vergönnt, die unbemerkten Tage,
Die fernhin rollen ohne Richt und Ziel,
Dem Dienst der hohen Himmlischen zu weihn;
Die einzelnen, die Wiesenblümchen gleich
Der Fuß des Wanderers zertritt und knickt,
Zum Kranz gewunden um der Göttin Haupt,
Zu weihen und verklären. Sie und mich.
. . .
Wie bin glücklich, daß nun heut der Tag,
Und daß der Tag so schön, so still, so lieblich. (*Waves*, 1.5–13)[27]

Because this is the only world that she has known, it becomes the only life that she can imagine for herself. It is one of beauty, idleness, tranquility, and service to the goddess. What Hero's words also disclose is a failure to engage fully with the depth of this reality. She wants to go through life without thought, without noticing, with a dedication to those on high that never surpasses the superficial—a life without distraction. Indeed, Hero has already given over her imagination superficially to the idea of the sacred life that is in touch with the divine. "Schaust du mich schon al eine von den Euren? / Ward es dir Kund, daß jene muntre Hero, / Die du wohl spielen sahst an Tempels Stufen, / Daß sie ergreifend ihrer Ahnen Recht, / Die Priester gaben von Urväterzeit / Dem hehren Heiligtum—daß sie's ergreifend / Das schöne Vorrecht, Priesterin nun selbst" (*Waves*, 1.17–23).[28] Hero is fully caught up in the myth of her family as an institution with its own deeply rooted religious customs that transcend marriage. She already sees herself as part of a line of descent that is ancient and derived from her forefathers. This "Vorrecht" or privilege is now hers to grasp. It is with some interest that Hero continues to speak but in the third person: "Und heute, heut: an diesem, diesem Tage. / Auf jenen Stufen wird das Volk sie sehn, / Den Himmlischen der Opfer Gaben spendend. / Von jeder Lippe ringt sich Jubel los, / Und in dem Glanz, der Göttin dargebracht, Strahlt auf der Priestrin Haupt—" (*Waves*, 1.24–28).[29] She first presents herself as an object—"dieses Festes Gegenstand"—and later in the same monologue, refers to herself in the third-person as "she." Hero is primed to be an object, something that is not an "I." While her purpose is a serious one, Hero treats it with a whimsy that does not acknowledge the duty and attention that the priestess must possess; the role has its own direction and goals that Hero ignores in her opening monologue focusing only on how satisfying her life will be once her days are unfettered by the cares of the world. It is only in conversation with the priest that we fully understand the difficulty of the office and the expectations that she must meet.

Although not divided into strict scenes, the interactions between Hero and the priest are important moments in Act 1 that are demarcated by their content. The priest tries to impress upon Hero that the life of the priestess is a hard one that is lonely and that she should find a suitable female companion to help her bear the burden of the office (*Waves*, 1.116–20). Hero, not understanding her uncle's meaning, replies lightly:

Ich kann nicht finden, daß Gesellschaft fördert;
Was Einem obliegt muß man selber tun.
Denn, nennst du einsam einer Priestrin Leben?
Wann war es einsam hier im Temple je? (*Waves*, 1.121–24)[30]

When she declares that the life of a priestess is not a lonely one and that there are always people in the temple and something to be done (*Waves*, 1.125–35), the priest responds: "Du hast mich nicht gefaßt" (*Waves*, 1.136).[31] Hero fails to comprehend the very real privations of her role as priestess and does not suffer any uneasiness about that new life. Indeed, she declares that what one does not understand cannot cause any desire; she is happy as she is: "Was man nicht faßt, erregt auch keine Verlangen. Laß mich so wie ich bin, ich bin es gern" (*Waves*, 1.137–38).[32] Her flippant response shows a young woman who does not understand the import of the role that she is about to enter or that she may indeed have desires that are as yet unknown to her. She goes about as if it were just a slight adjustment of the self to a new way of being rather than a major shift that is a decisive break with her already small and constrained existence. Hero cannot process how much her life will change once she is consecrated to the goddess even as her uncle tries to make her understand the extremity of that shift: "Doch kommt die Zeit und ändert Wunsch und Neigung" (*Waves*, 1.139).[33] Those two terms—"wish" and "inclination"—traffic in meanings that are about desire and the concept of composure. Even the priest recognizes that Hero might be susceptible to other ways of being as her preferences evolve over time. Hero's fatalistic view of the course of human life also shows the reader a glimpse of the Hero who does appreciate what she is losing in her life:

Man klagt ja täglich, daß der Unverständ'ge
Beharrt und bleibt, man tadl' ihm wie man will;
Weshalb nun den Verständ'gen unverständ'ger
Und beständ'ger glauben als den Tor?
Ich weiß ja was ich will und was wir wählten,
Wenn wählen heißen kann, wo keine Wahl. (*Waves*, 1.140–45)[34]

First, Hero refutes her uncle's words of advice and advances another view of life wherein one—the sensible person or the fool—complains and struggles daily but still suffers and stays in his place. For her, life is not about happiness but rather about endurance. Second, Hero makes a declaration about the concept of choice. Hero's pessimism is a subconscious one that only rises to the surface when she is forced to confront the features of her life, or, any life. When there is no decision to be made because there is no such thing as choice, what does it even mean to "make a choice" about anything in this world.[35] One could then believe that Hero accepts her coming role as priestess because she knows that there was no other choice to be made. Here, we might pause to consider *Sappho* and the choices that the poetess made in her life, decisions which led to her ultimate downfall. Hero claims that she first came to consciousness out of the long slumber of her childhood and found her existence and her own true self in the temple where she discovered a goal and a purpose: "Aus langer Kindheit träumerischen Staunen / Bin hier um Bewußtsein erst erwacht. / Im Tempel, an der Göttin Fußgestelle / War mir ein Dasein erst, ein Ziel, ein Zweck" (*Waves*, 1.155–58).[36] As readers, we wonder how this statement about first gaining "ein Ziel, ein Zweck" in the goddess's temple might be in tune or in discord with Hero's earlier statement about choice.[37] In his study, Konrad Schaum rightly states that: "Sie ist nicht bereit, ihren Beruf für eine ausgesprochen spiritualistische und kontemplative Haltung anzusehen, im 'schönen Vorrecht' einer gehobenen sozialen Stellung zu verharren und den göttlichen Willen aus 'Zeichen und Orakeln' zu deuten"[38]—suggesting that Hero is not prepared for the position of priestess due to a lack of requisite skills. The high priest also advises Hero to be less self-absorbed and accept her calling in a unselfish manner ("Nur hüte dich, daß so beschränktes Streben / Ein Billiger möge selbstisch nennen" [*Waves*, 1.165–67]).[39] These analyses resonate with the priest's words about "Wunsch" and "Neigung," and much later, with the term "Sammlung." How does consciousness function in a space where there is no choice? When there is only one goal and one purpose?

In this drama, traditional notions of the family are estranged in deference to religious ideology. Hero's relationship with her parents and her feelings about domestic life for a woman are other leitmotifs that Grillparzer develops. The family becomes an instrumental concept that underscores the tension between Hero and domestic principles. Hero depicts a tumultuous household in which her father acted as tyrant, her mother suffered in silence, and her brother tormented her (*Waves*, 1.199–210). The priest—her father's brother—tells her that her parents have traveled to see her consecration but not before he startles her with the false news that they had instead come to take her home to a waiting bridegroom. Although Hero's father speaks the first lines of their encounter, Hero only has words for her silent mother. Taking her mother to the side, Hero stands between her mother and father allowing her to speak freely without having to see her husband's face. In one of her boldest statements that speak to both gender and language, Hero tells her mother, "Im

Tempel hier hat auch die Frau ein Recht, / Und die Gekränkten haben freie Sprachen" (*Waves*, 1.279–80).⁴⁰ In the same breath, Hero rebukes her mother for wanting to take her home and marry her off:

Nun aber sag, ob ich dich erriet:
Nicht gleichen Sinn mit deinem Gatten kamst du,
Und wäre dir der freie Wunsch gewährt,
Du führtest gar die Tochter mit dir heim.
Aus ihres Glückes sturmbeschützer Ruh
In deiner dunkeln Sorgen niedre Hütte? (*Waves*, 1.283–88)⁴¹

When Hero speaks with her mother, a feminist sensibility comes through. Still, it appears as an individual act of defiance rather than a call to reform the structure of the social world in which women are subordinate to men. This minor narrative performance of rebellion against the cultural and gendered norms embedded in the tradition of marriage marks her as both willful and willing to take the risk of exiling herself from the family to enter into the sacred space, which she believes holds more opportunity for self-fulfillment. However, while she may escape from one unlivable space, she is about to enter another that will also prove to be equally unrealizable. Thus, her willfulness is an activity, an event that moves her from one kind of impossibility to another form of the impossible. Hero remains largely unaware of the power of her words in this drama. Her language is not as lapidary as that of either Sappho or Medea, but she does use language to advance an understanding of herself at times in the drama. At this moment, she is not exemplary in how she understands the power of language. She speaks freely without considering the impact of the transgressive nature of her language. When she talks about choice, companionship, mood, or duty, Hero does not have an exceptional gift for appreciating how those concepts organize her thoughts; the language that Hero has at her disposal for expressing those concepts in deep and meaningful ways is underdeveloped. She stays on the surface of every dialogue. Yet, by the end of the drama, Hero does not speak as a shallow or superficial woman about her love for Leander. These are the only instances in the text where we see the depths of her feeling rising to the level of language that is neither forced nor compulsory.

Narrating the family drama as a source of despair, her mother informs Hero that her brother has left the home abandoning his wife and children to seek unknown adventure with other like-minded men (*Waves*, 1.300–304). This is the privilege of being male. Her brother can flee his situation once it becomes untenable for him. Hero's response refuses the unspoken obligation to return home and marry because the son, her brother, is no longer there. "Doch ist nicht er, sind da noch Hundert andre, / Von gleichem Sinn und störrisch wildern Wesen. / Das ehrne Band der Roheit um die Stirn, / je minder denkend, um so heft'ger wollend" (*Waves*, 1.307–10).[42] The mother's only reply is that "Das Weib ist glücklich nur an Gattenhand" (*Waves*, 1.320).[43] One must wonder how much happiness Hero's mother experiences at the side of her husband. Although unable to speak openly to Hero while in her husband's presence, the mother is still devoted to the institution of marriage. There are no other options for her since the decision has been made since her birth. For her, the idea of "Wahl" (choice) does not exist. She has been prepared for marriage and children and there is no other possibility open for her. Hero harshly chastises her mother: "Das darfst du sagen, ohne zu erröten? / Wie? Und mußt hüten jenes Mannes Blick, / Des Herren, deines Gatten? Darfst nicht reden, / Mußt du schweigen, flüstern, ob du gleich im Recht, / Ob du die Weisre gleich, stillwaltend Beßre? / Und wagst zu sprechen mir ein solches Wort?" (*Waves*, 1.321–26).[44] Again, this is one of Hero's outspoken personal condemnations of marriage. It is not an objective speech about the demerits of marriage but rather one that gets to the deep level of that institution based on the experiences of her own mother.[45] Language is the place where female agency is frequently policed through acts of male institutional power as it the case with Hero's mother. In this case, Hero's words to her mother are defiant of male control over what a woman is allowed to say. The mother, unable to step outside of her domestic role, is shocked at Hero's speech and claims that "they" have stolen her pious child from her and turned her into a vain and selfish one with their teachings (*Waves*, 1.328–31). Walking away from her mother, Hero moves toward Aphrodite and says, "Ich aber will mit heiterm Sinne wandeln / Hier an der Göttin Altar, meiner Frau. / Das Rechte tun, nicht weil man mirs befahl, / Nein, weil es recht, weil ich es so erkannt. / Und Niemand soll mirs rauben und entziehen. Wahrhaftig" (*Waves*, 1.332–36).[46] Hero asserts a radical female autonomy with inflammatory words as she distances herself from her mother's very conventional views about marriage and the kind of life that is suitable for a woman. Although she is restrained in other ways that are directly connected to her role as a priestess, Hero will not be regulated by the physical and linguistic proscriptions of marriage. The provocation that Hero advances is one that refutes the world of domesticity and the conventional family for an existence in the sacred sphere where she believes that she can be agentic. Hero summarily rejects traditional family structures: she expresses opposition to marriage in conversation with her mother; she refers in negative terms to her own mother's marriage; she indirectly engages in a critique of marriage through the wayward brother who has deserted his wife and children; and she will not return home to marry as her mother suggests.

Act 1 of *The Waves of Sea and Love* demonstrates what it means to be integrated in a family or kinship model as well as in a set of religious practices.

Both acts of incorporation represent the collapse of possible forms of life for Hero. Immediately, we are cognizant of the ways in which religious practice and kinship are intertwined in this drama. While the normalization of exclusion and expulsion seems to be clear in *Sappho* and *Medea*, there is a challenge in the way in which Hero is with a dual gesture brought into the fold of family and religion and simultaneously exiled from the social world. Personal identity becomes a cultural event in Hero's situation. This twofold gesture is aimed at keeping her sense of self bound to that of religious practice and virtuous behavior. What Grillparzer might be asserting in this drama is his continued ambivalence about the nature of virtue and the privileges that it confers in opposition to those which the world offers. The office of the priestess is valued for what it represents but holds no intrinsic worth for what it actually is. That is, Hero is denied all freedom of speech and movement that is not determined by her status as priestess. While she may speak, she cannot interpret herself outside of a certain discursive context or semantics. Are the concepts of composure and distraction similar to performative gender and its production and reproduction in the material and discursive domains? Judith Butler puts forth an argument about the "I" and the struggle to express its meaning through the language at hand—the language of composure and distraction, in this case. This "I" is what Hero finally becomes as she laments the loss of Leander at the close of the drama. Might it be that the "I" only emerges in a discourse of loss in which the linguistic usage is simultaneously normative and noncompliant. Butler writes, "I am not outside the language that structures me, but neither am I determined by the language that make this 'I' possible. This is the bind of self-expression, as I understand it. What it means is that you never receive me apart from the grammar that establishes my availability to you."[47] Hero's "I" does not exist outside of the discourse which produced her but this "I" is also not completely compelled by that discursive construction. In another statement, Hero feels both like herself but also strange—a possible conflict between composure and distraction: "Hier fühl' ich mich und hier fühl' ich ein Fremdes— / Mein Wesen sind hindangibt und besitzt" (*Waves*, 1.153–54).[48] This availability, what I think of as composure and distraction, is only grasped in the language of the difficult "I." It appears but cannot be maintained and encouraged to become something that extends beyond the morphology of her world.

BECOMING THE PROBLEM

Tightly composed, but with little dramatic tension, Grillparzer's play does possess moments in which a certain amount of action articulates a way forward. That path may be fraught, but it does offer something tangible to grasp.

Occurring immediately after the tense exchange between mother and daughter, a dove's nest, one of Aphrodite's symbols, is discovered in the bushes surrounding the temple. The priest orders it removed against the wishes of both Hero and her mother. Addressing the mother and Hero, he tells them why the dove is not permitted to be in the temple:

Nun also denn zu dir. Schwachsinnig Weib,
Was kommst du her, zu stören diese Stunde?
Und staunst ob dem was du doch längst gewußt,
Der heil'gen Ordnung dieses Götterhauses.
Kein Vogel baut beim Tempel hier sein Nest.
Nicht girren ungestraft im Hain die Tauben,
Die Rebe kriecht um Ulmen nicht hinan,
All was sich paart bleibt ferne diesem Hause,
Du Jene dort fügt heut sich gleichem Los (*Waves*, 1.350–58).[49]

The vigilant priest addresses a variety of concerns in this short but important speech. First, he reprimands the mother for disturbing the order of the temple on this sacred day. Second, he says that no bird is allowed to build its nest in the temple nor may vines even wind their way around trees. Third, anything that forms a couple must remain far away from the temple. Finally, he says that today is the day that Hero must obey these same constraints that he has outlined. He will not stray from the rules of the temple and asserts his dominance not only as a man but also as a religious figure. As he says this, Hero strokes the dove and says to it: "Du armes Tier, wie streiten sie um uns!" (*Waves*, 1.359).[50] There are competing voices for Hero: the claims of the priest and that of the mother are at cross purposes. Hero tries to comfort the dove with words that also apply to her—poor creature that she also unknowingly is. It is only after some time that Hero gives up the dove to the servant and says, "Du nimms und trag es hin, und gibt ihm Freiheit, / Die Freiheit wie das Tier sie kennt und wünscht" (*Waves*, 1.381–82).[51] Hero has relinquished the dove in order to give it the freedom for which every animal wishes, herself included, even if Hero does not fully comprehend her captive state. Her desire to be free from the institution of marriage is as strong as her desire to be free from the constraints of the temple. The intrusion of the dove into the holy space runs parallel to Leander's later trespass into the temple. The presence of both the dove and Leander symbolizes distraction for they hold Hero's attention to the extrinsic world and away from the consecrated internal one.

In his tirade against the mother, the priest invokes the celestial Aphrodite to whom the temple is dedicated and chastises Hero's mother for her inferior understanding of the sacred office to which her daughter has been educated to enter. While the priest continues his harangue, he also enjoins Hero's mother to take her daughter with her home: "Was braucht die Göttin dein und deines Kinds?" (*Waves*, 1.361–62)[52] and in his passion says:

Geh hin und bette sie in Niedrigkeit,
In der du selbst, dir selbst zur Qual, dich abmühst.
Sie sei die Magd des Knechtes der sie freit,
Statt hier auf leichter Bahn, nach eignem Ziel.
Die Einz'ge sie des dürftigen Geschlechts,
Ein Selbst zu sein, ein Wesen, eine Welt
Bist du die Mutter doch! Du, Hero, folge!
Die Torheit ruft. Folg ihr als Mensch, als Weib! (*Waves*, 1.371–79)[53]

The priest's analysis of the kind of life that Hero would lead should she return home is both severe and discerning. He understands what marriage to a man means for a woman. The priest upholds the special nature of a life devoted to the goddess, one that is eminent and opens a world to Hero that is elevated but also flush with a freedom that is expansive as long as it is contained. The distinguished life that is Hero's to have is one that linguistically removes her from the world of the pejorative "Weib" and inscribes her into one where she can be an "ein Selbst," "ein Wesen," "eine Welt." The priest offers much—a transfigured existence for Hero, one where the appalling demands of domesticity will not touch her. His language plays in the realm of gender as much as Hero's does. Although the priest is cognizant of what traditional marriage and children do to women, he does not demonstrably consider what harm a life as a priestess might hold. He sees no harm because he is caught up in the lofty religious aspects of the role without a thought about the deprivations of that sacred office for a woman and his own privileged status as a man and priest.

As Hero and her mother leave the scene, one is left with the sense that this talk of freedom, independence, and transcendence cannot be fulfilled in the ways that either Hero or the Priest imagine. For with each utterance about freedom, an opposite and competing revelation is made. The priest tells Hero's father that, "Der freie Wahl ist schwacher Toren Spielzeug. / Der Tücht'ge sieht in jedem Soll ein Muß / Und Zwang, als erste Pflicht, ist ihm die Wahrheit" (*Waves*, 1.414–16).[54] In many ways, this echoes Hero's earlier words to the priest about how choice is not in question when there is no choice to be made. Yet the priest has a much more lethal version of Hero's words. The priest's final lines about "Zwang" (compulsion) and "Pflicht" (duty) are among the many instances in which his words are brutal and uncompromising about the kind of life to which he ascribes.

Once the ceremony commences, Hero successfully renounces love as she turns to the statue of Amor: "Der du die Liebe gibst, nimm all die meine.

/ Dich grüßend nehm' ich Abschied auch von dir" (*Waves*, 1.495–96).⁵⁵ However, when she stands by the statue of Hymen, Hero is able to only partially speak the words to him. She is unable to recall the aphorism abjuring Hymen once she sees Leander in the distance. Instead, she begins to repeat the same words that she had just delivered to Amor. This moment is one left unfinished and we never learn what those words of renunciation to Hymen were.⁵⁶ Since Hero does not reject the god of marriage, her consecration remains incomplete. Confused and distracted she spreads too much incense into the sacrificial fire and causes a high flame to shoot up representing a new passion that has been ignited in her. At the close of Act 1 with the failure to renounce Hymen, Hero's resolve for the sacred life appears to have dissolved when she sees Leander for the first time. According to the stage directions, Hero practiced subterfuge (she pretends to tend to her shoe) in order to turn and gaze at him.⁵⁷

The action in the first act establishes a set of relationships that revolve around gender thinking through a series of encounters between Hero and the other characters in the drama—Janthe, the Priest, the mother, the goddess, and the figures of Amor and Hymen. Hero's own monologues are attempts to uncover meaning in the events of her life. Her provocative statements about female life and its risks are important to recall as we move through the drama as they appear to fall to the side after Act 1. Like *Sappho* and *Medea*, this drama functions in much the same way—how to leave a life of consequence. In this case, Hero gradually displays openness to the unraveling of her existence as priestess, a role that she had only earlier that day embraced. Her early and thorough rejection of the domestic realm of marriage for the life of the chaste priestess is very quickly called into question. This rejection of marriage for the sacred life is a decision that was made for her. This was no active or self-motivated choice that was made. As part of her family lineage, the girl-child is selected and trained to be the priestess. Hero is descended from a family that has provided the priestess of Aphrodite to Sestos since "Urväterzeit." Reaching back into her ancestry, Hero understands that she is part of a female genealogy but perhaps what eludes her is that these girls, her aunts, and great aunts, were selected at a young age for this position and raised to have only one wish, which was to serve the goddess. It is only in Act 3, that the priest first mentions Hero's aunt who owned the lyre, an heirloom, that is in Hero's inner rooms in the tower: "Dies Saitenspiel sogar, ein altes Erbstück / Von deines Vaters Schwester und der meinen, / Einst Priesterin wie du an diesem Ort" (*Waves*, 3.911–13).⁵⁸ We also discover that Hero has been in training in the temple for seven years (*Waves*, 3.920–23). There appears to be an archival absence of female figures in this drama. They were certainly there but have disappeared without a word. What did her female ancestors think or want for themselves? Did they want to serve? Was it a privilege for them? It isn't addressed in Grillparzer's work and is an undeveloped question about how the course of female lives in this drama is made inevitable from an early age through this generational legacy. There is an untidiness to this unknown history, an inherited one, an Erbstück.[59]

MYTHIC REALITIES

In Act 2, Hero dressed as she was at the start of the drama—that is, without her priestly garb that would signify her new status—appears and sings the myth of Leda and the Swan:

Da sprach der Gott
Komm her zu mir,
In meine Wolken
Neben mir. (*Waves*, 2.707–10)[60]

Sie aber streichelt
Den weichen Flaum. (*Waves*, 2.728)[61]

While for her, the song appears innocent, and without meaning, her uncle has forbidden her from singing it. The priest perceives the forbidden nature of this highly erotic song.[62] The story of Leda and the Swan is a well-known one. Zeus, as is his usual practice, comes down from Mount Olympus in the guise of a swan to seduce, in this instance, the mortal Leda. The blatant desire of Zeus for Leda and the resulting consummation of that lust is the source of the priest's reluctance to have Hero sing such an overtly sexual song: a young woman seduced by what, at first, appears to be an innocuous bird. This pairing of innocence with the sexual brings us back to the confusion over the dove from Act 1: whatever "couples" is not allowed to be in the temple. Because Hero is not permitted to mate with anyone, the mere presence of the dove and the singing of the erotic myth are affronts to the goddess and the office of the priestess. The presence of Leander and Naukleros while Hero is singing these erotic lyrics reminds the modern reader that we are in the space of not yet realized desire and also doubly in the world of myth. Hero and Leander are themselves mythic beings: their tragic history known since antiquity and passed down to the present moment. However, Hero is also telling us about a mythic incident in which a god seduces a woman, another mythic history that is also known to us. To return to the imbrication of myth and sex in the drama, Grosz in *Volatile Bodies* had already declared that desire crosses over into boundaries that are not meant for it. It causes the desire not to desire to become sexual. Hero doesn't know how to step outside of myth-thinking, yet she also does not understand that she is thinking and acting myth as a manifestation of desire.

When she sings of Leda and the swan, Hero is unable to articulate why this song is meaningful enough to cause her to repeat it throughout the drama. Thus, this failure to understand the sensual implications of Leda and the swan is an important signpost of Hero's paucity of interpretative skills. Although gender and language as they are exposed in the myth of Leda and the Swan are central to the drama, they seem to be secondary to Hero's understanding of her own personal story.[63] In Act 3 while in her tower, Hero again invokes the song and her own ignorance of why she sings it:

Und Leda streichelt
Den weichen Flaum.
Das ew'ge Lied! Wie kommts mir nur in Sinn?
Nicht Götter steigen mehr zu wüsten Türmen,
Kein Schwan, kein Adler bringt verlaßnen Trost.
Die Einsamkeit bleibt einsam und sie selbst. *Waves*, 3.1043–1048.[64]

For the third time in Act 4, Hero again invokes the myth after she has already consummated her relationship with Leander. After the priest says that a stranger was observed at the tower the previous evening, Hero suggests that perhaps a supernatural being had come down from high:

Nun Herr, vielleicht der Überird'schen Einer!
Du sprachst ja selbst: in altergrauer Zeit
Stieg oft ein Gott zu sel'gen Menschen nieder.
Zu Leda kam, zum fürstlichen Admet,
Zur strengverwahrten Danae ein Gott.
Warum nicht heut? Zu ihr; zu uns, zu wem du willst (*Waves*, 4.1403–8).[65]

She uses the reasoning that perhaps it was a visit by a celestial creature that disturbed the tower the night before. However, Hero now understands the meaning of the song and, for her, Leander is this god that has come down ("Zu ihr; zu uns, zu wem du willst"). In Act 4, Hero falls asleep dreaming of Leda, a dream in which she welcomes the swan to her in an ultimate act of sensual tranquility, a displacement of her welcoming of Leander to her:

Und, o, dein Rauschen und der Blätter Lispeln,
Wie Worte klingt mir: von ihm mir, ihm, von ihm.
Breit aus die Schwingen, hülle sich um mich.
Um Stirn und Haupt, den Hals, die müden Arme,
Umfaß, Umfang! Ich öffne dir die Brust. (*Waves*, 4.1809–13)[66]

Earlier, the primary tension in the play was how Hero understands herself in light of her new role as the virginal priestess to Aphrodite. She does not yet realize that there may be a conflict about how she behaves as a priestess in training and how she must act as the consecrated priestess. As the priestess of Aphrodite, Hero no longer has to fear the female duty to marry and reproduce the family structure as the subordinate one in the domestic realm. However, she still has to submit to the values and norms of the sacred, which are determined by another man, the high priest. While Hero may disobey the social category, she is still bound by the religious norm. Thus, her use of language is one that minimizes or does not fully understand the importance of this shift. She does know that what she is refusing in the domestic realm is something that would have been constraining. However, Hero does not understand the life that she is entering is also one where she must give up much in order to be part of that sacred system. The importance of her new life in these structures of traditional organization and classification gives shape to Hero's self-presentation. She has been assembled for a set of practices whereby she has to conform to the requirements of the new relationship with the goddess. She leaves one form of figuration behind only to enter into a completely confining one that even dictates the language for her to think about herself. This is where composure and distraction come into play and the tension between these two competing ideals manifests themselves. While composure has a defined orderliness to it, distraction is much more unstable and volatile. Composure is constructed around the suppression of distraction and the external disorder implied in this distraction.

THE STATUS OF COMPOSURE

Act 3, the pivot on which this drama rotates, opens with a lengthy description of Hero's inner room within the tower while in conversation with the priest. The priest emphasizes how the new living quarters are separate and isolated from the rest of life (*Waves*, 3.894–906). We are meant to understand the physical composition of her new surroundings outside of the temple now that she has become the priestess. The lamp—a primary leitmotif of the drama—is placed on a tall stand in her chamber. Deeply invested in settling Hero into her new existence, her uncle is disappointed in Hero's reaction to her new life and to the living quarters. Her response is not one that is impressed with or even cognizant of the physical trappings or the existential meanings that saturate her room. The priest, with some degree of dismay, wants Hero to be enthusiastic about her new station in life:

Ich dachte dich erfreuter mir am Abend
Des sel'gen Tags, der unser Wünschen krönt.
Was wir gestrebt, gehofft, du hast, du bist es;
Und statt entzückt, find' ich dich stumm und kalt. (*Waves*, 3.928–31)[67]

The delight (Entzückung) that her uncle wishes her to express for the vocation, or rather, her calling, is indicative of the high esteem in which he holds the role. The verbs "streben" (to strive) and "hoffen" (to hope) are goal oriented; they are about something purposeful and wanted—a desire or a wish. And Hero now has the thing; she is the thing. The wishes that the priest believes they have achieved are actually his alone since Hero appears uninterested in the deeper significance of the new life that she has accepted. Because he also holds an exalted position in the temple, it is this privileged role that the priest is at pains to cultivate in Hero and uphold as part of the family story. Her silence in the face of this life is a refusal to accommodate herself to the privilege of those fulfilled wishes. Hero is very practical but also dismissive in her retort to her uncle's disappointment, a response that signals a labile state:

Du weißt, mein Ohm, wir sind nicht immer Herr
Von Stimmungen, die kommen, wandeln, gehen,
Sie selbst erzeugend und von nichts gefolgt. (*Waves*, 3.932–34)[68]

If, as Hero believes, moods cannot be controlled, if they are subject to changing whimsies and are acts of self-creation, then how can she be properly prepared for a life of restraint and repose when even she cannot guarantee that her moods will remain consistent? It is this lack of stability that signals Hero's unconscious inability to fully commit to the new life and thus to the necessity of composure. The priest had intimated only hours earlier, "Doch kommt die Zeit und ändert Wunsch and Neigung" (*Waves*, 1.139).[69] Hero, in her own words, must now contend with the capriciousness of wishes and inclinations that cause an imbalance in moods—this Zerstreuung or distraction.

Hero again denies her uncle's call to attend to her new office with all seriousness, but she makes a distinction here that is important for our understanding of her movements going forward. Hero tells her uncle:

Doch gönne mir nur eine Nacht der Ruh,
Des Sinnens, der Erholung, und, mein Ohm,
Du wirst mich finden, die du sonst gekannt.
Der Ort ist still, die Lüfte atmen kaum;
Hier ebben leichter der Gedanken Wogen,
Der Störung Kreise fliehn dem Ufer zu,
Und Sammlung wird mir werden, glaube mir. (*Waves*, 3.938–44)[70]

Hero uses "Sammlung" or composure for the first time in the drama when she requests a night of reprieve for peace, reflection, and relaxation, all examples of the kind of repose that the expression invokes.[71] The priest is immediately enthusiastic about her use of the word since it fulfills all of his expectations about the form of life that is required and wanted. She has spoken the magic word that allows him to be effusive about the life that she will now live in retreat and quiet contemplation:

Sammlung? Mein Kind, sprach das der Zufall bloß?
Wie, oder fühltest du des Wortes Inhalt.
Das du gesprochen, Wonne meinem Ohr?
Du hast genannt den mächt'gen Weltenhebel
Der alles Große tausendfach erhöht,
Und selbst das Kleine näher rückt den Sternen.
Des Helden Tat, des Sängers heilig Lied,
Des Sehers Schaun, der Gottheit Spur und Walten,
Die Sammlung hats getan and hats erkannt,
Und die Zerstreuung nur verkennts and spottet.
Sprichts so in dir? Dann, Kind, Glück auf!
Dann wirst du wandeln hier, ein selig Wesen. (*Waves*, 3.945–56)[72]

The priest endows the term "Sammlung" with the power to transfigure and transcend, but it also constrains and limits how a person can conduct the self. It is meant for poets and prophets. It is a disciplined, heroic, and performative category that recognizes only a certain form of life—one that is elevated, separate, and disinterested in the external. However much the priest holds up Sammlung as the epitome of a valuable life, it still remains subject to the influences of distraction. As a sanctified creature, Hero must now bend her will to the abstract concept of composure. The substance of the word does not have the same depth of meaning for Hero that it has for the priest:

Und wie der Mann, der Abends blickt gen Himmel.
Im Zwielicht noch, und nichts ersieht als grau,
Farbloses Grau, nicht Nacht und nicht erleuchtet;
Doch schauend unverwandt, blinkt dort ein Stern
Und dort ein zweiter, dritter, hundert, tausend,
Die Ahnung einer reichen, gotterhellten Nacht,
Ihm nieder in die feuchten, sel'gen Augen.
Gestalten bilden sich und Nebel schwinden,
Der Hintergrund der Wesen tut sich auf,
Und Götterstimmen, halb aus eigner Brust
Und halb aus Höhn, die noch kein Blick ermaß— (*Waves*, 3.958–68)[73]

The priest is ecstatic: forms take shape and fog recedes. An entire world that was once concealed is revealed to man. Once in the dark and without hope or inspiration, man is now suffused with the light of the stars and even the voices of the gods are his to both hear and to speak. Again, as she did in Act 1, Hero refuses the lofty idealization of her role as priestess but this time she also does so in a repudiation of the composure that the priest has just described:

Du weißt, mein Ohm, nicht also hohen Flugs
Erhebt sich mir der Geist. So viel nicht hoffe!
Allein was not, und was mir auferlegt,
Gedenk' ich wohl zu tun. Des sei gewiß. (*Waves*, 3.969–71)[74]

Hero will do what is mandated as priestess but she will go no further. She willfully denies the possibility of an elevated existence. She will not fully meet the task of her office but rather will deviate from its obligations. Hero will not be pushed in the proper direction, the right path. She has become a problem; she tells the priest what she will do and what she will not do. In fact, Hero urges her uncle to not hope for too much. This reflects her words early in Act 1 when she tells the priest, "Laß mich so wie ich bin, ich bin es gern" (*Waves*, 1.138).[75] This also echoes her words to her uncle about not being guided by a prophetic voice (*Waves*, 1.184–85). However much the priest engages in a rhapsodic appreciation of composure, he also cautions Hero about the world of distraction that might be her lot should she sink down into the province of action where she might become entangled in the stresses of life. Yet, he ends on a note that turns that world of fruitless striving into one of reward:

Doch wessen Streben auf das Innre führt,
Wo Ganzheit nur, des Wirkens Fülle fördert,
Der halte fern vom Streite seinen Sinn,
Denn ohne Wunde kehrt man nicht zurück,
Die noch als Narbe mahnt in trüben Tagen. (*Waves*, 3.982–86)[76]

It is the "Doch" that brings the priest back to the ideal of composure and the person who seeks out the mature interior world of self-fulfillment that leads to a "Ganzheit," a principle which implies completeness in itself, wanting of nothing. The priest insists that once one has entered the common world, it would be difficult to retrieve composure without scars. This testimony about the urgency of composure is how the priest understands the cultural vocabulary of this new existence.

It is also in Act 3 that Hero understands that it is the presence of Leander and Naukleros, his friend, in the grove earlier that day that caused the priest to be angry with her (*Waves*, 3.1003–1005). She imagines an existence where she is neither Hero nor a priestess consecrated to the goddess. If she were neither and had no obligation to the goddess, Leander would have pleased her as a mate. She acknowledges the attraction that she feels for Leander and how she must avoid it: "Ich weiß nunmehr, daß, was sie Neigung nennen, / Ein Wirkliches, ein zu Vermeidendes, / Und meiden will ichs wohl.—Ihr Götter! / Wie vieles lehrt ein Tag, und ach, wie wenig / Gibt und vergißt ein Jahr.—Nun, er ist fern / In ganzen Leben seh' ich kaum ihn wieder / Und so ists abgetan.—Wohl gut!" (*Waves*, 3.1010–16).[77] When we look back on the priest's words from Act 1 ("With change of times one's [wishes and] inclinations change."), it becomes clearer that he had some sense that Hero's commitment to the office could falter and that her emotions were not infallible. That is, they are capable of error—of wandering from the proper path. Although Hero appears to give up on the possibility of ever having Leander, the longing that is embedded in her speech is distinct.

Unable to sleep in her tower on her first night as priestess, Hero picks up her lamp and places it near the window where she speaks to herself about the waves in the Hellespont where only her lamp throws light into the darkness like a shining star (*Waves*, 3.1026–35). The lamp's significance becomes increasingly important and its light turns the course of the drama toward its tragic end. When Leander suddenly appears at the window of the tower, Hero is in disbelief (*Waves*, 3.1061–65). She allows Leander to enter her chamber where he confesses that he had plunged back into the sea from Abydos, his home across the Hellespont, to swim back to her with no guide but the light of the lamp to scale the tower to see her. Hero tells him once more, "Ich bin verlobt zu einem strengen Dienst, / Und liebeleer heischt man die Priesterin. / Ehgestern, wenn du kamst, war ich noch frei, / Nun ists zu spät. Drum geh und kehr nicht wieder" (*Waves*, 3.1127–30).[78] Hero repeats herself from Act 2 using almost the exact same words.[79] If only she were free. If only he had come before yesterday. These conditional words do not inspire confidence in Hero's dedication to her new role as the "liebeleer" (loveless) priestess.

Guarding the grounds, the temple warden who has seen the shine from her lamp in the window, is now suspicious as he walks through the tower. After he fails to discover anything amiss, Hero is angry with Leander about his trespass and the potential discovery of his presence in her chamber by the temple warden:

Was kamst du her? nichts denkend als dich selbst,
Und störst den Frieden meiner stillen Tage,
Vergiftest mir den Einklang deiner Brust?
O hätte doch verschlungen dich das Meer,
Als du den Leib in seine Wogen senktest! (*Waves*, 3.1170–74).[80]

This is a yet unknown but ominous portent of the future for Leander. Yet, it is a moment in which one could say that Hero is concerned about her own Sammlung which Leander has disturbed before it even has the opportunity to be something beyond a thought. Although she tries to deny Leander, Hero is weak in the face of desire for him. After she finally tells him that he can come back the next night, Leander continues his romance of Hero and Act 3 ends with the two lovers in the chamber of the tower. There is a discursive aspect to the consummation of their love. Her desertion of propriety is a willful act that Hero may not perceive as such. The moment of undecidability when Leander enters her room in the tower is quickly overcome by Hero's reluctance to let him go. In doing so, Hero is herself dismantled. At this point Hero could have made Leander leave but her reluctance to do so has undermined her very existence. Hero's will has acquired the status of a moral event in the drama that must be overseen and managed.

A WILLFUL PRIESTESS

Grillparzer's contemporary audience decried Acts 4 and 5 of the drama even as they heaped acclaim on the first three acts. It is not particularly difficult to understand their dislike of the turning point and resolution of the drama. The great love story ends with the death of the two lovers through the devious acts of the priest and the temple warden. The priest sees a moral danger in Hero's willfulness, and his role as the defender of their religious practices compels him to use direct and harsh intervention to take charge of Hero's will.

In her struggle with the authority of tradition, Hero becomes trouble or, rather, she becomes otherwise than she was supposed to be. The intrigue that will lead to the tragic end begins the next morning after Leander has made it safely back to Abydos. Here, it is the priest and the temple warden who are the focal points as they try to decipher the mystery of the commotion in the tower from the previous evening. The temple warden is suspicious of Hero for he saw the stranger jump into the sea just steps away from where Hero stood. He is sure that Hero has somehow transgressed but is unable to provide proof. But it is the lamp's shine from the tower window that tells him that she was awake all night. The temple warden documents for the priest the wildness of the night and also what he heard in the tower. It is at once an elemental but also a sensual depiction of the previous evening:

Bis zum Morgen.
Und oben wars so laut und doch so heimlich,
Ein Flüstern und ein Rauschen hier und dort;
Die ganze Gegend schien erwacht, bewegt.

In dichtsten Laub ein sonderbares Regen,
Wie Windeswehen, und wehte doch kein Wind.
Die Luft gab Schall, der Boden tönte wider
Und was getönt und widerklang war: nichts.
Das Meerstieg rauschend höher an die Ufer,
Die Sterne blinkten, wie mit Augen winkend,
Ein halbenthüllte Geheimnis schien die Nacht.
Und dieser Turm war all des dumpfen Treibens
Und leisen Regens Mittelpunkt und Ziel. (*Waves*, 4.1302–14)[81]

The temple warden cannot let go of his suspicions around Hero, the figure jumping into the sea, and the shine of her lamp. Interrogating both Janthe and Hero, the priest begins to doubt his niece. Now in league with the temple warden, the priest also has misgivings about Hero and the man who was observed swimming to Abydos from Sestos. The priest, growing increasingly distressed, is troubled by Hero's complacency and her lack of alarm about the appearance of the light in her tower and the signal that it sends to anyone who might look to it. At the same time, Hero is also gaining clarity about her situation and its fragility:

Ich sehe wohl, um mich geht Manches vor.
Das mich betrifft, und nah vielleicht und nächst,
Doch fass' ichs nicht und düster ist mein Sinn.
Ich will darüber denken. (4.1444–47)[82]

Although Hero now acknowledges that there is something amiss, she cannot grasp it because her mind is dulled from exhaustion and her need to sleep after her night with Leander. However, this is also a reference to the previous suggestion by the priest that she has not grasped his meaning about what the life of the priestess entails. The commotion and the priest's agitation are about her but Hero cannot fully understand it even if she acknowledges it. After sending the tired priestess to carry out tasks for her sacred office in order to distract her (*Waves*, 4.1468–75, 4.1476–84), the priest is clear in purpose and resolute in what he must do. His fury at Hero is palpable, and he is bound to vengeance for any man who would dare seek her out. He wants the guilty one dead but must find the indisputable proof first:

Erforschen jedes Zeichen, das der Tat
Der noch verhüllten, dunkeln Fußtritt zeigt.
Kommt die Nacht und siehst du wieder Licht –
Und doch wer weiß, ob wir uns getäuscht?
Ist Zutraun blind, sieht Argwohn leicht zu viel:

Zum mindesten befehl' ich dir zu zweifeln,
Bis ich dir sage: glaubs! (*Waves*, 4.1519–25)[83]

Committed to finding out the secret, the priest will stop at nothing in order to discover the truth of the light in Hero's tower. His severity and vigilance will not be tempered by any affection for his niece and remains poised to capture the guilty party. While the priest has placed the lamp in the window of her chamber in order to lure the unsuspecting swimmer to the tower, the exhausted Hero has fallen asleep on a bench outside of the tower dreaming of Leander embodied as the swan. A storm is approaching and the priest hopes that the absence of light from the lamp caused by the strong wind will reveal to him who has been visiting the tower: "Von Turme strahlt das Licht. Der Götter Sturm verlösche deine Flamme" (*Waves*, 4.1816).[84] This extinguishing of a flame is the cause to revisit Hero's consecration the previous day. By using too much incense, Hero had ignited a large flame that caused her consecration to remain incomplete. Thus, her rejection of Hymen was unfinished because she could not utter the correct words with which to abjure him. The priest, now transformed into a vigilante, closes Act 4 with these words:

Nun, Himmlische, nun waltet eures Amts!
Die Schuldigen hält Meer und Schlaf gebunden,
Und so ist eures Priesters Werk vollbracht;
Das Holz geschichtet und das Beil gezückt,
Wend' ich mich ab. Trefft Götter selbst das Opfer. (*Waves*, 4.1830–34)[85]

The light of the lamp that the priest has placed in the window of Hero's tower is extinguished by the wind from the storm. There is no guiding light for Leander's swim in the evening to visit Hero in her tower and he drowns in the Hellespont. Although the priest suggests that it is the heavenly powers who discovered the identity of the transgressor, it was the priest who played the central role. He has set in motion what he believed was necessary in order to preserve the moral ideal of the sacred office. However, he will not take ultimate responsibility for what will happen since it is the gods, he insists, that meted out the actual punishment for "das Opfer," the sacrifice or, in Leander's case, the victim. When Leander's corpse is revealed, the priest can only exclaim, "Gerechte Götter! / Ihr nahmt ihn an. Er fiel von Eurer Hand!" (*Waves*, 5.1904–5).[86] It is clear that the priest does not hold himself accountable for the death of Leander and perhaps believes that it was truly the gods who had taken the young man's life.

Act 5 rushes to its tragic end without a fully realized sense of purpose. Hero and Janthe have found Leander's body under some brush and the priest remains jubilant in his victory. He has lost much of his self-possessed and stoic demeanor in exchange for a vengeful one that shows no human remorse but rather a satisfaction that his plan has been fully realized. Without considering Hero, the priest is already preparing to send Leander's body back to Abydos with Naukleros, who has appeared in search of his missing friend. In a heated exchange with his niece, the priest is harsh but prepared to bury the secret of Hero and Leander:

Die Götter laut das blut'ge Zeugnis gaben.
Wie sehr sie zürnen, und wie groß dein Fehl;
So laß in Demut uns die Strafe nehmen.
Das Heiligtum, es teile nicht die Makel,
Und ew'ges Schweigen decke was geschehen (*Waves*, 5.1926–30).[87]

Instead of gratitude, Hero is violent in her recriminations. Her refusal to be as the priest wants marks her as willful and defiant. Instead of silently moving on and accepting her role as priestess, Hero expresses anger at both her uncle and herself. Returning to the concept of Sammlung, Hero has most obviously abandoned any effort to keep herself composed: "Ausschreien will ichs durch die Welt, / Was ich erlitt, was ich besaß, verloren, / Was mir geschehen, und wie sie mich betrübt. / Verwünschen dich, daß es die Winde hören / Und hin es tragen vor der Götter Thron. / Du warst, du legtest tückisch ihm das Netz, / Ich zog es zu, und da war er verloren" (*Waves*, 5.1933–38).[88] This desperate need to cry out to the world in lament at the loss of her lover demonstrates her all-consuming grief but also her refusal to remain silent and conceal the secret of Leander at the moment when the priest would have her bury it. While addressing Naukleros, Hero again says that it was she and her uncle that did the deed (*Waves*, 5.1944–53). Hero's grief is palpable and she speaks some of the most eloquent lines in the drama in the final act about her true feelings and instincts. Vanished is the young girl, who lived on the whimsy of the fickle mood, with no firm opinions about the conditions of her life. What we now have in her stead is a woman who understands her loss and whose anger is sharp, clear, and, in many ways, composed:

Sag: er war Alles! Was noch übrig blieb,
Es sind nur Schatten; es zerfällt; ein Nichts.
Sein Atem war die Luft, sein Auge die Sonne,
Sein Leib die Kraft der sprossenden Natur,
Sein Leben war das Leben, deines, meins,
Des Weltalls Leben. Als wir ließen sterben,
Da starben wir mit ihm. (*Waves*, 5.1974–80)[89]

Hero is publicly mourning Leander but also paving a way to vocalize a more constrained response to his death. Hero's speech gives Leander's life a rich meaning in which she endows him with the qualities of harmony and completeness. The loss of him, his every breath, his eyes, and his body creates a void in the world, which also pulls her down into its abyss. Here, I suggest that Hero's story embodies an expansion of discourse, one which becomes increasingly transgressive since the one who does not obey is willful.[90] Hero's willfulness, her refusal to adjust herself to the new circumstances of her life, is in direct conflict with the ideals of composure. Instead her behavior is very much aligned with the willful subject. Hero rejects the category of composure and throws herself into the fray of distraction and disobedience and away from her calling as priestess. Hero's love for Leander and the breaking of the sacred vows she took are forms of willfulness: "Willfulness might be required to act when you do not have the right to act."[91] How can we understand Hero's character as part of this willful archive? Sara Ahmed's description of willfulness is full of possibility for thinking about Hero's decision to take Leander as her lover and abandon her newly gained life as a priestess. The impossibility of her position is also about knowability. What can be known with any certainty about a life which is inflected by a gendered and religious structure? Does will then become the expectation of not being degraded to a thing or not to be coerced by an external power?

The priest is so forcefully bound to his religious calling that there is nothing he will not do to protect it. Wishing to conceal the death of Leander and return Hero to her sacred life, the priest tells the temple warden, "Die Bräuche muß man halten, sie sind gut. / Und nun zu ihr! Entfernt die Störung erst, / Legt mild die Zeit den Balsam auf die Wunde. / Ja, dieses Gefühl, im ersten Keim erstickt, / Bewahrt vor jedem zweiten die Verlockte / Und heilig fürderhin—" (*Waves*, 5.1997-2002).[92] Without comprehending the cruelty of his words and still bound to tradition and customs, the priest cannot speak without resorting to empty platitudes about the goodness and necessity of customs. He speaks of a future in which Hero, still serving as priestess, will have forgotten this first "Störung" (disturbance) and never again stray from her sacred role.

Hero's death is produced discursively. It is recounted by Janthe, the servant girl who shows that her allegiances are with Hero. Gathering strength, Hero is led by Janthe to the throne of Aphrodite where she tells the priest that Hero is dying—her heart is beating too quickly. The priest will not listen. Janthe is the only one who recognizes that Hero is on the verge of death as her prostrate figure lies on the steps leading to the temple. With Janthe by her side, Hero dies on the steps with little commotion. It is only Janthe's words that indicate that Hero has died. As the boat begins its journey to Abydos with Leander's body, Janthe tells the priest, "Es braucht kein Meer, der Tod hat gleiche Macht. / Zu trennen, zu vereinen. Komm und schau / So sehn die Toten aus in diesen Landen" (*Waves*, 5.2102–4).[93] Calling the rowers back, Janthe commands them to bury Hero and Leander together.

A POLITICS OF REFUSAL

Grillparzer gave voice to the Zerstreuung (distraction) that Hero speaks and acts while also sounding the claims of Sammlung (composure) out of the mouth of the priest. This is true if we believe that the dramatist was ventriloquizing Hero and the high priest in differing modes. By telling the story of composure and the search for it, Grillparzer is, in fact, suggesting that there is no way for Hero to achieve composure and another way must be made. The drama functions, in many ways, as a theorization of distraction. For composure is never realized, it is only described and anticipated as an ethical category or one that tries to enact a literary understanding. What moves this text forward is the ever-expanding display of distraction.

The female figures are animated by Grillparzer across all three dramas but what happens to their stories in his voice? Hero's performance is one that is instantiated by Grillparzer. If it is in self-interest that one speaks, then can we say that Grillparzer was speaking his own self and his own distraction when writing *Des Meeres und der Liebe Wellen*? It might be the case that Grillparzer was trying to articulate something about his own poetic practice and his inability to focus his energies on that enterprise entirely. Earlier when speaking about ventriloquism, I suggested that when Grillparzer spoke for the other, it was a denial of the agency of this someone who is spoken. Perhaps Grillparzer is projecting his own voice and is engaged in a reading of himself even as he reads Hero. Could it be the case that this was an elaborate impersonation of his own self and his struggle with Sammlung through the figure of Hero?

The priest can only express the idea of Sammlung in speech; he cannot practice it. However much he would wish for it, the priest's citation of the conventions of composure cannot make it appear. There is a politics to his evocation of Sammlung and its difficulties are that it cannot be negotiated. The priest's ethical posture belies his reliance on the myth of composure. It becomes a practiced space that is filled with the condition of its possibility. Yet that possibility remains largely hidden. The establishment of the concept of composure creates a tension with that of distraction. Can these two be reconciled? Is there a way to have a composed Zerstreuung or a more distracted Sammlung? Does composure exist at a symbolic level or is there something substantial and material about it? Composure is about virtue and becoming virtuous. A cultural vocabulary surrounds it and bolsters it up as a literary and ethical idea. Does this mean that composure is a performative category that only materializes once it has a language to sustain it?

Returning for a moment to Judith Butler, can we say that the idea of Sammlung is socially constructed and that its linguistic construction is an idea based on conformity to a virtuous life and its repetition. A virtue that does not imply change or transformation but keeps its practitioners locked in an unhealthy relationship with their own minds without offering something concretely sufficient to sustain life. And not merely life, but rather a life that is livable. How do ideas about livable lives inflect the literary choices that Grillparzer creates for Hero? Is his ventriloquism of her something more than a way to theorize Sammlung or even his failure to attain composure in his own life? However much he wants to tightly collect himself into a whole and single-minded entity without external distractions, Grillparzer cannot make that into a livable life, a life that can be survived by Hero. This is why Hero's near undetected death is important. It demonstrates that the difference between composure and distraction is not as distant as one might expect. Their linguistic boundaries slide into each other. Hero has achieved a kind of composure after seeing the corpse of Leander. It is not the composure of self-possession but rather that of refusal. Hero's is a refusal—even if unconscious—to be organized by the economy of either domesticity or that of the sacred. Here, one might want to think about how the concept of Sammlung writes out of existence the type of person that Hero has become and how she moves in that world as a female figure. She is one who cannot capture the logic of composure whose operation would shut down the possibilities for her to express the person that she truly is—one who is neither fully committed to nor understands the very concept of composure.

What does the strict obedience to the ideal of composure do to women's voices? What does the failure to achieve composure mean for women's experiences of life? As a counterweight, I suggest that distraction can function as a model of resistance and willfulness in this drama. It is the manner in which Hero repudiates the claims of the category of composure in favor of desire and love. Love being one of those distracting aspects of human life that prevents the active achievement and cultivation of composure.

Might it not be of interest to move through Hero's drama as one about female flight in the wake of the compulsory? The force of convention and its authority is eluded and Hero becomes the errant and willful subject. Here, I want to pick up Sara Ahmed's *Willful Subjects* with its deeply engaged discussions of the origins of will, willful, and willfulness that tackle thinkers from Augustine and Pascal to Arendt and Foucault. While I am not writing about the history of willfulness, I think it is instructive to return to Hero's story in the wake of ideas about the "willful subject," one of whom Hero appears to be. To return to a phrase that I took up in the Introduction, "the feminist killjoy," I also want to retrieve, its close partner, the willful subject, to trace an idea of Hero. To quote Ahmed, "Feminist killjoys: willful women, unwilling to get along, unwilling to preserve an idea of happiness."[94] The feminist killjoy and the willful subject are inextricably linked in Ahmed and perhaps what is most compelling about this willful woman is that she is trouble: she is insistent and performative. She also turns herself and her willfulness into a narrative event that interrupts the flow of happiness and accord. Hero commits an error of will that leads to unhappiness.[95] Thus, happiness and willfulness are closely linked in Ahmed's thinking and that connection can also be pursued with Hero. Hero and, in many ways, Medea become the focus of male power due to their inordinate wills. They are willful women whose impulse is to disobey; they contain an excess of that unwanted feature.

The challenge of *The Waves of Sea and Love* is that the messiness of its situation is not revealed until the play ends. It is an untidy drama that obscures its disorderliness behind a placid and, at moments, prosaic quality. The characters do not reveal themselves in a satisfactory manner across the five acts. In particular, Hero remained a mystery—even to herself. Her willfulness was a quiet disturbance, marks left on the pages of Grillparzer's drama. Hero's coming to consciousness is not easy to track but it does survive as willful once we consider her escape from the demands of both religious and domestic duties. This barely perceptible excess of female will is Grillparzer's achievement in the drama. It begins with Hero's appearance and her eventual disappearance. I am interested in the in-between spaces of that dis/appearance, those moments in which we recognize Hero's status as a female figure in flight who will not accept what is offered. She has become the wrong sort.

Thus, the story of Hero moves on will and desire, the erotics of wanting but also the erotics of fleeing. Hero strays from the direction that has been laid out for her and away from the path of what has been customarily known as the epitome of virtue and happiness. Her first wayward and feminist movement is foregoing the domestic realm of the nuclear family where marriage is the ultimate and only appropriate goal. Hero's second waywardness occurs as a consequence of her first permissive deviation. Although neither aimless nor irregular, the story of Hero suggests that she has erred in her ways by flouting the demands of her sacred role as the virgin priestess of Aphrodite by pursuing a sexual relationship with Leander. Her refusal to comply with these cultural imperatives marks her as willful—possessing, as Ahmed demonstrates in her study—an overflow of willfulness.

If Hero calls ideas about feminine behavior, practice, and customs into question, she becomes a site of quiet resistance by rejecting the apparent stability of the ordinary way of doing things. She refuses the civic and religious worlds that surround her and that have organized her. Unfinished though they are, female-directed modes of resistance have shaped Hero's project. These kinds of oppositions are a consequence of leaving a life. While the extravagant violence in *Sappho* and *Medea* expressed a kind of unending desire, the greater reality of desire might be the imperceptible death. What Grillparzer did in this drama was to render an old plot in uncertain or problematic ways that were, in many ways, unremarkable. Grillparzer did not end any of his dramas with consolation and unity but rather he made things less certain, more subjunctive, as narratives based on deviation and refusal.

NOTES

1. The first plan for the revision of the myth was first made in 1819 immediately after the work on *Sappho* was completed.
2. What is particularly fascinating about Ovid's *Letters of Heroines* is their premise: twenty-one epistolary poems written by mythic women abandoned or mistreated by their lovers. *Heroines* contains letters from "Sappho to Phaon," "Medea to Jason" and "Hero to Leander" (as well as "Leander to Hero"). Grillparzer was a great admirer of Ovid's work and wrote a series of poems, *Tristia ex Ponto*, modeled on Ovid's exile poems, *Letter from the Black Sea* or *Epistulae ex Ponto*. See Ovid, *Heroides*, trans. Harold Isbell (London: Penguin Books, 1990).
3. Musaeus, *On the Loves of Hero and Leander* (London: F.B. for Humphrey Mosley, 1647).
4. Cy Twombly, the abstract expressionist, did a series of paintings based on Hero and Leander called "Hero and Leandro" in the early 1980s. Cy Twombly, *Hero and Leandro, 1981–1984*, paintings in four parts, oil, crayon, and graphite on canvas; Cy Twombly, *Hero and Leandro (To Christopher Marlowe)*, 1985, oil paint and oil based house paint on canvas, 202 × 254 cm.
5. Anselm Kiefer, *Des Meeres und der Liebe Wellen*, 2011, mixed media and gyneaecological instrument on photograph, 107 × 327 cm, White Cube Hoxton Square, London, UK.
6. Manuel Baumbach, "Hero and Leander," in *Brill's New Pauly Supplements I, Volume 4: The Reception of Myth and Mythology*, ed. David van Eijndhoven, Christine Salazar, and Francis G. Gentry (Leiden: Brill, 2010), 348. Along those same lines, Baumbach also notes that "[w]hen considering the reception history of this myth, it is important to note that ancient tradition comprised a distinct narrative with no significant variants of content. The stimulus to later reception thus lay partly in 'translating' this material into various literary genres and artistic and musical forms of expression. The reception history of H. and L. includes folk songs, epics, ballads, dramas, parodies, operas, symphonic poems, comedies and works of art. On the other hand, it also lay in the more creative direction of interpolating the missing details in the myth, inventing matters of the protagonist's origins or the reasons for their secret affair." Baumbach, "Hero and Leander," 348.
7. Another central assertion is that "a major key to the tale's success in literature is the simplicity of its core development. It includes: the protagonists' falling in love; Leander's swim and their first night; his death in the storm; and Hero's suicide."

Silvia Montiglio, *The Myth of Hero and Leander: The History and Reception of an Enduring Greek Legend* (New York: I.B. Tauris, 2018), 6–7.

8. Baumbach, "Hero and Leander," 348.

9. Much of the scholarship on *The Waves of Sea and Love* in some form references the similarities between Shakespeare's play (or the Yorkshire tragedy) and *The Waves of Sea and Love*. One of the earliest comparisons was Hans Braun 1916 dissertation, *Grillparzers Verhältnis zu Shakespeare* (Nürnberg: Gedruckt bei H. Lotter, 1916), especially pp. 94–100. For early assessments of Grillparzer's connection with Shakespeare's play, see A. E. Zucker, "Shakespeare and Grillparzer," *Modern Language Notes* 31, no. 7 (November 1916): 396–99, and Douglas Yates, "Grillparzer's Hero and Shakespeare's Juliet," *Modern Language Review* 21, no. 4 (October 1926): 419–25. Alan Menhennet's article, in general, treats the connection between Grillparzer and Shakespeare on history (the History plays) and the representation in drama. Alan Menhennet, "Grillparzer, Shakespeare, and Historical Drama," *German Life and Letters* 44, no. 3 (1991): 208–20.

10. Butler, *Gender Trouble*, xxx.

11. I understand the difficulty with using the word 'human' because it is historically an exclusionary term meant to identify some as human and others as not. Gender is also implicated in the use of 'human' since it and claims about race, ethnicity, nationality and sexuality have all been invoked at various times to exclude and restrict groups from membership in a 'human' community entitled to rights and participation.

12. Elizabeth Grosz, *Volatile Bodies: Toward a Corporeal Feminism* (Bloomington: Indiana University Press, 1994).

13. Grosz, *Volatile Bodies*, viii.

14. See Brigitte Prutti, *Unglück und Zerstreuung: Autobiographisches Schreiben bei Franz Grillparzer* (Bielefeld: Aisthesis Verlag, 2016).

15. Whitaker, "The Concept of 'Sammlung' in Grillparzer's Works."

16. Whitaker, "The Concept of 'Sammlung' in Grillparzer's Works," 94.

17. Shortly after the completion of the drama, Grillparzer wrote the poem "An die Sammlung" (1833). In his apostrophe to "Sammlung," Grillparzer extols the virtues of composure against that of distraction which Whitaker takes up in his article. Whitaker writes, "In this poem, 'Sammlung' appears as a coordinating, cohesive, directing force, subduing those human energies which would dissipate themselves in pointless, undirected activity, and guiding the errant impulses. It welds the undirected forces of man's nature into a powerful, concentrated current of energy directed towards a single, clear goal." Whitaker, "The Concept of 'Sammlung' in Grillparzer's Works," 95. In his further analysis of the poem, Whitaker uses as his examples for Grillparzer's concept of composure, the dramas of Sappho and Hero, and the drama, *Libussa* (1848), a seeress.

18. E. E. Papst, *Des Meeres und der Liebe Wellen* (London: Edward Arnold, 1967), 12.

19. Papst, *Des Meeres und der Liebe Wellen*, 14–15.

20. Gisela Stein, *The Inspiration Motif in the Works of Franz Grillparzer* (The Hague: Martinus Nijhoff, 1955), 78–85, 132–38.

21. Lorenz, *Grillparzer: Dichter des sozialen Konflikts*, 52. "Hero is neither predetermined by her spiritual and intellectual gifts to be an exceptional figure."

22. Lorenz, *Grillparzer: Dichter des sozialen Konflikts*, 51. "Thematically *The Waves of Sea and Love* belongs to the much earlier *Sappho*. Dialectically, it is the complement. Grillparzer had already contemplated the Hero-and-Leander theme in 1819, immediately after *Sappho*."

23. Lorenz, *Grillparzer: Dichter des sozialen Konflikts*, 52. "She wants to escape the fate of women, one which she sees before her in the figure of her morally broken, humiliated and demoralized mother."

24. Lorenz, *Grillparzer: Dichter des sozialen Konflikts*, 53. "Hero believes that with the priesthood she has chosen self-determination. Since her goddess is her 'wife,' she imagines that she is under female protection and overlooks the male priestly apparatus."

25. Brigitte Prutti, *Grillparzers Welttheater: Modernität und Tradition* (Bielefeld: Aisthesis Verlag, 2016), 24. "The gender theme is central to Grillparzer's dramas and it concerns the cultural gender of the protagonists in the double sense of gender and genealogy and the role of sexuality and eroticism in the constellations of different dramatic relationships and problems."

26. Prutti, *Grillparzers Welttheater*, 154. Grillparzer "puts a young girl at the center of his love drama and unfolds the conflict of this figure between a yearning for autonomy and an erotic fusion of desires. He locates the individual psychological conditions of these contradictory wishes in the repressive gender order of the modern nuclear family, which the heroine of his play seeks to escape by deciding on the virginal priesthood."

27. "I am allowed to consecrate my days, / That roll unnoticed on without a goal, / To the high service of our heavenly goddess, / My lonely days that, like the meadow flowers, / Trampled upon by wandering feet and crushed, Are now a wreath upon the goddess' head / Transfiguring, consecrating her and me . . . How happy I that this should be the day, / And such a beautiful and tranquil day!" *Waves*, 1.5–13.

28. "Do you view me as one of yours already? / Did they inform you, the lighthearted Hero. / Whom you saw playing on the temple's steps, / That she, pretending to her forbears' right. / Who've furnished priests to serve this sanctuary / From dim antiquity—that she pretending/ To this rare privilege, is now herself priestess." *Waves*, 1.17–23.

29. "Today, today, upon this very day? / The crowd shall see her standing on those steps. / Dispensing sacrifices to the gods, / From every lip shall acclamation burst, / And in the splendor offered to the goddess / The priestess' head shall shine—" *Waves*, 1.24–28.

30. "I do not think companionship will help: / What one must do, is best done by oneself. / How can you call as priestess's life lonely? / When was I ever lonely in this temple?" *Waves*, 1. 121–124.

31. "You have not grasped my meaning." *Waves*, 1.136.

32. "What is not grasped arouses no desire. / Leave me just as I am, I'm happy so." *Waves*, 1.137–138.

33. "With change of times one's [wishes and] inclinations change." *Waves*, 1.139.

34. "We grumble daily, human senselessness / Will still endure however much we rail; / Then why believe the sensible to be / More senseless and more fitful than the fool? / I do not know what I would, what we choose, / If where there's no choice, you can call it choosing." *Waves*, 1.140–45.

35. This brings us back to Sappho and the idea of choice in her life—the domestic sphere of love or the public as famous poetess and leader of Mytilene.

36. "From the long, dreamy wonderland of childhood / I first, in this place, woke to consciousness. / Here, in the temple, at the goddess' feet, / At last I found myself, my aim in life." *Waves*, 1.155–58.

37. A reader is hard-pressed not to think about Kant's essay, "What is Enlightenment?" (1784), given Hero's statements about waking from a dream-like state. Immanuel Kant, "What Is Enlightenment?" in *The Philosophy of Kant: Immanuel Kant's Moral and Political Writings*, trans. and ed. Carl J. Friedrich (New York: The Modern Library, 1993), 145–53.

38. Konrad Schaum, *Grillparzer-Studien* (Bern: Peter Lang, 2001), 237. "She is not prepared to regard her profession as a decidedly spiritualistic and contemplative attitude, to remain in the 'beautiful privilege' of an elevated social position and to interpret the divine will from 'signs and oracles.'" Schaum, *Grillparzer-Studien*, 237.

39. "You must beware lest such a narrow aim / May rightly be regarded as self-centered." *Waves*, 1.165–67.

40. "Within this temple women too/ Have rights; and the oppressed may freely speak." *Waves*, 1.279–80.

41. "Now tell me if I rightly guessed your mind; / You did not come here sharing Father's views. And. were you free to have your wishes granted, / You'd gladly take your daughter home with you/ Far from her haven here, safe from the storms, / In the mean hut of your dismal cares?" *Waves*, 1. 283–88.

42. "So he is there no more? With such good news, / Thrice-willingly I'd go back with you! / Yet, if he's not, a hundred more are there / Of the same stamp, with head-strong savage ways. . ." *Waves*, 1. 307–10.

43. "A woman's happiness is by her husband's side [A woman to be happy must be wed]." *Waves*, 1.320.

44. "Can you say that to me and still not blush? / What have to look to that man's every glance, / Your lord and master's? Never dare to speak; / Still silent, whispering, even when you're right? / When you're wiser, calmer, more efficient? / How can you dare to tell me such a thing?" *Waves*, 1.321–26.

45. In "Grenzgänge in Franz Grillparzers Trauerspiel 'Des Meeres und der Liebe Wellen,'" Ulrike Tanzer contends that Hero's statements are laudatory and indicate a budding need for emancipation and for a rethinking of woman's place in society. See Ulrike Tanzer, "Grenzgänge in Franz Grillparzers Trauerspiel 'Des Meeres und der Liebe Wellen,'" in *Grenzgänge und Grenzgänger in der österreichischen Literatur: Beiträge des 15. Österreichisch-Polnischen Germanistentreffens Kraków 2002*, ed. Maria Klanska, Krzysztof Lipinski, Katarzyna Jastal, and Agnieszka Palej (Kraków: Wydawnictwo Uniwersytetu Jagiellonskiego, 2004), 77–86.

46. "But I will wander with my mind serene / Here by my lady Aphrodite's altar; / Do what is right, not since I am commanded, / But since it is right, and I see it so;

/ And none shall rob me of this and deprive—In sober truth!" (*Waves*, 1.332–36). McCarthy-Rechowicz reads these last two lines in terms of Kantian philosophy, specifically from his essay, "What is Enlightenment?": "Grillparzer has put her in Hero's mouth what Kant defined as the motto of the Enlightenment: 'Sapere aude! Have courage to use your *own* understanding!" McCarthy-Rechowicz's reading of *The Waves of Sea and Love* is especially engaged with Kantian philosophy and Grillparzer's selective use of it. He gives special significance to light and the lamp as metaphors which evoke rationality and goes on to discuss the differing ways in which Hero and the priest understand 'Unmündigkeit," reason or rationality, and independent thought. McCarthy-Rechowicz, *Dramatic Heroines*, 105–7, 110.

47. Butler, *Gender Trouble*, xxvi.

48. "Here I feel me, and here an alien substance—/ My being gives itself and takes possession . . ." *Waves*, 1.153–54.

49. "And now let me tell you, you feeble woman, / Why did you come sowing dissension here? / Why show surprise at what you know's our rule, / The sacred order of our holy temple? / No bird may nest here in this temple's grove, / Nor with impunity may ring doves coo; / No climbing tendril may embrace the elms. / And all that couples must stay far away, / And she too must submit to the same fate." *Waves*, 1.350–58.

50. "Poor creature, how they quarrel over us!" *Waves*, 1.359.

51. "Take it away and give it back its freedom, / The freedom every animal desires." *Waves*, 1.381–82.

52. "The goddess has no need of you nor her [your child]." *Waves*, 1.361–62.

53. "Then go, find her some undistinguished mate, / Exhausting yourself in the painful process; / Make her the hand-maid of the boor who woos her; / Instead of independent, radiant here, / The one of her exiguous kin / To be herself, a being, a whole world. / But since you wish it, she is free, then take her! / You are her mother still. You, Hero, follow! / Folly is calling, follow like a woman!" *Waves*, 1.371–79.

54. "Free choice is but the plaything of weak fools; / The wise man sees in every "shall" a "must." Compulsion, as first duty, is his truth." *Waves*, 1.414–16.

55. "You, who vouchsafe love, take from me all mine. / In greeting you, I take my leave of you." *Waves*, 1.495–96.

56. In an interesting and not completely unexpected moment, Naukleros compares Leander to Hymen in Act 2: "Kein Amor mehr, doch Hymens treues Bild" (Eros no more, but Hymen's very image). *Waves*, 2.586. Thus, Hero has not only not rejected the god of marriage but also finds herself enamored of one who is the very image of this god.

57. Naukleros provides a long description of how the new priestess would have done better to swear to love rather than reject it (*Waves*, 2.621–624) and he also depicts the moment when Hero sees Leander for the first time at the ceremony. Naukleros reads Hero's behavior at the moment of her consecration as a desiring action: "Da stockte sie, die Hand hing in der Luft; / Nach dir hin schauend stand sie zögernd da, / Ein, zwei, drei kurze, ew'ge Augenblicke. / Zuletzt vollbrachte sie ihr heilig Werk. / Allein noch scheidend sprach ein tiefer Blick. / Im herben Widerspruch des frost'gen Tages, / Der sie auf ewiglich verschließt der Liebe: / »Es ist doch

Schad« und »Den da möchte' ich wohl«. . ." ([And] she approached, disseminating incense; / She stood stone-still, her hand limp in the air; / Gazing at you, she stood there hesitating, / One, two, three brief, and everlasting moments. / At last she went on with her sacred task. But even in parting her eyes plainly said, / In harsh breath of the day's cold chastity, / That shuts her out for evermore from love: 'Ah, what a pity, that one is my man. . .'). *Waves*, 2.642–49.

58. "Even this lyre here, an ancient heirloom/ From your paternal aunt, my own dear sister, / Who once was priestess in this place like you." *Waves*, 3.911–13.

59. There is a long unknown history of dead women in Hero's family story—female figures who also consecrated their lives to the goddess as an expression of family honor and legacy. What happened to these priestesses—this lineage? Hero's inheritance is a curious one since it is about abnegation rather than about a fully realized existence. Hero receives her inheritance and only after receiving this legacy realizes it is not what she wants. She becomes errant once she gives into her desire for Leander. Her desire for him is not her willed inheritance.

60. "Then spoke the god; / Come hither to me/ In my clouds, / Beside me." *Waves*, 2.707–10.

61. "But she is stroking / The silk-soft down." *Waves*, 2.728.

62. Heinz Politzer offers a compelling analysis of the Leda and the Swan motif in Heinz Politzer, *Franz Grillparzer oder das Abgründige Biedermeier* (Vienna: Fritz Molden, 1972), 216–18, 224.

63. Heinz Politzer writes: "'Das ewge Lied' birgt ein Doppelsinn. Einmal spricht sich in diesem „ewig" das unwillige Staunen des Mädchens darüber aus, daß sich ihr diese Zeilen immer wieder ungereimt aufdrängen—sie auch am Morgen nach der Liebesnacht wiederkehren. Dann aber deutet diese 'Ewigkeit' des Lieds auch in die Zeitlosigkeit des Mythos, der in ihm Gestalt geworden ist. Stets wiederkehrend wie das Lied ist auch die Leidenschaft, von der ist kündet. Zwischen der sehnsüchtigen Hero und der Schwanenbraut Leda hat sich eine 'mythische Identifikation' eingestellt." Politzer, *Franz Grillparzer oder das Abgründige Biedermeier*, 217. See "Tragik des Mittelmaßes: *Des Meeres und der Liebe Wellen*" in Politzer, *Franz Grillparzer oder das Abgründige Biedermeier*, 210–29.

64. "And Leda's stroking/ The silk-soft down. / Th'e eternal song! Why does it haunt me so? No more do gods assail the wildest towers; / No swan, no eagle comforts the forlorn; /Now solitude stays ever solitary." *Waves*, 3.1043–48.

65. "Perhaps, sir, one of the immortals! / Yourself you used to say: in ancient days / A god would often come down to blessed mortals / To Leda and Admetus, stricken prince, / And strictly guarded Danae came a god; / Why not today? To her? To us? To whom you will?" *Waves*, 4. 1403–8.

66. "And, oh, your rustling and the whispering leaves / Sing in my ears "we are from him, him, him, from him" / Spread out your wings, enfold them all around / My brow and head, my neck, my weary arms, / Embrace me tight, I bare my breast to you —" *Waves*, 4. 1809–13.

67. "I thought to find you merrier on the evening / Oft the auspicious day that crowns our wishes. / What we have striven, hoped for, you have, are that, / And you're cold and dumb and not delighted." *Waves*, 3.928–31.

68. "Uncle, you know, we are not always master / Of every mood that comes and roves and goes. / Just self-creating without consequence." *Waves*, 3.932–34.

69. "With change of times one's [wishes and] inclinations change." *Waves*, 1.139.

70. "Yet grant me but one night of sweet repose, / Refreshing meditation, and, dear Uncle, / You'll find me just the same as you have known. / This place is still, there's scarce a breath of air; / The waves of thought more lightly ebb away, / With all disturbance rippling to the shore, / And, be sure, I shall once more find composure." *Waves*, 3.938–44.

71. Hero would like to think of herself as someone who can achieve composure but her words suggest someone who is distracted by the things of the world. One example is her inability to understand why the myth of Leda and the Swan and its erotic sensibility might be anathema to the priest, her uncle, but have such a hypnotic influence on her imagination. For his part, the priest is ready to uphold the necessity of composure and quiet self-possession in its strictest form by censoring Hero at every point of error. He is disappointed in her lack of enthusiasm about her new role: her refusal to rise to the occasion of the prophetic practice that other priestess' have had and her inability to absorb the ancient customs of her family in a way that demonstrates that she is aware of the privilege that has been conferred upon her. While Hero might believe that she strives for composure, she, in fact, represents distraction. Her mind is elsewhere. This dispersal of the self is important to think about in how Hero manages the space around her. The temple, the grove, the tower are all places in which Hero must manage the demands of composure against the appeal of distraction. This is in terms of how she relates to Janthe, to her uncle the, priest, to her parents, and to Leander.

72. "Composure? What this but some slip, my child? / Or did you feel the meaning of the word/ You have just uttered, music to my ear / You've named the mighty leaven of the world/ That buoys all greatness a thousandfold aloft / And even bears the trivial toward the stars. / The hero's feat, the poet's sacred song, / The prophet's vision, the divinity's trace, / All this, composure quickens and salutes—While dull distraction but mistakes and mocks. Then, child, be of good cheer! / For you shall wander here, a blessèd being." *Waves*, 3.945–56.

73. "Just like the man who heavenward looks at evening, / In the dim twilight, seeing only gray, / Drab gray, and neither night nor trace of light, / Yet vaguely gazing, spots a twinkling star/ And then a second, third, a hundred, thousands— / Rich harbingers of a divine illumined night—with blessed tears in his uplifted eyes. / Beings take shape and faëry mists dissolve, / The background of existence opens up, / And heavenly voices, half from one's own breast / And half from the wide infinite above—" *Waves*, 3.958–68.

74. "Uncle, you know, my mind does not presume / To soar to such heights. Do not hope so much! / But be sure I intend to be most faithful / To all my duties and my obligations." *Waves*, 3.969–71.

75. "Leave me just as I am, I'm happy so." *Waves*, 1.138.

76. "But he who struggles for self-fulfillment, / Where only wholeness spells mature achievement/ Must keep his mind far from the common strife, / For one does

not return from this unscathed; / The very scars remain as sharp reminders." *Waves*, 3.982–86.

77. "But by this time I know what's called attraction / Is very real and is to be avoided; / Avoid it then I will. You, kindly gods! / How much one day may teach and ah, how little / A year may give, forget—well, he is gone, / I'll hardly see him more in all my life, / And so it's over. Ah! Well!" *Waves*, 3.1010–16.

78. "I am committed to a rigorous service, / Exacting lovelessness from the priestess:/ Had you come one day earlier I were free; / It's now too late. So go, and come no more." *Waves*, 3.1127–30.

79. "No man alive may hope to seek my hand, / For duty bids me live without a husband. / Had you come yesterday, I were still free: / But I have vowed today, and mean to keep it." *Waves*, 2.786–89.

80. "Why did you come? Thinking but of yourself, / Disturbing all my halcyon innocence, / And poisoning the concord in my breast? / Ah, would the roaring sea had swallowed you/ When you had merged your body in its waves!" *Waves*, 3.1170–74.

81. "Till morning / And up there so much noise and yet so secret, / A whispering and a rustling everywhere / The entire area seemed awake, astir: / Mysterious movements in the thickest foliage / Like puffs of wind where yet no wind was puffing; / The air was alive with sounds the ground reechoed, / And all the sound and fury turned to nothing. / The sea rose roaring higher on the shore, / The stars were twinkling with their beckoning eyes, / The night appeared a secret half unveiled. / And this tower was the center and the goal / Of all the dull commotion, gentle stirring." *Waves*, 4.1302–14.

82. "I plainly see around me much is happening / That touches me perhaps most intimately, / I cannot grasp it and my mind is dark. / I'll sleep upon it [I want to think about it]." *Waves*, 4. 1444–47).

83. "[And] search out every sign that will disclose / The dark trace of the deed, still unrevealed / When night comes and you see the light again— / And yet, who knows, if we are not mistaken? / If faith is blind, suspicion sees too much: / The very least, I order you to doubt / Until I say: 'Believe!'" *Waves*, 4.1519–25.

84. "The light beams from the tower, May the gods' storm, promptly put out your flame." *Waves*, 4.1816.

85. "Now, heavenly powers, you execute your office! / The culprits are held down by sea and sleep; And so your priest's work is accomplished now. The wood is piled up and the hatchet drawn, / I turn aside. Perform your sacrifice!" *Waves*, 4.1830–34.

86. "O you righteous Gods! / You've taken him. He fell through your own hands!" *Waves*, 5.1904–5.

87. "The Gods have borne aloud their bloody witness, / How great their anger and how grave your wrong, / So let us humbly take our punishment; / What's sacred must be wholly without stain, / May eternal silence bury what has happened." *Waves*, 5.1926–30.

88. "I'll shout it out aloud through the wide world, / What I have suffered, what possessed, what lost, / What has befallen, how they have pursued me. / I'll loudly curse you, that the winds shall hear / And bear my curses to the gods' high throne.

/ You were the one who spread the wicked net / That I pulled tight, and so he was destroyed." *Waves*, 5.1933–38.

89. "Say he was everything: what now remains. / Is but a fleeting shadow, but a void. / His breath was the pure air, his eye the sun, / His limbs the quickening power of burgeoning nature: His life was life itself: your life, my life, / We too all died with him." *Waves*, 5.1974–80.

90. Ahmed, *Willful Subjects*, 137.

91. Ahmed, *Willful Subjects*, 141.

92. "We should pay heed to customs, they are good. / And now to her! With her disturbance gone, / Time's healing balsam shall allay her wound. / Yes, this first passion smothered in the bud, / Preserves her heart beguiled from any second; / And henceforth sacred—" *Waves*, 5.1997–2002.

93. "No sea is needed, death has equal power/ To part or unite. Then come and see! / This is how those who die look on this earth." *Waves*, 5.2102–4.

94. Ahmed, *Willful Subjects*, 2.

95. Ahmed, *Willful Subjects*, 4.

Conclusion

Language is a cultural, political, and religious mechanism that structures the way that identity and subjectivity are verbalized and performed as gendered categories in *Sappho, Medea,* and *Des Meeres und der Liebe Wellen.* As critical operations, gender and language are the ways in which the tragic is presented in *Gender and Identity in Franz Grillparzer's Classical Dramas.* In my treatment of Grillparzer's three heroines, I thought about the way that language functions as a site in which they voice themselves in ways that refute normative models of a "female way" of being in the world. Sappho, Medea, and Hero defied the ways in which women were expected to articulate themselves as they struggled with restraints on their self-expression. The work of gender, practices of inclusion and exclusion, and the amplification of discourse were the three modes around which this project was organized. I unpacked Grillparzer's dramas by exploring the management of art and life, exile and kinship, and desire and duty.

Grillparzer's texts, while rich and strong, were also desolate and defenseless. His writing could not support Sappho, Medea, and Hero's efforts to change the courses of their lives. Grillparzer chose to represent female figures who were well-known in the antique repertoire. In the classical versions of these stories (with the exception of Sappho whose story is recreated biography) they cannot represent themselves fully in language because the accepted conventions and patterns of language do not have room for them. Grillparzer also encountered the same problem in his revisions—there was no discursive space for him to successfully practice the idea of an internally constructed identity.

As its point of departure, I offered a reading of Franz Grillparzer's classical plays that asked questions about narrative activity, ventriloquial crisis, and what feminist speech sounds like. I understood Grillparzer's method of identity formation and its instability as the primary manner in which the female figure expressed herself in a world that was ambivalent or even hostile to her. At play with ideas about gender and its manifestation, this study was interested in how each protagonist constituted her identity as discursively produced and intentional in its opposition to the power structures encircling her. The restrictive social milieu that each inhabits stretches its way into all other openings and confounds the poetess, witch, and priestess who would enter those spaces of sociality to speak about the conditions of their lives. What was at stake for Grillparzer was how narrative performance created those spaces in which Sappho, Medea, and Hero could refute the processes of a conventional and constricting world. What was important to Grillparzer was not suffering and redemption but rather what caused those situations to develop.

I examined what the female figures say (or are allowed to say) about themselves and also explored the types of independent choices they were able to make, whether formal or informal, overt or covert, or legal or ritual. The content of their speech was about desire; they wanted to express themselves as desiring subjects. This excess of both voice and desire point to the alterity represented by the women in the dramas. Grillparzer's achievement was to create a space in which these desires were voiced—even if that space of longing was already determined, and the tragic conclusions of the ancient materials were known to us as modern readers.

Since Grillparzer expresses narrative alterity in all three dramas, one goal of this study was to show the narrative value of lives when others understand them as figures of difference. Sappho, Medea, and Hero became three distinct ways to formulate descriptions of worlds. How might these identities be reconciled or, at least, spoken together as a difficulty? Their difficulty was a way to produce knowledge as they navigated hostile spaces. The premise of this study going forward was that each drama offered an aesthetic experience, that it was written to do something, that it had a function and an underlying structure that allowed a reader to make interpretative attempts, and, finally, that the texts allow previously unrepresented or unrepresentable experiences to become visible. Even if newness comes into the world via novel interpretative modes, the appearance is not necessarily able to be articulated given the limitations of language to accommodate and make sense of what was formerly only imaginary or perceptual. Hence, the readings that I carried out are constituted as critically permissive and strategic. They are tactical devices that offer the outlines of a method for analyzing social, political, and religious practices that seek to construct and then silence the figure of the female.

I wanted to think about these analyses of Grillparzer's dramas as interventions that take up a certain form of feminist reasoning as motivation. As Sara Ahmed wrote in *Living a Feminist Life*:

> If feminists are willful women, then feminism is judged as a product of those who have too much will or too much of a will of their own. This judgment is a judgment of feminism as being wrong, but also an explanation of feminism in terms of motivation: the act of saying something is wrong is understood as being self-motivated, a way of getting what you want or will.[1]

Grillparzer also takes up these materials about female action and dispute at moments where social norms about gender are actively thought in everyday life, political spaces, and social interactions. Feminist thinking can also happen in those very places in which "feminist" is not recognized as such: "Feminism involves a process of finding another way to live in your body. We might learn to let ourselves bump into things; not to withdraw in anticipation of violence. Of course I am describing a difficulty; I am describing how ways of resolving problems can enact the problems we are trying to resolve."[2] The work of Grillparzer illustrates how the claims of a normative gender position are impossible to refute but are also difficult to shape. Grillparzer's dramas function as a form of contestation, explaining their own existence while creating distinct levels of narrativity. This variance was intended to uncover a multitude of readings of the ancient materials that once appeared to be complete—that is, there was no more to be added to these ancient stories. Instead, Grillparzer produces fissures in each of his dramas that disrupt what was once believed to be solved by older or other simultaneous accounts. He breaks apart the older narratives and demonstrates that there is something fragmentary, disguised, and violent that alters our understanding of these three protagonists' stories. Grillparzer's readings of these dramas—that is, his reinterpretations—are fractures that cause both a division and a disintegration of narrative certainty, which then become a reformulation of liminal spaces inhabited by women.

Grillparzer's nineteenth-century dramas are open to feminist readings in ways that think about female life as a center of literary activity even if they are considered to be decentered discourses. The urgency of the female voice in Grillparzer's classical works indicates that he was interested in forms of action that could be conveyed through speech. The social and political positioning of the three protagonists is contingent upon the movement of various available narratives. Grillparzer's conceptualization and investigation of female subjectivities take up these available narrative formulations from the ancient world and create an informal theory of culture using gender as the fulcrum. This decentering of discourse is one of the most significant features of Grillparzer's writing since it allows structures of power to be displayed and lived out. The forms in which stories are told stage the female figure as central to the recuperation of female realities under the aegis of the classical tragedy.

Serving as cultural documents, *Sappho*, *Medea*, and *The Waves of Sea and Love* offer us a way of thinking of gender as a social organization that Grillparzer ventriloquized in order to consider female identity and the values at work in its construction. While the textual strategies are different across each drama, Grillparzer chose the figure of the female to articulate ideas about the gendered roles of the artist, the witch, and the priestess. These strategies also provide a reading of Grillparzer's work that is at play with ideas about a feminist voicing of the outsider as female—the other of society, the willful subject.

This project offered a gender performative interpretation of Grillparzer's dramas that understood them as effects of a discourse. By invoking these three female figures in drama, Grillparzer calls these identities into being and inaugurates them as subjects. While the three are fundamentally unstable discursive productions, Grillparzer's work remains, for me, a way to think through that discursive practice as potentially subversive rather than conservative. Even if he did not name it as such, Grillparzer's works are theoretical exercises that look at exclusionary practices around the idea of the female and gender through the dramatization of difference which is central to his ventriloquism.

While I remain interested in the way that ideas about feminism can be woven through the individual dramas, an overarching preoccupation for each chapter was how Grillparzer reimagined these three very different antique figures as outbursts of a feminist impulse coming to the surface. How did their attempts to construct their identities through speech in opposition to the possibilities that their cultures and contexts allowed them inform each drama's direction? In *Sappho*, we have a poetess who is already in possession of a strong lyrical voice. However, the voice that she wishes to cultivate— the domestic one—is soon revealed to be impossible for her to achieve. In *Medea*, we encounter a witch who is excluded from the social experience of the world. She is marked by a difference that is both gendered and ethnic. In *The Waves of Sea and Love*, Hero neither understands the world that she is giving up nor the one she is about to enter. Each drama is an articulation of melancholy and disaffection that triggers a crisis or turning point.

The final chapter on *The Waves of Sea and Love* ended with a discussion of composure (Sammlung) and distraction (Zerstreuung), and I want to return to those two ideas since, in the end, they inform the ways in which we can also read *Sappho* and *Medea*. Composure is quiet and contained. It will not be moved by the world around it and competes forcefully with the qualities of distraction. Composure is shape; it has a form. It has its own rules and restrictions that have no regard for the thoughtlessness of distraction. However, both are equally powerful and aggressive. Composure is silence, or rather, composure silences; its core achievement is that it produces silence. It quiets voices that would otherwise sound aloud agitation, confusion, or perplexity about the conditions of the world. It is withdrawn and recessive. Composure has no need for distraction's wild exuberance or inordinate passion since distraction has proven itself to be troublesome and disconcerting. One meaning of distraction now obsolete is "drawn apart or pulled to pieces." One could claim this is how each of the female figures experiences her life. A life that is in a violent struggle with keeping itself held together but which must contend with forces whose very existence threatens the ideal of composure. Pulled to pieces. Uncomposed. Drawn apart.

Hero is caught between competing claims on her life that threaten to upset any equanimity she might have once wished for. Held between the domestic realm and that of the sacred, Hero can only realize the one by renouncing the other. However, once she claims the religious domain as her own, she is now caught between that world and the new one of love for Leander. However, it is composure (her role as priestess) that is in contest with distraction (her passion for Leander). Medea's sense of composure is lost almost as soon as the first drama of the trilogy commences, and it is this loss that seduces Medea away from her calling as princess and witch once Jason arrives on Colchis. Her efforts to regain self-possession fail at every attempt. In Medea, we see that it is language that offers her a way to contextualize her deeds in a manner that attempts to gain composure after a series of horrific events. Sappho is caught between the composure of her life as a poetess, divorced from the cares of the world, and her wish to enjoy domestic bliss with Phaon. Sappho shows us that her search for balance is impossible given her identities as woman and as artist. She cannot descend from the heights of the poetic to the conventional world. It is one that leads her away from her calling into the despair of rejected love—a distraction that ultimately results in her suicide.

I would even go as far as to claim that composure or its promise is a form of politics—a way of organizing and regulating bodies for certain purposes in society. It might also be the case that distraction or even willfulness is also a form of politics that troubles proper categories for moving around in the world. Turning once more to Sara Ahmed: "We tend to notice categories when we come up against them: when they do not allow us to flow through space. Willfulness might be an experience of coming up against."[3] Hero has come up against the formal structure of composure, which prevents her from expressing her most authentic self. She knows that she has avoided the category of the domestic realm but has now come up against something that she had initially thought was good and proper. We can also apply this to Sappho and Medea. Sappho is celebrated for her poetic prowess, but once she tries to retreat to another form of life, she realizes that there is no path there for her that would allow a both/and existence. In her attempt to transgress the shutting out of love by Phaon, Sappho loses her composure and violates her own artistic and moral principles. In her final testimony, Sappho recognizes that she cannot choose choice and that her willfulness is only a partial remedy to this lack of choice. Medea must contend with a series of men who use her to enrich their own lives. It is only by defying them—"coming up against"—that Medea can act with agency and become willful—so much so that she lays waste to everything around her.

At stake in this study was the narrative value of lives when they are understood as figures of difference; the language that defines those eccentric lives; and the limits of that language's expressive quality for the experiences of the perceptual and the imaginary. Is language up to the task of knowing and then telling "reality" when it is most urgently needed, when the failure of telling is the effacement of lives and the erasure of the linguistically plural? I was not able to answer all questions that I posed at the start of this project. One notable example was if Grillparzer's specific use of ventriloquism to give voice to marginalized others (female figures in classical antiquity) was a success? If so, in what sense? Can ventriloquisms, like other gender performances, be more or less coherent? If so, does this question come into play in Grillparzer's ventriloquisms? Does ventriloquism also become a "place where theory takes place," as I noted in the introduction about literature as a space for theoretical formation?

This study examined how Grillparzer animated the female figures from the antique world through new formulations of old materials in the nineteenth century. I do not presume that Grillparzer's structures are cohesive or consistent but rather that they are alive as specters whose peculiar narrativity requires accommodation, a slight adjustment to the manner of looking, the redirection of the oblique gaze in the direction of the figurations of three women—out of bounds, inordinate in their desires, and excessive in their needs. The historical Sappho knew this only too well:

Someone, I say, will remember us in the future.[4]

Sappho's fragment (even if we may want to read it as complete) is a two-part proclamation, a linguistic structure that is about subject formation and continuity that also embraces the stories of Medea and Hero in its formulation. The first part is declarative while the second part is proleptic. The emphatic and resolute "I say" vibrates with the certainty of discovery in the present tense voice. "I say" resides in that space of a bold willfulness. Flanked by what looks to be a complete sentence, "Someone will remember us in the future," is an assertion that reaches for or out to another time. One that is not yet formed for this "someone." What does it is mean to remember in this instance? To remember is to have previously known or perceived. It supposes something that has been held in the memory and must only be recovered through the reminding of. This "us" can be productively used to suggest a unity that gives an account of the stories of Sappho, Medea, and

Hero as a shared experience, one that is also about recognition. It is about persistence and memorialization—inscribed in some form. Is remembering an activity or is it a situation? And can it be addressed to a future someone who will do it justice? Is remembering sufficient? Can it be done with integrity? However much one wants to articulate a certain moment, a presence, a person from the past, there is a necessary discontinuity between loss and retrieval. Grillparzer's dramas conjure Sappho, Medea, and Hero but is his recovery and reimagination of the materials enough to do the work that Sappho's fragment announces? While his narrative structures across the three dramas may sometimes be inconsistent, Grillparzer is the "someone" in this moment who responds to Sappho's declaration to "remember us."

NOTES

1. Ahmed, *Living a Feminist Life*, 74.
2. Ahmed, *Living a Feminist Life*, 30.
3. Ahmed, *Willful Subjects*, 150.
4. Sappho, fragment 147, in Sappho, *Greek Lyric, Volume I: Sappho and Alcaeus*, ed. and trans. David A. Campbell (Cambridge, MA: Harvard University Press, 1982).

Bibliography

Aeschylus. *The Libation Bearers*. Translated by Richmond Lattimore. In *Aeschylus I: Oresteia; Agamemnon, The Libation Bearers, The Eumenides*. Vol. 1 of 9, *The Complete Greek Tragedies*. Edited by David Grene and Richmond Alexander Lattimore. Chicago: University of Chicago Press, 1953.

Ahmed, Sara. "Feminist Killjoys (and Other Willful Subjects)." *Scholar and Feminist Online* 8, no. 3 (Summer 2010). http://sfonline.barnard.edu/polyphonic/ahmed_01.htm.

Ahmed, Sara. *Living a Feminist Life*. Durham, NC: Duke University Press, 2017.

Ahmed, Sara. *The Promise of Happiness*. Durham, NC: Duke University Press, 2010.

Ahmed, Sara. "A Willfulness Archive." *Theory & Event* 15, no. 3 (2012). https://muse.jhu.edu/article/484421.

Ahmed, Sara. *Strange Encounters: Embodied Others in Post-Coloniality*. London: Routledge, 2000.

Ahmed, Sara. "Whose Counting?" *Feminist Theory* 1, no. 1 (April 2000): 97–103.

Ahmed, Sara. *Willful Subjects*. Durham, NC: Duke University Press, 2014.

Alcoff, Linda. "The Problem of Speaking for Others." *Cultural Critique* 20 (Winter 1991–1992): 5–32.

Apollonius of Rhodes. *Argonautica*. Translated by R. C. Seaton. Cambridge, MA: Harvard University Press, 1988.

Austin, J. L. *How to Do Things with Words*. Oxford: Clarendon Press, 1962.

Baker, Christa Suttner. "Unifying Imagery Patterns in Grillparzer's *das goldene Vließ*." *MLN* 89, no. 3 (April 1974): 392–403.

Bakhtin, Mikhail M. *The Dialogic Imagination: Four Essays*. Edited by Michael Holquist. Translated by Caryl Emerson and Michael Holquist. Austin: University of Texas Press, 1981.

Baumbach, Manuel. "Hero and Leander." In *Brill's New Pauly Supplements I, Volume 4: The Reception of Myth and Mythology*, edited by David van Eijndhoven, Christine Salazar, and Francis G. Gentry. Leiden: Brill, 2010.

Beauvoir, Simone de. *The Second Sex*. Translated by H. M. Parshley. New York: Vintage, 1973. Originally published as *Le deuxième sexe*. Paris: Gallimard, 1949.

Bernd, Clifford Albrecht. "Grillparzer: Austrian Playwright or Weimarian Classicist? An American Perspective on *König Ottokars Glück und Ende*." In *Aneignungen, Entfremdungen: The Austrian Playwright Franz Grillparzer (1791–1872)*, edited by Marianne Henn, Clemens Ruthner, and Raleigh Whitinger, 111–18. New York: Peter Lang, 2007.

Bhabha, Homi. *The Location of Culture*. New York: Routledge, 1994.

Black, Max, ed. *Philosophy in America*. Ithaca: Cornell University Press, 1965.

Blundell, Sue. *Women in Ancient Greece*. London: British Museum Press, 1995.

Braun, Hanns. *Grillparzers Verhältnis Zu Shakespeare*. Nuremberg: H. Lotter, 1916.

Brown, Laura S. "Not Outside the Range: One Feminist Perspective on Psychic Trauma." In *Trauma: Explorations in Memory*, edited by Cathy Caruth, 100–12. Baltimore, MD: Johns Hopkins University Press, 1995.

Butler, E. M. *The Tyranny of Greece Over Germany: Study of the Influence Exercised by Greek Art and Poetry Over the Great German Writers of the Eighteenth, Nineteenth and Twentieth Centuries*. Cambridge: Cambridge University Press, 1935.

Butler, Judith. *Antigone's Claim: Kinship Between Life and Death*. New York: Columbia University Press, 2000.

Butler, Judith. *Bodies That Matter: On the Discursive Limits of "Sex."* New York: Routledge, 1993.

Butler, Judith. *Gender Trouble: Feminism and the Subversion of Identity*. New York: Routledge, 1990. Reprinted with prefaces from 1990 and 1999. New York: Routledge, 2010. Page references are to the 2010 edition.

Byron, Lord George Gordon. "Written After Swimming from Sestos to Abydos." In *Selected Poems of Lord Byron*, edited by Susan J. Wolfson and Peter J. Manning. New York: Penguin Classics, 2006.

Calderón de la Barca, Pedro. *Life Is a Dream (La vida es sueño)*. Translated by William E. Colford. Woodbury, NY: Barron's Educational Series, 1958.

Campbell, David. *Greek Lyric, Volume I: Sappho and Alcaeus*. Cambridge, MA: Harvard University Press, 1982.

Caruth, Cathy, ed. *Trauma: Explorations in Memory*. Baltimore, MD: Johns Hopkins University Press, 1995.

Caruth, Cathy. *Unclaimed Experience: Trauma, Narrative, and History*. Baltimore, MD: Johns Hopkins University Press, 1996.

Clauss, James Joseph, and Sarah Iles Johnston. *Medea: Essays on Medea in Myth, Literature, Philosophy, and Art*. Princeton, NJ: Princeton University Press, 1997.

Daviau, Donald G. "Biedermeier. The Happy Face of the Vormärz Era." In *The Other Vienna: The Culture of Biedermeier Austria; Österreichisches Biedermeier in Literatur, Musik, Kunst und Kulturgeschichte*, edited by Robert Pichl and Clifford A. Bernd, 11–27. Vienna: Lehner, 2002.

Dunham, T. C. "Symbolism in Grillparzer's *das Goldene Vließ*." *PMLA* 75, no. 1 (March 1960): 75–82.

Easterling, P. E. *The Cambridge Companion to Greek Tragedy*. Cambridge: Cambridge University Press, 1997.
Euripides. *The Medea*. Translated by Rex Warner. In *Euripides I: Alcestis, The Medea, The Heracleidae, Hippolytus*. Vol. 3 of 9, *The Complete Greek Tragedies*. Edited by David Grene and Richmond Alexander Lattimore, 59–112. Chicago: University of Chicago Press, 1955.
"The Fable of the Golden Fleece." *Ballou's Monthly Magazine*, October 1892.
Fichte, Johann Gottlieb. *Grundriß des Familienrechts (als erster Anhang des Naturrechts)*. In *Grundlage des Naturrechts nach Prinzipien der Wissenschaftslehre*, 298–365. Hamburg: Meiner, 1960. Originally published in 1796.
Foley, Helene P. "The Conception of Women in Athenian Drama." In *Reflections of Women in Antiquity*, edited by Helene P. Foley, 127–68. New York: Gordon and Breach, 1981.
Foley, Helene P. *Female Acts in Greek Tragedy*. Princeton, NJ: Princeton University Press, 2001.
Foley, Helene P., ed. *Reflections of Women in Antiquity*. New York: Gordon and Breach, 1981.
Garner, Richard. *From Homer to Tragedy: The Art of Allusion in Greek Poetry*. New York: Routledge, 1990.
Goethe, Johann Wolfgang. *Johann Wolfgang Goethe. Klassische Dramen: Iphigenie Auf Tauris / Egmont / Torquato Tasso*. Edited by Dieter Borchmeyer and Peter Huber. Deutscher Klassiker Verlag, 1995.
Goethe, Johann Wolfgang.*Verse Plays and Epic*. Translated by Cyrus Hamlin and Frank Glessner Ryder. Princeton, NJ: Princeton University Press, 1987.
Goff, Barbara E. *Citizen Bacchae: Women's Ritual Practice in Ancient Greece*. Berkeley: University of California Press, 2004.
Goldblatt, David. *Art and Ventriloquism: Critical Voices in Art, Theory and Culture*. London: Routledge, 2006.
Gouge, Olympe de. *Déclaration des droits de la femme et de la citoyenne*. Paris: Editions Mille et une nuits, 2003. Originally published in 1791.
Graf, Fritz. "Medea, the Enchantress from Afar: Remarks on a Well-Known Myth." In *Medea: Essays on Medea in Myth, Literature, Philosophy, and Art*, edited by James J. Clauss and Sarah Iles Johnston, 21–43. Princeton, NJ: Princeton University Press, 1997.
Grillparzer, Franz. *Medea: Vollständiger Text*. Dichtung Und Wirklichkeit. Edited by Marie Luise Kaschnitz. Vol. 18. Frankfurt am Main: Ullstein, 1966.
Grillparzer, Franz. *Plays on Classic Themes*. Translated by Samuel Solomon. New York: Random House, 1969.
Grillparzer, Franz. *Franz Grillparzer Werke in sechs Bänden* [Franz Grillparzer Works in Six Volumes]. Edited by Helmut Bachmaier. Frankfurt am Main: Deutscher Klassiker Verlag, 1986.
Grillparzer, Franz. *Dramen 1817–1828*. Vol. 2 of *Franz Grillparzer Werke in sechs Bänden*, edited by Helmut Bachmaier. Frankfurt am Main: Deutscher Klassiker Verlag, 1986.

Grillparzer, Franz. *Dramen 1828–1851*. Vol. 3 of *Franz Grillparzer Werke in sechs Bänden*, edited by Helmut Bachmaier. Frankfurt am Main: Deutscher Klassiker Verlag, 1986.

Grosz, Elizabeth A. *Volatile Bodies: Toward a Corporeal Feminism*. Bloomington: Indiana University Press, 1994.

Gubitz, Friedrich Wilhem. *Sappho. Monodrama*. Berlin: Maurersche Buchhandlung, 1816.

Gustafson, Susan E. *Absent Mothers and Orphaned Fathers: Narcissism and Abjection in Lessing's Aesthetic and Dramatic Production*. Detroit, MI: Wayne State University Press, 1995.

Gutzwiller, Kathryn. "Seeing Thought: Timomachus' Medea and Ecphrastic Epigram." *American Journal of Philology* 125, no. 3 (Autumn 2004): 339–86.

Hall, Edith. "The Sociology of Athenian Tragedy." In *The Cambridge Companion to Greek Tragedy*, edited by P. E. Easterling, 93–126. Cambridge: Cambridge University Press, 1997.

Halliwell, Stephen, trans. *The Poetics of Aristotle*. Chapel Hill: University of North Carolina Press, 1987.

Harrigan, Renny Keelin. "Woman and Artist: Grillparzer's *Sappho* Revisited." *German Quarterly* 53, no. 3 (May 1980): 298–316.

Harry Houdini Collection and McManus-Young Collection (Library of Congress). *Ventriloquism Explained: And Juggler's Tricks, Or Legerdemain Exposed: With Remarks on Vulgar Superstitions: In a Series of Letters to an Instructor*. Amherst, MA: J. S. and C. Adams, 1834.

Hebbel, Friedrich. *Hebbels Werke in Drei Bänden*. Edited by Joachim Müller. 4 Aufl ed. Berlin: Aufbau-Verlag, 1971.

Henn, Marianne, Clemens Ruthner, and Raleigh Whitinger, eds. *Aneignungen, Entfremdungen: The Austrian Playwright Franz Grillparzer (1791–1872)*. New York: Peter Lang, 2007.

Herodotus, ed. *Histories IV*. Translated by Michael A. Flower and John Marincola. Cambridge: Cambridge University Press, 2002.

Heyse, Paul. *Medea. in: Gesammelte Werke Von Paul Heyse*. Berlin: Wilhelm Hertz, 1899.

Hippel, Theodor Gottlieb von. *Über die bürgerliche Verbesserung der Weiber*. Berlin: Voss, 1792.

Hölderlin, Friedrich. 1895. *Hölderlins Gesammelte Dichtungen*. Edited by Berthold Litzmann. Stuttgart: J.G. Cotta, 1895.

Homer. *The Iliad*. Edited by Bernard Knox. Translated by Robert Fagles. New York, NY: Penguin, 1990.

Homer. *The Odyssey*. Edited by Bernard Knox. Translated by Robert Fagles. New York: Penguin, 1996.

Irigaray, Luce. *This Sex Which Is Not One*. Translated by Catherine Porter. Ithaca, NY: Cornell University Press, 1985. Originally published as *Sexe qui n'en pas un* (Paris: Minuit, 1977).

Jahnn, Hans Henny. *Medea: Tragödie*. Leipzig: Schauspiel Verlag, 1924/1926.

Jennings, Lee. "Biedermeier." In *A Concise History of German Literature to 1900*, edited by Kim Vivian, 240–61. Columbia, SC: Camden House, 1992.

Kant, Immanuel. "What is Enlightenment?" In *The Philosophy of Kant: Immanuel Kant's Moral and Political Writings*, translated and edited by Carl J. Friedrich, 145–53. New York: The Modern Library, 1993.

Kaschnitz, Mary Louise. *Medea: Dichtung und Wirklichkeit*. Frankfurt am Main: Verlag Ullstein, 1966.

Kiefer, Anselm. *Des Meeres Und Der Liebe Wellen*. 2011. Mixed media and gynaecological instrument on photograph, 107 × 327 cm. White Cube Hoxton Square, London, UK.

Klanska, Maria, Krzysztof Lipinski, Katarzyna Jastal, and Agnieszka Palej, eds. *Grenzgänge und Grenzgänger in der österreichischen Literatur: Beiträge des 15. Österreichisch-Polnischen Germanistentreffens Kraków 2002*. Kraków: Wydawnictwo Uniwersytetu Jagiellonskiego, 2004.

Kleinschmidt, Gert. *Illusion Und Untergang. Die Liebe Im Drama Franz Grillparzers*. Lahr/Schwarzwald: Schauenburg, 1967.

Kleist, Franz. *Sappho. Ein dramatisches Gedicht*. Berlin: Vossiche Buchhandlung, 1793.

Kleist, Heinrich von. *Penthesilea: A Tragic Drama*. Translated by Joel Agee. New York: Harper Collins, 1998.

Kottman, Paul A. "Art and Necessity: Rethinking Lessing's Critical Practice." In *Rethinking Lessing's "Laocoon": Antiquity, Enlightenment and the 'Limits' of Painting and Poetry*, edited by Avi Lifschitz and Michael Squire, 327–44. Oxford: Oxford University Press, 2017.

Kristeva, Julia. *Powers of Horror: An Essay on Abjection*. Translated by Leon S. Roudiez. New York: Columbia University Press, 1982. Originally published as *Pouvoirs de l'horreur: Essai sur l'abjection* (Paris: Éditions du Seuil, 1980).

Lefkowitz, Mary R. *Women in Greek Myth*. 2nd ed. Baltimore, MD: Johns Hopkins University Press, 2007.

Lessing, Gotthold Ephraim. *G.E. Lessings Gesammelte Werke*. Leipzig: Göschen, 1855.

Lessing, Gotthold Ephraim. *'Laocoon': An Essay upon the Limits of Painting and Poetry, With Remarks Illustrative of Various Points in the History of Ancient Art*. Translated by Ellen Frothingham. Boston: Roberts Brothers, 1887. Originally published 1766.

Lifschitz, Avi, and Michael Squire. "Introduction." In *Rethinking Lessing's "Laocoon": Antiquity, Enlightenment and the 'Limits' of Painting and Poetry*, edited by Avi Lifschitz and Michael Squire, 1–58. Oxford: Oxford University Press, 2017.

Lorenz, Dagmar C. G. "Grillparzer's Attitude toward the State, the Nation and Nationalism." In *Aneignungen, Entfremdungen: The Austrian Playwright Franz Grillparzer (1791–1872)*, edited by Marianne Henn, Clemens Ruthner, and Raleigh Whitinger, 1–20. New York: Peter Lang, 2007.

Lorenz, Dagmar C. G. *Grillparzer: Dichter des sozialen Konflikts*. Vienna: Böhlau, 1986.

Lü, Yixu. *Medea unter den Deutschen: Wandlungen einer literarischen Figur*. Freiburg im Breisgau: Rombach, 2009.

Lütkehaus, Ludger, ed. *Mythos Medea: Texte von Euripides bis Christa Wolf*. Stuttgart: Reclam, 2007.

Marlowe, Christopher. *The Complete Poems and Translations*. Edited by Stephen Orgel. New York: Penguin Classics, 2007.

McCarthy-Rechowicz, Matthew. *Franz Grillparzer's Dramatic Heroines: Theatre and Women's Emancipation in Nineteenth-Century Austria*. Cambridge: Legenda, 2018.

McDonald, Marianne. "Medea as Politician and Diva: Riding the Dragon into the Future." In *Medea: Essays on Medea in Myth, Literature, Philosophy, and Art*, edited by James J. Clauss and Sarah Iles Johnston, 297–323. Princeton, NJ: Princeton University Press, 1997.

McInnes, Edward. "Psychological Insight and Moral Awareness in Grillparzer's *Das goldene Vliess*." *Modern Language Review* 75, no. 3 (July 1980): 575–82.

Menhennet, Alan. "Grillparzer, Shakespeare, and Historical Drama." *German Life and Letters* 44, no. 3 (1991): 208–20.

Montiglio, Silvia. *The Myth of Hero and Leander: The History and Reception of an Enduring Greek Legend*. New York: I.B. Tauris, 2018.

Musaeus. *On the Loves of Hero and Leander*. London: F.B. for Humphrey Mosley, 1647.

Naumann, Walter. "Grillparzer: Der Dichter und Die Sprache." *Monatshefte* 45, no. 6 (November 1953): 337–54.

Ovid. *Heroides*. Translated by Harold Isbell. London: Penguin Books, 1990.

Ovid. *Metamorphoses*. Translated by Charles Martin. New York: W. W. Norton & Co., 2005.

Ovid. *The Poems of Exile: Tristia and the Black Sea Letters*. Translated by Peter Green. Berkeley: University of California Press, 2005.

Papst, E. E. *Des Meeres Und Der Liebe Wellen*. London: Edward Arnold, 1967.

Pichl, Robert, and Clifford A. Bernd, eds. *The Other Vienna: The Culture of Biedermeier Austria; Österreichisches Biedermeier in Literatur, Musik, Kunst und Kulturgeschichte*. Vienna: Lehner, 2002.

Politzer, Heinz. *Franz Grillparzer oder Das abgründige Biedermeier*. Vienna: Fritz Molden, 1972.

Powell, Anton. *Euripides, Women, and Sexuality*. London: Routledge, 1990.

Prutti, Brigitte. *Grillparzers Welttheater: Modernität Und Tradition*. Bielefeld: Aisthesis Verlag, 2013.

Prutti, Brigitte. *Unglück und Zerstreuung: Autobiographisches Schreiben bei Franz Grillparzer*. Bielefeld: Aisthesis Verlag, 2016.

Reeve, William C. "Grillparzer's *Die Ahnfrau:* Das Leben Ein Traum." *Modern Austrian Literature* 39, no. 1 (2006): 1–26.

Reynolds, Margaret, ed. *The Sappho Companion*. New York: Palgrave for St. Martin's Press, 2002.

Rilke, Rainer Maria. *The Selected Poetry of Rainer Maria Rilke*. Translated by Stephen Mitchell. New York: Random House, 1982.

Roe, Ian F. *Franz Grillparzer: A Century of Criticism*. Columbia, SC: Camden House, 1995.
Rogowski, Christian. "Erstickte Schreie. Geschlechtliche Differenz Und Koloniales Denken in Grillparzers Medea-Trilogie *Das Goldene Vließ*." *Jahrbuch Der Grillparzer Gesellschaft* 21, no. 3 (2003–2006): 32–50.
Rusten, Jeffrey S. *Dionysius Scytobrachion*. Opladen: Westdeutscher Verlag, 1982.
Ruthner, Clemens. "Argonaut und Tourist: Repräsentationen der Fremde(n) bei Franz Grillparzer." In *Aneignungen, Entfremdungen: The Austrian Playwright Franz Grillparzer (1791–1872)*, edited by Marianne Henn, Clemens Ruthner, and Raleigh Whitinger, 49–68. New York: Peter Lang, 2007.
Sappho. *Greek Lyric, Volume I: Sappho and Alcaeus*. Edited and translated by David A. Campbell. Cambridge, MA: Harvard University Press, 1982.
Sappho. *Sappho: A New Translation*. Translated by Mary Barnard. Berkeley: University of California Press, 1986. Originally published in 1958.
Sappho. *If Not, Winter: Fragments of Sappho*. Translated by Anne Carson. New York: Alfred A. Knopf, 2002.
Sappho. *Sappho: Poems and Fragments*. Translated by Stanley Lombardo. Indianapolis, IN: Hackett Publishing Company, 2002.
Sappho. *Sappho*. Translated by Robert Chandler. London: J. M. Dent, 1998.
Schaum, Konrad. *Grillparzer-Studien*. Bern: Peter Lang, 2001.
Schiller, Friedrich. *Schiller's Sammtliche Werke*. Vollstandige Ausgabe. Stuttgart: Cotta, 1867.
Schlesier, Renate "Sappho." In *Brill's New Pauly Supplements 2, Vol. 7, Figures of Antiquity and their Reception in Art, Literature and Music*. English edition by Chad M. Schroeder (2016). http://dx.doi.org/10.1163/2468-3418_bnps7_SIM_004732. Originally published as *Historische Gestalten der Antike: Rezeption in Literatur, Kunst und Musik*, ed. Peter von Möllendorf, Annette Simonis, and Linda Simonis (Stuttgart: J. B. Metzlersche Verlagsbuchhandlung und Carl Ernst Poeschel Verlag GmbH, 2013).
Searle, John R. "What Is a Speech Act?" In *Philosophy in America*, edited by Max Black, 221–39. Ithaca, NY: Cornell University Press, 1965.
Seneca. "Medea." In *Seneca: Six Tragedies. Oxford World's Classics*. Translated by Emily Wilson. Oxford: Oxford University Press, 2010.
Sengle, Friedrich. *Biedermeierzeit: Deutsche Literatur im Spannungsfeld zwischen Restauration und Revolution, 1815–1848*. Stuttgart: J. B. Metzler, 1971–1980.
Shakespeare, William. *The Tragedy of Antony and Cleopatra*. Edited by Michael Neill. Oxford: Oxford University Press, 2009.
Sophocles. *Antigone*. Translated by Elizabeth Wyckoff. In *Sophocles I: Antigone, Oedipus the King, Oedipus at Colonus*. Vol. 8 of 9, *The Complete Greek Tragedies*. Edited by David Grene and Richmond Alexander Lattimore, 158–203. Chicago: University of Chicago Press, 1954.
Stein, Gisela. *The Inspiration Motif in the Works of Franz Grillparzer*. The Hague: Martinus Nijhoff, 1955.
Stephan, Inge. *Medea: Multimediale Karriere Einer Mythologischen Figur*. Köln: Böhlau, 2006.

Storsve, Jonas, ed. *Cy Twombly Exhibition*. Munich: Sieveking Verlag, 2017.
Tanzer, Ulrike. "Grenzgänge in Franz Grillparzers Trauerspiel 'Des Meeres und der Liebe Wellen.'" In *Grenzgänge und Grenzgänger in der österreichischen Literatur: Beiträge des 15. Österreichisch-Polnischen Germanistentreffens Kraków 2002*, edited by Klanska, Maria, Krzysztof Lipinski, Katarzyna Jastal, and Agnieszka Palej, 77–86. Kraków: Wydawnictwo Uniwersytetu Jagiellonskiego, 2004.
Tasso, Torquato, Ugo Foscolo, and Francesco Domenico Guerrazzi. *La Gerusalemme liberata*. Firenze: F. Le Monnier, 1853.
Vivian, Kim. *A Concise History of German Literature to 1900*. Studies in German Literature, Linguistics, and Culture. Columbia, SC, USA: Camden House, 1992.
Weissman, Dirk. "When Austrian Classical Tragedy Goes Intercultural: On the Metrical Simulation of Linguistic Otherness in Franz Grillparzer's *The Golden Fleece*." *Critical Multilingualism Studies* 5, no. 3 (2017): 52–74.
Welcker, Friedrich Gottlieb. *Sappho, von einem herrschenden Vorurtheil befreyt*. Göttingen: Vandenhoek und Ruprecht, 1816.
Wellbery, David. "*Laocoon* Today: On the Conceptual Infrastructure of Lessing's Treatise." In *Rethinking Lessing's "Laocoon": Antiquity, Enlightenment and the 'Limits' of Painting and Poetry*, edited by Avi Lifschitz and Michael Squire, 59–85. Oxford: Oxford University Press, 2017.
Whitaker, Paul K. "The Concept of 'Sammlung' in Grillparzer's Works." *Monatshefte* 41, no. 2 (February 1949): 93–103.
Williamson, Margaret. "A Woman's Place in Euripides' *Medea*." In *Euripides, Women, and Sexuality*, edited by Anton Powell, 16–31. London: Routledge, 1990.
Winckelmann, Johann Joachim. *Gedanken über die Nachahmung der griechischen Werke in Der Malerei und Bildhauerkunst*. Dresden und Leipzig: Im Verlag der Waltherischen Handlung, 1756.
Winckelmann, Johann Joachim. *Johann Winckelmanns Geschichte der Kunst des Alterthums*. Dresden: In der Waltherischen Hof-Buchhandlung, 1764.
Winkler, Markus. *Von Iphigenie zu Medea: Semantik und Dramaturgie des Barbarischen bei Goethe und Grillparzer*. Tübingen: Max Niemeyer Verlag, 2009.
Wollstonecraft, Mary. *A Vindication of the Rights of Woman: An Authoritative Text, Backgrounds, and Contexts Criticism*. 3rd ed. Edited by Deidre Shauna Lynch. New York: Norton, 2009. First published as *A Vindication of the Rights of Woman with Strictures on Political and Moral Subjects* (London: J. Johnson, 1792).
Woolf, Virginia. *Mrs. Dalloway*. New York: Harcourt, Brace & Company, 1925.
Yates, Douglas. "Grillparzer's Hero and Shakespeare's Juliet." *Modern Language Review* 21, no. 4 (October 1926): 419–25.
Yates, Douglas. *Franz Grillparzer: A Critical Biography*. Oxford: Basil Blackwell, 1946.
Zeitlin, Froma I. *Playing the Other: Gender and Society in Classical Greek Literature*. Chicago, IL: University of Chicago Press, 1996.
Zeitlin, Froma I. "Playing the Other: Theater, Theatricality, and the Feminine in Greek Drama." *Representations* 11 (Summer 1985): 63–94.

Zucker, A. E. "Shakespeare and Grillparzer." *Modern Language Notes* 31, no. 7 (November 1916): 396–99.

Zweig, Max. *Dramen: Der Abgrund; Medea in Prag; Die Entscheidung Lorenzo Morenos; Israel, was Nun?* Edited by Eva Reichmann. Paderborn: Igel Verlag Literatur, 1949;1997.

Index

abjection, 29n52
Absyrtus, 77, 100n19
Achilles, 103n58
agency, 138; female, 1, 108, 121; and language, 121
Ahmed, Sara, 2, 4–5, 23–24, 24n3, 31, 37–39, 51–52, 56, 60–61, 72, 82, 87, 95, 152–53; alien, figure of, 97n5; crisis, idea of, 71; and feminism, 70; feminist killjoys, 3, 9, 57, 139–40; white male structures, 103n51; and willfulness, 57, 137, 139–40, 155
Aietes, 75–77, 81, 88–89, 100n20, 103n59
Alcaeus of Mytilene, 29n43
Alcoff, Linda, 27n21, 27n22
alterity, 14, 69, 72, 96, 152; as gendered, 1, 10
Amor, 116, 124–25
Antigone: as defiant figure, 79–80; as discursive, 87
Antigone's Claim (Butler), 79
Aphrodite, 38, 56–57, 108, 111–13, 116, 123–25, 128, 137, 140
appropriation, 10, 13
Arendt, Hannah, 139
Argonauts, The, 75–76, 79
Argonauts, The (Grillparzer), 79, 89, 91, 96–97, 103n59; as revenge drama, 77

Aristotle, 62n2
Art and Ventriloquism (Goldblatt), 12
Athens (Greece), 20; public and private spheres, distinction between, 74
Attic tragedies, 18, 73
Augustine, 139
Austria, 6, 24n6

Bakhtin, Mikhail, 13–14
Baudelaire, Charles, 28n42
Baumbach, Manuel, 141n6
Beauvoir, Simone de, 15
belonging, 2, 18, 21, 49, 72, 95–96
Bernd, Clifford Albrecht, 26n13
Bhabha, Homi: unhomed, as term, 82
Biedermeier, 6
Blundell, Sue, 28n40
Bodies That Matter (Butler), 2
Brown, Laura S., 105n77
Butler, Judith, 2, 14–15, 17, 27n31, 35, 52–53, 65n45, 80, 108, 122, 139; feminist impulse, legacy of, 79
Byron, Lord, 107

Calderón de la Barca, Pedro, 7, 104–5n76
Carson, Anne, 28n42
Christian, Barbara, 2
composure, 83, 113, 118, 129–31, 137–39, 142n17, 147n71, 156; and

distraction, 113–14, 122, 128, 137–39, 147n71, 154–55; internal, 114; politics, as form of, 155. *See also* Sammlung
Corneille, Pierre, 34
Creon, 79

Darimba, 75, 101n31
Der Gastfreund (The Guest), 74
Des Meeres und der Liebe Wellen (The Waves of Sea and Love) (Grillparzer), 1, 5, 19, 22–23, 36, 74, 107–9, 113–15, 121, 142n9, 143n22, 151, 157; aboutness, conveying of, 34; distraction, as theorization of, 138; duality of, 34; gender thinking, 125; and Kant, 144–45n46; lamp, primary leitmotif of, 128, 132–35; melancholy, articulation of, 154; myth of Hero and Leander, remaking of, 110, 141; precarity, 111; prosaic quality of, 140; religious practice and kinship, as intertwined, 122; ritual space of, 116
Die Ahnfrau (The Ancestress) (Grillparzer), 7
Die Argonauten (The Argonauts), 74, 88
"An die Sammlung" (Grillparzer), 142n17
Dionysis of Halicarnassus, 29n43
dislocation, 13, 20, 29n52, 82–83, 112
distraction, 113, 117, 123, 129–31, 137, 147n71; and composure, 114, 122, 128, 138–39, 142n17, 154–55; politics, as form of, 155; resistance, model of, 139; theorization of, 138. *See also* Zerstreuung
Droste-Hülshoff, Annette von, 6

Eteocles, 79
ethics, 35
Eucharis, 55, 59–60
Euripides, 13, 21, 73–75, 81, 88, 92, 104n69

female agency, 1, 108; and language, 121
femaleness: and exclusion, 70–71; language, use of, 70
femininity, 38, 70, 84–85, 100–101n23; social spaces, 14
feminism, 3–4, 32, 70, 82, 152–54
feminist theory, 3, 23–24; and subjectivity, 111
figuration, 11–12, 61; and visibility, 23
Foley, Helene, 18
Foucault, Michel, 139

Gastfreundschaft, 75
gender, 1, 5, 31, 40, 72, 124, 142n11, 153; as construction, 15; constructive work of, 70; as cultural phenomenon, 38; descriptive, 37; and difference, 3; erasure, subject to, 15; and identity, 11, 14; and kinship, 79; and language, 151; manifestation of, 152; normative, 37; as performance, 11; as performative act, 15–16, 35; as regulation of possibility, 70; as social organization, 154; unthinking of, 110
Gender Trouble (Butler), 2, 14–15, 35, 52, 108
German literary studies, 26n13
Goethe, Johann Wolfgang von, 5, 26n13, 34, 41, 97–98n6
Goethe, Johann Wolfgang von, 5, 26n13, 34, 41, 97–98n6
Goldblatt, David, 12–13
Golden Fleece, 73, 75, 79, 83, 90–93, 99–100n14; as prized object, 81; shifting significance of, 101–2n38; as source of power, 88
Golden Fleece, The, 73–74, 107–8; return of child, symbol in, 89
Gora, 81, 83–84, 87–88, 90, 101n31; lamentation, feminine act of, 89
Gordimer, Nadine, 82
Gotthelf, Jeremias, 6
Graf Fritz: vertical tradition, 99n11
Greece, 39–40

Grillparzer, Franz Seraphicus, 7, 9, 11, 18, 20–22, 26n14, 27n22, 31, 33–35, 46–47, 52–53, 61, 69–70, 72, 75–76, 79–81, 86, 92–97, 97–98n6, 100n19, 104n69, 107–11, 115, 119, 122, 126, 133, 141, 143n22, 157; appropriation, as central to work of, 10, 13; Biedermeier, association with, 6; Calderón de la Barca, influence on, 104–5n76; composure, significance of, 114, 138, 142n17; composure and distraction, 113–14; decentered figures, writing about, 10, 153; and discourse, 151, 153; as "discursively privileged," 27n21; discursive practice of, 154; dislocation, as central to work of, 13; and distraction, 113; dramas of, as contestation, 153; female figures, and gendered roles of artist, 154; female identity, formulation of, 14; female protagonists, utilization of, 74; and gender, 151; gender scripts, updating of, 14; heroines, language of, 28n36; and identity, 15–17, 19, 151–52; inclusion and exclusion, 151; and Kant, 144–45n46; lack of interest in, 26n13; language practice, use of, 32; liminal spaces, 153; narrative alterity, 152; narrative performance, 1, 152; outsider, as female, 154; power and relationality, 112; reader, role of, 10–11; subjectivity, appropriation of, 10; symbols, use of, 101–2n38; textual identity, 2; ventriloquism, use of, 12–14, 16, 23–24, 71, 73, 114, 138–39, 151, 154, 156; willfulness, dramatization of, 8; work of, attitudes toward, 36; work of, as feminist intervention, 3; work of, as oppositional, 24; "wrong sort," tendency toward, 5–6
Grosz, Elizabeth, 111, 126
Guest, The (Grillparzer), 75–76, 79, 89, 91, 96–97

Gutzwiller, Kathryn, 98–99n10

Harrigan, Renny Keelin, 36, 64n28
H. D., 28n42
Hebbel, Christian Friedrich, 5
Hector, 103n58
Hegel, G. W. H., 79
Herder, Johann Gottfried von, 20
Hermes, 103n58
Hero, 1–3, 5, 14–16, 19, 21, 70, 107, 113, 135, 144n45, 144–45n46, 145n56, 145–46n57, 151, 154, 157; becoming, process of, 111; body of, as site of tension, 111–12; chastity, 109; and choice, 119; composure, 114, 130, 133, 136, 147n71; composure, rejection of, 137, 139; composure and distraction, conflict between, 122, 128–29, 131, 138, 155; as consecrated, 109; dead women, 146n59; death of, 137–39; desire and meaning, relationship between, 109; difference, as figure of, 152, 156; and discourse, 137; as discursive subject, 22–23, 108, 133; and distraction, 129, 131, 137–39, 147n71; dove, as symbol of distraction, 123; endurance, 118–19; energy, as embodiment of, 114; family, traditional notions of, 119–21; female autonomy, asserting of, 121; female flight, 139; female personhood, riskiness of, 111; feminist impulse of, 109, 120, 140; as feminist killjoy, 9; feminist will, 8; flight, desire of, 22, 110–11; gaze, reversal of, 108–9; grief of, 136; as harmed woman, 4; humanity of, 109–10; and identity, 122; interiority of, 112; and kinship, 110; knowability, 137; language, power of, 120; language, use of, 8–10, 119–20, 128; Leander, love for, 22, 111–12, 120, 123, 132–33, 136–37, 140, 155; Leda and Swan,

myth of, 126–27; as listener, 11; love, renouncing of, 124–25; marriage, condemnation of, 121, 123, 125; as mystery, 140; as object, 116–17; ordinary status of, 114–15; otherness of, 8; personal identity, 122; pessimism of, 119; as priestess, 8, 17, 23, 108–18, 122, 125, 128, 134, 137; quiet resistance of, 140; radicality of, 4; sacred function of, 111; sacred life, as form of escape, 109; Sappho, as countertext to, 115; sense of self, 116; speech patterns, 8; talking back, 13; as troublemaker, 4, 8, 22–23; ventriloquizing of, 114; virginal life, 8; as willful, 4, 8, 133, 136–37, 139, 140

"Hero" (Hölderlin), 107

Hero and Leander: myth of, 22, 107–8, 110, 126, 141n6, 141–42n7

"Hero and Leander" (Marlowe), 107

Hero and Leander (Musaeus), 107

"Hero and Leander" (Schiller), 107

"Hero and Leander" (Twombly), 141n4

Heroides (Ovid), 107

Hölderlin, Friedrich, 107

hospitality, 75

Hymen, 116, 125, 135, 145n56

identity, 2, 7, 29n52, 52, 74; and assimilation, 21, 22; and difference, 23; erasure, subject to, 15; female, 14, 19, 22, 154; and gender, 11, 14; gender, and discourse, 14; and language, 151; of other, 97n5; and self-concept, 92; social, 27n21; and subjectivity, 15; textual, 2; unknowability of, 54

Iliad, The (Homer), 103n58

Iphigenie auf Tauris (Goethe), 34

Irigaray, Luce, 27n31, 79

Janthe, 125, 134, 137–38, 147n71

Jason, 75–76, 78, 80, 102n43, 103n59, 104n69, 104–5n76, 155; and Medea, 7–8, 21–22, 77, 81, 83–96; multiple personas of, 92; as powerless, 94; shunning of, 91–92

Kant, Immanuel, 144n37, 144–45n46

Kiefer, Anselm, 107

kinship, 1, 8, 21, 49–50, 74, 86–87, 89–90, 96, 108, 110; and exile, 151; and gender, 79; and legitimacy, 75; political sovereignty, 80; religious practice, 122

Kleist, Heinrich von, 34, 53, 62n3

König Ottokars Glück und Ende (King Ottokar's Fortune and End) (Grillparzer), 7

Kottman, Paul A., 28n36

Kreon, 85–91

Kreusa, 84–88, 90–91, 94, 100–101n23

Kristeva, Julia, 29n52

Lacan, 79

lamentation, 89

language, 8, 28n36, 43–44, 48–49, 51, 55–58, 60, 70–72, 75–78, 85–87, 109, 122, 128, 155; coercive power in, 21–22; female agency, 121; female figures, 2–4, 12, 14–17; and figuration, 11; and gender, 1, 5, 11, 17, 40, 61, 119–20, 124, 127, 151; as gendered, 41; and identity, 151; limits of, 152, 156; literary history, 3; and meaning, 32, 39, 47; metaphorical, 89; and representation, 73–74; self, representing of through, 10; and subjectivity, 151; as teller of people, 74; theoretical practice, 9

Laocoon (Lessing), 16

Leander, 107–8, 110, 122, 125–27, 131, 134, 138–39, 145n56, 145–46n57, 146n59, 147n71; distraction, as symbol of, 123; drowning of, 135–37; and Hero, 22, 111–12, 120, 123, 132–33, 136–37, 140, 155

Leda and the Swan: myth of, 126–27, 147n71

Index 173

lesbian: as term, 28n40
Lessing, Gotthold Ephraim, 5, 16, 98–99n10; aesthetic imagination, 28n36
Letters of Heroines (Ovid), 141n2
Liebestod (The Waves of Sea and Love) (Grillparzer). See *Des Meeres und der Liebe Wellen* (The Waves of Sea and Love)
Life Is a Dream (La vida es sueño) (Calderón de la Barca), 104–5n76
Living a Feminist Life (Ahmed), 3–4, 51–52, 95, 103n51, 152–53
Location of Culture, The (Bhabha), 82
Lorenz, Dagmar, 6, 26n14, 36, 114–15, 143n22, 143n23, 143n24
Lü, Yixu, 104n69

Marlowe, Christopher, 107
materiality, 17
McCarthy-Rechowicz, Matthew, 24n6, 97–98n6, 144–45n46
McDonald, Marianne, 21
McInnes, Edward, 93
Medea, 2–3, 5, 11, 14–17, 62, 69, 73, 100n19, 100n20, 100–101n23, 101n31, 102n43, 104n69, 104–5n76, 108–10, 113, 120, 140, 151, 157; abjection, figure of, 21; alterity of, 96; banishment of, 86–87; betrayal of, 81, 83, 89; catharsis, as unachievable, 94; and causality, 90; and chest, 83, 88, 101–2n38; and crisis, 71, 80, 96; as dangerous stranger, 72, 78–80, 83; as defiant, 96; difference, as figure of, 152, 156; differences of, as multiple, 72; as discursive subject, 22–23, 80, 87; feminist consciousness of, 95–96; as feminist killjoy, 9; feminist will, 8; and gender, 72; gender difference, 80; as gendered other, 86; gender oppression, as victim of, 70; Greeks, socially abhorrent to, 21; as harmed woman, 4; humanity, denial of, 8; and identity, 72, 82, 86, 88, 92; inclusion and exclusion, strategy of, 110; as insurrectionary power, 94; and Jason, 7–8, 21–22, 77, 81, 83–96; kinship, lack of, 86; kinship norms, and resistance, 80, 87, 89–90; language, use of, 8–10, 70–73, 75–78, 85–87, 155; as marginalized, 20n52, 71–72, 94, 96; myth of, 96–97; otherness of, 8, 85, 88; as outsider, 71, 78, 84, 94, 96; as political figure, 80; private and public, doubling of, 82; radicality of, 4; representation of, 77, 80, 87–88; revenge of, 76, 80, 87, 89–93; as rogue female figure, 79; and rupture, 77, 78; self-presentation, insistence on, 77, 87–88; social belonging, yearning for, 72; speech patterns, 8; as sympathetic, 80; talking back, 13; as textual riddle, 72; trauma, figure of, 94, 95; as troublemaker, 4, 8, 22–23, 72; as uncivilized, 21, 87; as unhomed, 81–84, 94; unhomely, forgetting of, 83; ventriloquism of, 71; as victim, of socially inscribed structures, 72; as victim and victimizer, 96; white male structures, 103n51; as willful, 4, 8, 72, 75, 85, 87, 140, 156; as witch, 8, 21, 23, 70–72, 76–77, 93
Medea (Euripides), 21, 73–75, 81, 88, 92
Medea (Grillparzer), 1, 7–8, 21–23, 69, 79–81, 83, 86–87, 89, 91–92, 94–95, 97–98n6, 104n69, 109–10, 112, 122, 125, 140–41, 151, 154, 157; aboutness, conveying of, 34; alterity, 72; as descriptive, 73; as discourse, between present and past, 74; discursive framing of, 70; duality of, 34; female speech in, as defiant and unwanted, 94; feminist impulse in, 70; gender, constructive and deconstructive work of, 70; humanism of, 97; inclusion

and exclusion, 70; language, and
representation, 73–74; management
of crisis, shift in, 96; melancholy,
articulation of, 154; myth of,
reimaging of, 96–97; representation
and language, as central to, 74; as
trilogy, 73–74; ventriloquial moment
in, 72–73; wrongness, recognition
of, 70
Melitta, 33–34, 46, 52, 55–56, 60,
84–85; identity of, 50; monologue
of, 49–51
memory: and remembering, 156–57
Menhennet, Alan, 142n9
Metternich, Klemens von, 25n11
Molière, 34
Mörike, Eduard, 6
Morrison, Toni, 82
Mrs. Dalloway (Woolf), 9, 22, 95
Müller, Heiner, 13
Musaeus, 107

Naukleros, 126, 131–32, 136, 145n56,
145–46n57
Naumann, Walter, 36

otherness, 8, 61, 69–70, 85, 88
Ovid, 107, 141n2

Papst, E. E., 114
Pascal, Blaise, 139
Pelias, 86
Penthesilea, 53
Penthesilea (Kleist), 34, 53, 62n3
performativity, 14; as repetition and
ritual, 52
Peritta, 75, 100n20
Phaon, 22, 33–35, 40–45, 50–52, 54,
155–56; monologue of, 46–49;
Sappho, rejection of, 55–59
Philoctetes (Sophocles), 16
Phryxus, 75–78, 81, 83, 89–90, 99–
100n14
Poetics (Aristotle), 62n2
polis, 94

Polyneices, 79
Pope, Alexander, 28n42
precarity, 35, 50, 86, 111
Priam, 103n58
Prutti, Brigitte, 97–98n6, 115, 143n25,
143n26

Racine, Jean, 34
recognition, 156–57
Reeve, William C., 7
Renaissance, 107
representation, 3, 27n31, 77, 80,
87–88; of female figures, 1, 10,
15–18, 69; as impression, of a life,
36; and language, 32, 73–74; male
authentication, 14; and recognition,
21; self-representation, 23, 31;
visibility, granting of, 14–15
Restoration, 25n11
Rhamnes, 38–40, 59–60
Rilke, Rainer Maria, 107
Roe, Ian F., 26n16
Römische Elegien (Goethe), 6
Rossetti, Dante Gabriel, 28n42

Sammlung, 113, 115, 130, 133, 136,
138, 142n17, 154; definition of, 114;
as socially constructed, 139. *See also*
composure
Sappho, 2–3, 5, 7, 11, 14–17, 19, 28n42,
29n43, 33, 35–36, 42, 62, 63n12, 70,
108–9, 112–13, 120, 144n35, 151–
52, 157; as alienated, 38; as alienated
poetess, 23; autonomy of, 37, 43;
balance, impossibility of, 155; as
cultural outsider, 39; difference,
as figure of, 152, 156; discourse,
amplification of, 110; as discursive
subject, 22–23, 51; dwelling of, as
mixed space, 38; exceptional status
of, 40, 43; feminist impulse, 51; as
feminist killjoy, 9, 57; feminist will,
8; genders, inequity between, 53;
gender thinking, 50–53; as harmed
woman, 4; Hero, as countertext

to, 115; as historical figure, 20;
identity of, 21, 32, 41, 43, 45, 48,
50, 52, 54, 57–60; language, use of,
8–10, 32, 39–41, 43–44, 47–49, 51,
55–58, 60–61; otherness of, 8, 61;
radicality of, 4; rejection of, 55–59;
self-representation, 31; as sexless,
40; speech patterns, 8, 41, 43–44;
suicide of, 34, 46, 59–61, 155;
talking back, 13; as transgressive,
40; as troublemaker, 4, 8, 22–23;
unraveling of, 52; as willful, 4, 8,
57, 156
Sappho (Grillparzer), 1, 7, 20, 22–23,
35, 38, 69–70, 84, 85, 109–10, 112,
115, 122, 125, 140–41, 143n22,
151, 157; aboutness, conveying of,
34; Act 1, stage directions, 63n14;
Act 2, 46; critical response to, 36;
discourse, 21, 62; duality of, 34;
feminism in, 32; feminist impulse,
62; gender in, 21, 31, 37, 40, 43,
62; inclusion and exclusion, 21,
31, 62; as knowledge project, 62;
melancholy, articulation of, 154;
performativity, problem of, 52;
subjectivity of, 61; unities in, 34;
ventriloquism in, 32–33
Schaum, Konrad, 119, 144n38
Schicksalstragödie (fate tragedy), 7
Schiller, Friedrich, 5–6, 26n13, 41, 107
Schlesier, Renate, 20
Searle, John, 65n45
Second Sex, The (Beauvoir), 15
Seneca, 13, 104n69
Sophocles, 79
speech acts, 65n45
Stein, Gisela, 114
Swinburne, Algernon Charles, 28n42

Tanzer, Ulrike, 144n45
temporality: and ventriloquism, 34

Torquato Tasso (Goethe), 34
Tragedy of Antony and Cleopatra, The,
69
trauma, 94; feminist analysis of,
105n77; as knowing and not
knowing, 95, 97
Twombly, Cy, 107, 141n4

"Uber Laokoon" (Goethe), 6
unhomed, 81, 83, 94; as term, 82
United States, 26n13
unrepresentable: idea of, 27n31

ventriloquism, 13–14, 16, 23–24, 33,
71–73, 114, 138–39, 151, 154,
156; gender alterity, 10; gender
performance, as mode of, 11;
metaphor of, 11; and temporality,
34
*Volatile Bodies: Towards a Corporal
Feminism* (Grosz), 111

Weissman, Dirk, 73, 98n9
Wellbery, David, 16, 28n36
Whitaker, Paul K., 113, 142n17
"Whose Counting?" (Ahmed), 23–24
"Willfulness Archive, A" (Ahmed), 57
Willful Subjects (Ahmed), 56–57,
60–61, 139
Williamson, Margaret, 74
Winckelmann, Johann Joachim, 25n9
Winkler, Markus, 97–98n6
Winterson, Jeanette, 28n42
Wolf, Christa, 13
Wollstonecraft, Mary, 4, 25n7
women's rights, 4
Woolf, Virginia, 9, 95
"Written After Swimming from Sestos
to Abydos" (Byron), 107

Zerstreuung, 113, 138. *See also*
distraction

About the Author

Alicia E. Ellis is associate professor of German at Colby College. Her research interests include German literature from 1789-1919, comparative literature, diasporic and Black Atlantic Studies, women's and gender studies, and African American and Caribbean literatures. She has lectured and written on Derek Walcott, Heinrich von Kleist, ETA Hoffmann, Heinrich Heine, and Christa Wolf. Ellis has also published work on Edwidge Danticat, Andrea Levy, and Sam Selvon.

www.ingramcontent.com/pod-product-compliance
Lightning Source LLC
Chambersburg PA
CBHW020122010526
44115CB00008B/938